ChaseDream GMAT 备考系列丛书

GMAT™
Focus Edition
阅读理解
长难句精讲 第❸版

毕 出　王钰儿 ◎ 编著

机械工业出版社
CHINA MACHINE PRESS

GMAT阅读理解着重考查考生对于文章词句的理解能力、对段落及语句间逻辑结构的把握能力，以及利用文章所提供的信息做出合理推断的能力。阅读理解考题会利用不同题型来体现对于这些能力的考查。本书正是以这些题型作为基础编写的：全书共五章，内容涉及阅读长难句所需的语法基础、长难句详解、理解文章的技巧、阅读考题不同题型的问法与解读，以及最后的实战练习。本书语言简练，让考生从了解阅读理解的题型含义及考查重点开始，进而掌握阅读理解中各种题型的考法及变化，最后可以快速而准确地答对阅读理解考题。作者在书中揭示了 GMAT 阅读考题真正的考查重点，避免了一些书籍基于现象总结的弊端，具有强大的可推广性和适应性，力求做到内容专而不广，叙述简洁，通俗易懂。

本书适用于所有已经参加过或者准备参加 GMAT 考试的考生，也适用于喜好研究 GMAT 考试的同仁。

图书在版编目（CIP）数据

GMAT 阅读理解：长难句精讲 / 毕出，王钰儿编著. —3 版. —北京：机械工业出版社，2024.4
（ChaseDream GMAT 备考系列丛书）
ISBN 978-7-111-75483-1

Ⅰ.①G… Ⅱ.①毕… ②王… Ⅲ.①英语 – 阅读教学 – 研究生 – 入学考试 – 自学参考资料　Ⅳ.① H319.37

中国国家版本馆 CIP 数据核字（2024）第 065204 号

机械工业出版社（北京市百万庄大街 22 号　邮政编码 100037）
策划编辑：苏筛琴　　　责任编辑：苏筛琴
责任校对：尹小云　　　责任印制：单爱军
保定市中画美凯印刷有限公司印刷
2024 年 7 月第 3 版第 1 次印刷
184mm×260mm · 20.25 印张 · 1 插页 · 493 千字
标准书号：ISBN 978-7-111-75483-1
定价：78.00 元

电话服务　　　　　　　　　网络服务
客服电话：010-88361066　　机 工 官 网：www.cmpbook.com
　　　　　010-88379833　　机 工 官 博：weibo.com/cmp1952
　　　　　010-68326294　　金 书 网：www.golden-book.com
封底无防伪标均为盗版　　　机工教育服务网：www.cmpedu.com

特别鸣谢
INSEAD 欧洲工商管理学院对本书提供的帮助。

Special thanks to
INSEAD The Business School for the World.

INSEAD
The Business School for the World

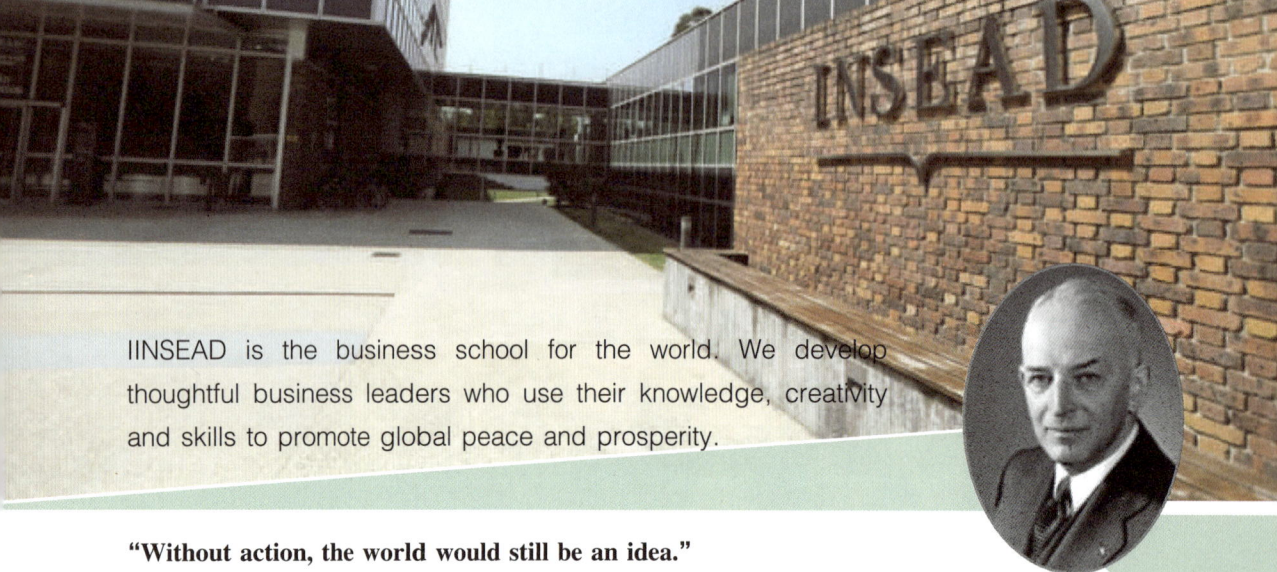

IINSEAD is the business school for the world. We develop thoughtful business leaders who use their knowledge, creativity and skills to promote global peace and prosperity.

"Without action, the world would still be an idea."
—Georges Doriot, INSEAD Founder
French-born American, pioneering venture capitalist and Harvard Business School professor who founded the Chamber de Commerce de Paris.

Our Mission, Our Promise

We create a transformative learning environment in which people, cultures and ideas come together to promote prosperity and social progress.

Through academic research, we expand the frontiers of knowledge and shape business practice.

Through teaching, we develop responsible and analytical leaders who create value for their organisations and for society.

Through our entrepreneurial spirit, we champion innovative forms of management education that foster business as a force for good.

The Business School for the World

As one of the world's leading and largest graduate business schools, INSEAD offers participants a truly global educational experience. With locations in Europe (France), Asia (Singapore), the Middle East (Abu Dhabi) and North America (San Francisco) and alliances with top institutions, INSEAD's business education and research span the globe.

Fontainebleau
Europe Campus

Singapore
Asia Campus

Abu Dhabi
Middle East Campus

San Francisco
Hub for Business Innovation

Our 159 renowned faculty members from 41 countries inspire more than 1,300 students in our degree and PhD programmes. In addition, more than 11,000 executives participate in INSEAD's executive education programmes each year.

Faculty Figures
(as of 1 September 2023)

Total number of resident faculty*: **159**

Asia Campus	Europe Campus	Middle East Campus	San Francisco Hub
57	95	5	2

Number of nationalities	Number of women faculty	Number of new faculty
41	38	4

*Resident faculty refers to affiliate and boarding faculty

INSEAD Ranking

☐ First business school to be ranked #1 in three categories by the *Financial Times* (MBA, EMBA, and single-school EMBA)

☐ Ranked No. 1 in the world 3 times in the recent 6 years by the *Financial Times* Global MBA Ranking

☐ Ranked No. 2 in the world by QS WUR Ranking by Business & Management Studies Subject for the 6th consecutive year.

As of 2022, INSEAD ranks
#2
in terms of number of MBA graduates who are currently Chief Executive of an FT500 company.

INSEAD also ranks as one of Europe's
Top 10 unicorn universities
by Sifted, the new-media site for Europe's innovators and entrepreneurs backed by the *Financial Times*.

Institutional Partnerships

Our partnerships with three of the greatest international names in higher education confirm our reputation for our faculty, research and teaching.

INSEAD Full-time Degree Programmes

Master in Management
Launching global careers

The INSEAD Master in Managment (MIM) is a 14- to 16-month full-time programme designed to equip pre-experience students with a holistic set of skills to launch a successful global career. Conducted across the INSEAD Asia and Europe Campuses, with field trip options to the Middle East, China and the USA, the INSEAD MIM combines an innovative learning approach with problemsolving practical applications. The programme empowers the next generation of wellrounded and agile thinking individuals to make a positive impact in today's society.

Master in Management — MIM'24

Aimed at young leaders with a clear sense of direction when they finish their undergraduate studies. Students take a deep dive into business theory and gain complete set of management skills. The MIM programme also focuses on leadership in global business with international experience integrated into the course of study.

| 177 Students | 23 Average age | 38% Women | 36 Nationalities | 11 Average months of internship or work experience | 689 Average GMAT score | Dec 2024 Graduation |

MBA
Empower your future

The INSEAD MBA is an accelerated 10-month programme that develops successful, thoughtful leaders and entrepreneurs who create value for their organisations and communities. Be it a career switch, advancement or new business venture, the INSEAD MBA helps our graduates realize their professional aspirations. With no dominant nationality in the classroom, it opens up a world of new perspectives. Thanks to partnerships with schools such as Wharton, Kellogg and CEIBS, INSEAD students can exchange with globally renowned institutions. The ten months go by quickly—but their impact lasts a lifetime.

MBA

Designed for early to mid-career professionals, and featuring an accelerated 10-month curriculum, our MBA programme develops successful leaders and entrepreneurs.

MBA'23D
| 439 Students | 29 Average age | 35% Women | 68 Nationalities | 6.2 Average years of experience | 700 Average GMAT score | Dec 2023 Graduation |

MBA'24J
| 429 Students | 29 Average age | 37% Women | 66 Nationalities | 5.7 Average years of experience | 701 Average GMAT score | Jul 2024 Graduation |

Career Development

The INSEAD Career Development Centre (CDC) consists of a global team of educators and connectors committed to assisting students, participants and graduates in maximizing their career opportunities and increasing social mobility.

Career coaches, employer engagement specialists and operations professionals partner with students in their career journey: from inculcating a broad range of life-long career building skills to supporting the individual's journey in one-on-one coaching, as well as optional advisory sessions.

The CDC offers career education via online tools, workshops and webinars, covering a broad range of topics, including networking and building relationships, self-assessment tools, crafting a unique value proposition, CV writing, interviewing—both technical and professional—and salary negotiation.

Additionally, CDC hosts multiple on-campus events to create recruitment and networking opportunities. It is envisaged that these CDC resources will act as lifelong catalysts and accelerants for the career journeys of INSEAD students, participants and alumni.

Top MBA Recruiters 2023

#	Company	#	Company	#	Company
124 (43*)	McKinsey & Company	10	EY	4 (1*)	AlixPartners
83 (25*)	BCG	9	accenture	4 (1*)	Alvarez & Marsal
71 (18*)	BAIN & COMPANY	7 (3*)	Oliver Wyman	4	Amphenol
29 (9*)	strategy&	7	SAMSUNG	4 (1*)	Morgan Stanley
27 (5*)	KEARNEY	6	amazon	4	rbi
13 (6*)	Roland Berger	5	Lilly		

* The number of students returning to their former employers post-graduation.

Career Statistics by Degree Programme

MBA '22D and '23J

88%
Received offers 3 months post graduation

€113,400
Average base salary

50%
Changed country

80%
Accepted offers 3 months post graduation

48%
Changed sector

25%
Changed all three dimensions

57
Countries employed in

57%
Changed function

78%
Changed at least one dimension

Sectors of work

- 61% Consulting
- 9% Technology, Media & Telecom
- 14% Financial services
- 16% Other corporate sectors

INSEAD Alumni Network

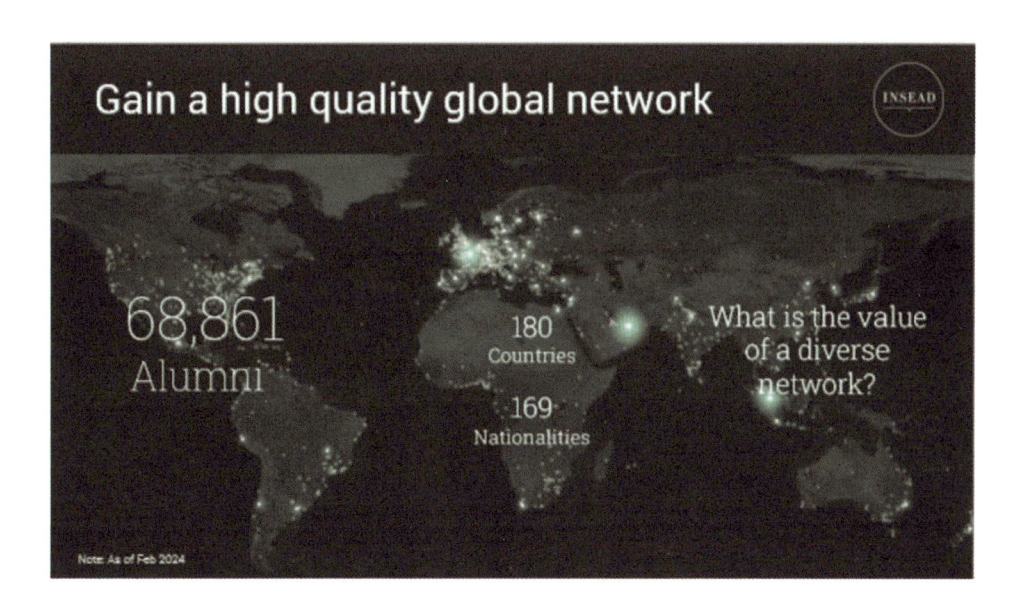

Gain a high quality global network

68,861 Alumni
180 Countries
169 Nationalities

What is the value of a diverse network?

Note: As of Feb 2024

INSEAD brings together people, cultures and ideas to develop responsible leaders who transform business and society.

INSEAD Europe Campus
Boulevard de Constance
77305 Fontainebleau Cedex, France
T +33 1 6072 4000

INSEAD Middle East Campus
Al Khatem Tower, ADGM Square
Al Maryah Island, P.O.Box 48049 Abu Dhabi, UAE
T +971 2 651 5200

INSEAD Asia Campus
1 Ayer Rajah Avenue
Singapore 138676
T +65 6799 5388

INSEAD San Francisco Hub
224 Townsend Street
San Francisco, CA, 94107 United States
T +1 888 546 7323

INSEAD 欧洲工商管理学院

The Business School for the World®

微信公众号　　官方微博

https://www.insead.edu/

ChaseDream 总编推荐序

阅读理解（Reading Comprehension，简称 RC）是一个我们从小考到大的题型。不管是中考、高考，或是英语四级、六级，还是托福、雅思，几乎所有考试都有 RC，但就是这种已经不能再熟悉的题型，到了 GMAT 这里似乎又变了样儿……

如果这时你还天真地认为单词、句式是搞定 GMAT RC 的不二法宝，那可就真是"图样图森破（too young too simple）"了。满篇词句全认识，凑到一起就是看不明白说的是什么；看懂了题目和选项，却仍然无法找出解题思路；细节题最简单了吧？可为什么在原文中就是找不到答案呢？多年的解题经验常常失效，已成为 GMAT 考生挥之不去的痛，甚至有人已经开始怀疑自己是否先天条件不足。

那么，阅读的问题究竟出在哪儿，又该如何解决呢？GMAT RC 又有哪些独创的问题呢？

向后翻，你会接触到一些全新的基础训练，它们将带你一步步走出 RC 困境。准备好了吗？

我们开始吧！

steven
ChaseDream 总编

前　言

很多 GMAT 考生都"惧怕"阅读。要想在阅读理解题型中表现得更好，考生们需要渡过两大难关：一是理解文章，二是抓准问题思路。

先从理解文章上说。一直以来，很多考生都有一个错误观点，即只要能认识一篇文章中绝大部分的单词，就能很好地理解文章。你上高中时，或许这个观点曾被你反复证实过，而在 GMAT 考试中，却经常会出现那种单词全认识但放在一起就不认识了的句子。这是因为 GMAT 文章中很多句子是"长难句"，其中涉及一些语法现象及层级关系，单纯地翻译词汇用处不大，自然会"看不懂"。那么，用什么方法才能轻松看懂这些句子呢？这个问题的答案，留给本书的"阅读长难句所需的语法基础"来回答。

再从抓准问题思路上来说。GMAT 的阅读考题与托福等纯英语考试不同，它不仅考查理解文意的能力，更多考查在理解文意的基础上进行推理的能力（例如：基于文章信息做出推断的能力）。因此，本书从第三章开始详述了这些推理能力以及基本的解题技法。

希望这本书能成为你在学习 GMAT 阅读理解这类考题道路上的垫脚石，踩着它，距离征服 GMAT 可以更近一些。

由于时间仓促，水平有限，本书难免会有不足和纰漏之处，欢迎读者朋友们批评指正，并且提出宝贵意见。若有意见请发送至：book@chasedream.com，感谢斧正。

毕出
于 2024 年春

目 录

INSEAD 欧洲工商管理学院
ChaseDream 总编推荐序
前言

00 绪论

01 第一章
阅读长难句所需的语法基础

1.1 阅读理解应拆分成"阅读 + 理解" // 006
1.2 什么是 GMAT 长难句 // 007
1.3 为什么要看懂长难句 // 008
1.4 为什么读句子要学语法 // 009
1.5 阅读长难句的语法基础 // 011
    1.5.1 简单句 // 011
    1.5.2 复合句 // 013
1.6 GMAT 长难句典型结构 // 021
    1.6.1 长成分 // 021
    1.6.2 省略 // 023
    1.6.3 倒装 // 023
1.7 句子读法—— 分层阅读 // 030

第二章
长难句详解

C 组 // 041

B 组 // 079

A 组 // 146

第三章
如何理解文章
——脑中具象化，纸上搭框架

3.1 将文章具象化 // 177

3.2 搭建逻辑框架 // 188

第四章
阅读考题

4.1 主旨大意题 // 201

4.2 支持观点题 // 208

4.3 推断题 // 214

4.4 应用题 // 219

4.5 评估题 // 222

第五章
阅读实战

第一组 // 236

第二组 // 255

第三组 // 273

第四组 // 291

绪论

阅读理解 (Reading Comprehension) 在 GMAT 考试的语文 (Verbal) 部分所占据的比重大概为 56.5%(13/23)，题目包含 3~4 篇文章，每篇文章 3～4 小题。

阅读理解考题主要考查 GMAT 考生如下四个方面的能力：

理解词义和句义；

理解要点和概念的逻辑关系；

从事实和陈述中做出推断；

理解文中出现的一些定量概念。

从这些考点上很容易发现，绝大部分的题目着重于考查考生对于文意的理解以及基于文意做出合理推断。让我们首先来看一篇中文的 GMAT 阅读文章，相信大家可以从中体会出 GMAT 阅读理解的命题方式（为了保证模拟效果，请在 6 分钟内完成）。

> 很多学者提出：经济发展，尤其是工业化和城镇化的发展，帮助了民主制的发展。根据这个原理，合乎逻辑的是：一旦经济发展提高了女性的经济能力，更多女性就会要求获得选举权。但是，这个经济发展理论并不足以解释一些特定的关于建立妇女选举权的历史事实。例如，为什么美国于 1920 年建立了妇女选举权，但是直到 1970 年瑞士才建立妇女选举权呢？要知道，在 1920 年，两个国家都已经良好地推行了工业化：在美国，超过 33% 的工人被不同的工业雇用，在瑞士这个数据是 44%。当然，我们也得承认，美国和瑞士在工业化等级和城镇化等级的协同性上还是有区别的：在 1920 年，只有 29% 的瑞士人住在拥有超过 10 000 名居民的城市里。但是，城镇化也不能完全解释建立妇女选举权的原因。例如，在 1920 年前的美国，只有城镇化较差的州才会承认妇女有选举权。相似地，早在瑞士承认妇女有选举权之前，城镇化较差的柬埔寨和加纳的女性就已经拥有投票权了。当然，一般来说瑞士的城镇化地区比非城镇化地区更早地通过了建立妇女选举权的法案。虽然城镇化和工业化看起来都不能完全解释为何建立妇女选举权，但是，这些地区还拥有一些可以帮助解释这个现象的其他特征，例如：相似的语言背景和强大的左翼政党。
>
> 1. 这篇文章的主要目的是：
>
>   (A) 对比关于妇女选举权的两种解释
>   (B) 说明某一个因素比另一个因素更能解释建立妇女选举权的原因
>   (C) 讨论一个理论的适用性，这个理论在试图解释建立妇女选举权的原因
>   (D) 澄清一个潜藏在关于妇女选举权的理论内部的假设
>   (E) 解释一个历史事件是如何同建立妇女选举权有机地联系在一起的

2. 下列哪项描述了文章所叙述的 1920 年以前美国的州的情况?

   (A) 那些并没有高度城镇化的州在承认妇女选举权方面进展缓慢。
   (B) 那些高度城镇化的州在决定关于国家选举权政策时是最有影响力的。
   (C) 那些城镇化程度最高的州更有可能拥有强大的左翼政党。
   (D) 那些城镇化程度最高的州并不一定是工业化程度最高的。
   (E) 那些城镇化程度最高的州还没有承认妇女选举权。

3. 下列哪一项是文章所说的关于瑞士的城镇化地区的情况?

   (A) 这些地区拥有一些除城镇化之外的其他特征,可以解释批准妇女获得选举权的原因。
   (B) 这些地区比非城镇化地区政治分歧更多。
   (C) 这些地区拥有一些像相似的语言背景和强大的左翼政党这样的非城镇化特征。
   (D) 因为城镇化加剧了观念的传播,所以这些地区的人民持有相似的观点。
   (E) 这些地区可以在对待妇女选举权的态度上与美国城镇化程度最高的州相媲美。

4. 下列哪项关于瑞士和美国 1920 年的城镇化情况是文章所提出的?

   (A) 相较于美国工人,更高比例的瑞士工人居住在城镇化地区。
   (B) 瑞士拥有超过 10 000 名居民的城市比美国更多。
   (C) 住在城镇化地区的瑞士人民比住在城镇化地区的美国人民更可能被工业雇用。
   (D) 瑞士的城镇化地区比同级别的美国地区更有可能具有强大的左翼政党。
   (E) 相对于瑞士人,更高比例的美国人居住在城镇里。

这是一篇翻译的 GMAT 阅读理解真题。它的难度在 GMAT 所有阅读理解考题中属于中等偏上。也就是说,如果你能答对难度同等于这篇阅读的大部分 GMAT 考题,你的成绩将不会低于 700 分。这几道题的答案是 (C)(E)(A)(E)。怎么样,你选对了吗?我调查了一些我的同事、朋友,包括上课的学生,发现绝大部分的人可以在规定时间内完成,并且做对至少 3 道题目。下面对这 4 道题目稍做解析。

第一题问的是文章的主旨。通读文章可知,最开始文章给出了一个经济发展理论,并且认为这个理论可以解释建立妇女选举权的原因。后文从多个角度阐释了这个理论在解释能力上的不足,并且提出一些其他可以解释建立妇女选举权的因素。由此可知,本题答案为 (C),即讨论一个理论的适用性。

第二题是一道推断类型的考题。文中给出了"例如,在 1920 年前的美国,只有城镇化较差的州才会承认妇女有选举权"。通过此句可知，在1920年前，城镇化较好的州没有建立妇女选举权。

第三题的 (C) 选项具有很强的迷惑性。的确，文中提到了"瑞士的城镇化地区拥有一些可以帮助解释这个现象的其他特征，例如：相似的语言背景和强大的左翼政党"，但是并没有说过相似的语言背景和强大的左翼政党等特征是非城镇化特征。

第四题相对比较容易，文中提到：当然，我们也得承认，美国和瑞士在工业化等级和城镇化等级的协同性上还是有区别的：在1920年，只有29%的瑞士人住在拥有超过10 000名居民的城市里。基于此句可知，1920年，一定有更高比例的美国人居住在城镇里。

当然，我们没法期待短期内能把英语的句子都看得和汉语一样熟练，但是，通过一定量的针对英语句子的阅读练习，绝大部分的考生可以在短期内将英语能力提升至满足 GMAT 考试阅读要求的水平。

因此，本书一共分为两大部分，第一部分（第一、二章）是对英语阅读的训练，即 GMAT 长难句训练；第二部分（第三、四、五章）是对 GMAT 阅读理解考题的训练。可以说，第一部分是基础，第二部分是实战。当然，长难句训练不仅对阅读理解有帮助，它对 GMAT 语文部分的其他考题均有很大帮助。之所以在这本书里讲长难句，主要是因为长难句障碍在阅读中体现得尤为明显（批判性推理的考题你甚至可以在考场上读两遍，但是阅读题目你很难有时间读两遍）。

下面，就让我们去征服长难句、征服阅读理解吧！

第一章

阅读长难句所需的语法基础

1.1 阅读理解应拆分成"阅读 + 理解"

"阅读理解（Reading Comprehension）"是一个词组，它应被拆分成"阅读"和"理解"两个部分："阅读"通常指的是能否读懂句子的字面意思；"理解"则通常指的是能否体会到其背后暗含的意思。

举一个简单的例子：

Team A won the competition. It is reported that unlike Team B, Team A used team-based decision-making, which increased the likelihood that the team adheres to plans, because each involved in the decision-making may be more committed to the chosen course of action.

根据文段，我们可以"推断"出如下两个句子：

(1) Team A is less likely to deviate from strategic plans because team members may be more devoted to plans.

此句正是原文的同义转换：adheres to plans 对应 is less likely to deviate from strategic plans；be more committed to 对应 be more devoted to。本句是对"阅读"的考查，即考生是否认识每一个单词，以及整句话表达的字面意思。

(2) Team B failed the competition, probably because it pursed an ineffective decision-making strategy rather than a team-based one.

此句蕴含了文段中没有明说的信息。通过文段第一句话"Team A won the competition."以及第二句话中的 unlike Team B，我们可以合理推断出 B 团队没赢得比赛，而且很可能是因为没有采取合适的决策。本句是对"理解"的考查，即考生是否能感知文章中没有明说却蕴含在字里行间的信息。

我们之前见过的大部分英语考试，如雅思、托福等语言类考试，更侧重于对"阅读"的考查，但 GMAT 考试更注重的是考生能否充分理解文段蕴含的所有信息，无论是明说的还是没有明说的。GMAT 阅读是一个充满挑战性的任务，但绝不是没有方法可循的。接下来本书将帮助你从"阅读"和"理解"这两个维度更好地备考阅读理解题型。

1.2 什么是 GMAT 长难句

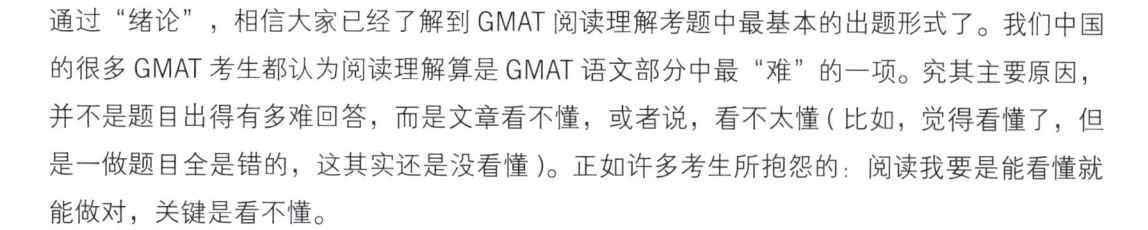

通过"绪论",相信大家已经了解到 GMAT 阅读理解考题中最基本的出题形式了。我们中国的很多 GMAT 考生都认为阅读理解算是 GMAT 语文部分中最"难"的一项。究其主要原因,并不是题目出得有多难回答,而是文章看不懂,或者说,看不太懂(比如,觉得看懂了,但是一做题目全是错的,这其实还是没看懂)。正如许多考生所抱怨的:阅读我要是能看懂就能做对,关键是看不懂。

看不懂的原因,无非两种:一种是单词不认识;另一种是单词虽然认识,但是连在一起就不认识了(即句子看不懂)。第一种原因较容易解决,找一本单词书背背就可以了。但是,认识单词仅仅是一个必要条件,很多考生会发现,就算是背了再多的单词,终归还是有不认识的,并且总是感觉这些不认识的单词是"重点词"。这是因为,当年英语老师们为了培养我们对英语的兴趣,或者说,让英语尽量简单化,让我们先背单词,然后把句中每个单词的中文意思"串"在一起,再用中文的逻辑填补一下空缺,最终掌握一句话的意思。自然,在这种阅读方法下,只要有一个或者几个单词不认识,想看懂这句话就非常困难了。退一步说,就算是词汇都认识,由于 GMAT 的阅读文章或多或少含有长句,我们也很难通过逐词翻译的方法看懂这些句子,一是没有人的脑容量大到可以同时处理 40 或者 50 个单词,更重要的是这样的阅读方式在句意的理解上很容易产生偏差。一句偏就可能句句偏,文章的意思就不知道偏到哪里去了。这就是第二种看不懂的原因——句意理解困难。

句子看不懂,肯定不是所有句子都看不懂。由于英语和汉语的语序有很多相似之处,所以简单的结构非常容易理解。看不懂的,无非就是 GMAT 考试中的"长难句"。

什么是长难句呢?顾名思义,GMAT 长难句就是在 GMAT 考试中,尤其是阅读考题中,出现的那些既长又不容易读懂的句子。这种句子对于考生掌握文章的主旨大意往往有着较强的阻碍作用,例如:

Five fledgling sea eagles left their nests in western Scotland this summer, bringing to 34 the number of wild birds successfully raised since transplants from Norway began in 1975.

这个句子"只"有 29 个词,还远远算不上 GMAT 的长句。但是,就是这个句子,应该也会让不少考生十分头疼。如果阅读功底不扎实,往往是读了后面忘了前面,就算是勉强撑着读下来,也难以掌握句意,更甭提与其他句子建立起逻辑联系了。

1.3 为什么要看懂长难句

这个问题其实很容易回答。

第一个原因是：GMAT 考试中几乎每篇文章都有或多或少的长难句。GMAT 阅读文章短的仅有 200 多个词，长的最多有 350 个词，一个长难句可能就占去了 50 个词左右，甚至能占去文章长度的 20%。可想而知，如果看不懂长难句，理解文意是有多么困难。

第二个原因是：GMAT 很喜欢在长难句部分设置"理解句意"[1]类的考题，例如：

> **原文：**
>
> The 1980 volcanic eruption of Mount Saint Helens, for example, sent mud and debris into several tributaries of the Columbia River. For the next couple of years, steelhead trout (a species included among the salmon) returning from the sea to spawn were forced to find alternative streams. As a consequence, their rates of straying, initially 16 percent, rose to more than 40 percent overall.
>
> Although no one has quantified changes in the rate of straying as a result of the disturbances caused by humans, there is no reason to suspect that the effect would be qualitatively different than what was seen in the aftermath of the Mount Saint Helens eruption.
>
> **题目：**
>
> Which of the following does the author mention as support for the view that environmental disturbances caused by human activity could increase straying rates?
>
> (A) The existence of salmon populations in rivers where the elimination of salmon habitat by human activity had previously made the fish extinct.
>
> (B) The results of studies measuring the impact on straying rates of habitat loss caused by human activity.
>
> (C) The potential for disturbances in one environment to cause the introduction of novel genes into salmon populations in neighboring areas.

---

1. 关于题型，我们将在后文详细讨论。

(D) The weaknesses in the view that the extinction of entire salmon populations is the only mechanism by which human destruction of salmon habitat reduces genetic diversity in salmon.

(E) The absence of any reason for believing that disturbances brought about by human activity would differ in their effects from comparable disturbances brought about by natural causes.

同样，本题也算不上 GMAT 阅读考题中最难的。我们可以看到，这道题目的答案其实就是原文第二段主句的同义改写。只不过，无论是原文中的句子，还是答案选项 (E) 的句子，都不是那么好懂，如果考生没有能力读懂两个句子，那么这道题目无论用任何技巧都无法回答正确。

实际上，很多 GMAT 阅读考题就是为了考查考生阅读长难句的能力。因此，可以说，想做好 GMAT 阅读题，必须先跨过阅读长难句这一关。

1.4 为什么读句子要学语法

那么，如何看懂长难句呢？这个答案也十分简单，即学会"按照语法成分读句子"。例如"绪论"中例题文章第三行的一句话：

但是，这个经济发展理论并不足以解释一些特定的关于建立妇女选举权的历史事实。

绝大多数人会把这句话提炼为：

这个理论不足以解释一个事实。

在使用母语时，我们的思维会"自动"摄取一句话的关键信息，在一定程度上忽略次要信息，从而使得我们的阅读非常有效。如果我们对这句话做一个标准的语法分析，则可以发现：

"理论"是主语，"不足以解释"是谓语动词，"事实"是宾语；被我们忽略的"一些特定的关于建立妇女选举权的历史"是定语。

在语法上，主、谓、宾、补是一个句子的"主干"，定语和状语是这个句子的修饰成分。由此可见，母语语言本身的逻辑会让我们提炼出主干并且减弱修饰部分对我们理解句意的影响，即有轻有重的阅读。但是，这一切在非母语的环境下很难发生，尤其是长句很难抓到重点，

009

该突出的信息没获取到，反而是"垃圾信息"堆了一片。

那么，难道母语非英语的我们就没法有效地阅读英语句子了吗？答案是否定的。为了让人类学会第二门语言，"语法"这门学科诞生了。它的目的是让人类学会除母语外的另一门语言，了解这门语言的构句规则，进而在阅读句子时模拟出母语的阅读感觉（当然，这些只是语法的目的之一，语法还能帮助人们交流、写作等）。可以说，只有掌握了英语语法，才能真正看懂英语句子。

就算汉语并非母语，我们也可以凭借对各个成分的判断（主、谓、宾、定、状、补）来准确找到那句汉语例句的主干，继而主次分明地理解这个句子。再看上文中出现过的这个英语例句：

Five fledgling sea eagles left their nests in western Scotland this summer, bringing to 34 the number of wild birds successfully raised since transplants from Norway began in 1975.

我们需要纯熟地掌握如下三个语法点才能很好地理解这个例句：

伴随状语；
特殊的定语从句；
倒装。

本句的主干为：

Five fledgling sea eagles left their nests in western Scotland.

主干的后面是一个伴随状语，可以看作一个特殊的状语从句，其主干为：

Five fledgling sea eagles bring to 34 the number of wild birds.

这个伴随状语中还存在一个倒装，还原为正常语序是：

Five fledgling sea eagles bring the number of wild birds to 34.

这是一个 SVOO 结构的简单句。该句的字面意思是：

五只雏鹰把野生鸟的数量带到了 34 只。

wild birds 的后面还有一个特殊的定语从句，在逻辑上其可以被看作：

wild birds that were successfully raised since transplants from Norway began in 1975

这句话完整的意思是：

五只雏鹰在今年夏天离开了它们在西苏格兰岛的巢穴，这五只雏鹰将于 1975 年开始的迁移活动（从挪威迁移）所成功养大的野生鸟类的数量提升到了 34 只。

由此可见，只要我们有能力正确区分复合句中的各种成分，就一定可以有效地快速理解句意。

说到这里，相信很多读者会问：让我先读一遍句子，然后再一点点慢慢分析，也许能分析得出来，但是如何在第一次读句子的时候就分清楚这些呢？毕竟，美国人通常不会把每个句子读两遍吧（就像我们阅读中文一样）。

实际上，语法并不是"马后炮"。我们只能"慢慢分析"，因为我们对语法概念比较陌生，加之没有养成正确的英语阅读习惯，自然在初次阅读时用不上语法。要想像母语使用者那样阅读，我们必须得熟悉语法概念，了解各种成分的"长相"。例如：

Five fledgling sea eagles left their nests in western Scotland this summer, bringing the number of wild birds to 34.

在读到第一个词组 Five fledgling sea eagles 时，由于它的前面没有任何连词，可知接下来要读的肯定是主句；读到逗号后面的 bringing 可知接下来出现的将会是伴随状语（现在名词短语出现在句末，且逻辑主语是主句主语，这种结构必然是伴随状语），约等于一个和主句主语相同的普通状语从句，是句子的"次级"信息。

只要我们能熟悉各种语法现象的"长相"，就可以在初次阅读时了解所读成分的"分量"，继而像母语使用者一样有轻有重地理解整个复合句。

1.5 阅读长难句的语法基础

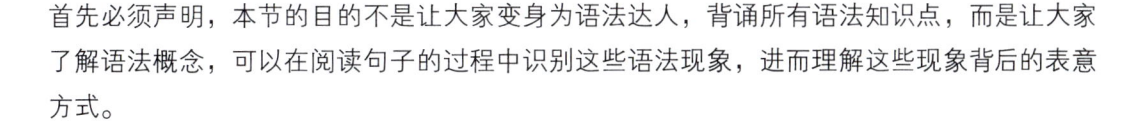

首先必须声明，本节的目的不是让大家变身为语法达人，背诵所有语法知识点，而是让大家了解语法概念，可以在阅读句子的过程中识别这些语法现象，进而理解这些现象背后的表意方式。

1.5.1 简单句

宏观上，英语句子可以分为两种——简单句和复合句。

依照动词特性的不同，简单句可以分为五种基本句型：

> 句型 1：主语 + 谓语 (SV)
>
> 句型 2：主语 + 谓语 + 宾语 (SVO)
>
> 句型 3：主语 + 谓语 + 补语 (SVC)
>
> 句型 4：主语 + 谓语 + 双宾语 (SVOO)
>
> 句型 5：主语 + 谓语 + 宾语 + 宾补 (SVOC)
>
> (S=Subject：主语；V=Verb：动词；O=Object：宾语；C=Complement：补语)

在简单句中，句型 1、2、3、4 都比较容易看出来，此处不再赘述，只是句型 5 需要格外留意。

在初高中时期，老师一定讲过关于宾补的用法及语义，但是很多人似乎并没有认真听讲，或者说，没想认真听讲。这个知识对于读懂较长的简单句非常重要。

要想讲清楚宾补的概念以及意义，先要讲清楚句型 3，例如：

The dog is a German Shepherd Dog.（这只狗是德国牧羊犬。）

和一般的动词不同，is 这个动词可以翻译为"是"，它并没有告诉我们关于 the dog 的任何信息。谓语部分的动词本身没有内容，所有叙述的工作完全落在后面的 a German Shepherd Dog 身上。动词 is 只是把主语 The dog 和后面的 a German Shepherd Dog 串联起来而已。又例如：

The dog is dangerous.（这只狗很危险。）

这个句子翻译为中文是"这只狗很危险"。请注意，在这句话的中文翻译中，动词"是"根本就没有出现。这个例子充分显示了"是"这个动词是空的，完全没有任何意义。

由于所有翻译为"是"的动词都是没有意义的，只能把主语和后面的叙述部分串联起来，所以这些词也叫作"连系动词/系动词 (link verb)"。跟在这种动词后面的部分，因为其代替了动词应该扮演的叙述角色——补足句子使其产生完整的意思，所以称为"补语"，这里也叫主语的补语，简称"主补"。

了解主语补语的句型之后，宾语补语的句型就容易理解多了。主语补语的句型，是用补语来告诉读者主语"是"什么，中间用各种各样的"是（系动词）"串联起来。宾语补语的句型则是用补语来告诉读者宾语"是"什么，中间暗示有一个"是"的关系存在。例如：

James makes the question hard.

宾语 the question 和宾语补语 hard 之间虽然没有"是"字，但是其暗示了这种关系的存在。

值得注意的是，宾补在语义上通常表达的是谓语动词作用在宾语上的结果，例句中的 hard 就是 makes 的结果，该例句可以翻译为：

詹姆斯让这个问题变得很困难。

有以下几种结构可以作为宾语补足语：

- 形容词
- 介词短语（或动词不定式）
- 现在分词（当感官动词做谓语时，此结构才可以为宾补）
- 副词

若这些结构表达的是谓语动词作用在宾语上的结果，则它们一定是宾语补足语。请注意，补语是句子的主干信息（五种简单句句型中出现过的成分有主、谓、宾、补。但凡是简单句中出现过的成分都是主干信息，没出现过的定语、状语都是修饰成分，是次级信息），不可忽略。

1.5.2 复合句

复合句分为合句和复句两类。

1.5.2.1 合句

所谓合句 (Compound Sentences)，实际上就是用对等连接词（主要是 and、or 或 but）连接句子中任意两个对等的部分，也可以连接两个对等小句，例如：

(1) George and I play cards.（乔治和我打牌。）
(2) George, Mary, and I are good friends.（乔治、玛丽和我是好朋友。）
(3) We always work and play together.（我们总是一起工作、一起玩。）
(4) I eat bananas and apples.（我吃香蕉和苹果。）
(5) We take our holidays in July or August.（我们在七八月份度假。）

实际上，上述例句均是对等小句的省略形式，例如：句 (1) 是由 "George play cards and I play cards." 省略而来的。在对称的两个小句内，由于经常会有重复的部分，所以较为常见的形式是上述例句的形式。

1.5.2.2 复句

复句 (Complex Sentences) 是由两个以上的小句构成的，包括主句和从句。

在阅读句子时，我们只要有能力正确识别主句和从句，肯定就可以有效地抓取句子的主要信息（主句），同时减轻次要信息（从句）在脑中的分量。

主句本身是一个独立的小句，从句则需要有连词或关键词引导，放在主句中做名词（名词性从句）、状语（状语从句）或形容词（定语从句）。简而言之，开头有连词的就是从句，没有连词的就是主句。

名词性从句

名词性从句可以分为两种：由陈述句改造而来的和由疑问句改造而来的。

陈述句改造为名词性从句很简单，只需要在一个小句前面加上一个无意义的从属连接词 that，然后将其放在另一个小句中名词出现的位置上即可，例如：

(1) The study shows X.
(2) People are unhealthy.

将 (2) 前加入一个 that，形成 that people are unhealthy，并且填入 (1) 中 X（宾语）的位置，形如：

The study shows that people are unhealthy.（研究表明人们是不健康的。）

疑问句改造为名词性从句可以按照疑问句的类型分成两种——特殊疑问句 (information questions) 和一般疑问句 (Yes or No questions)。

由特殊疑问词 (who、which、what、when、why、how、where 等) 引导的疑问句成为特殊疑问句。对于这些疑问句来说，疑问词可以充当现成的从属连接词，所以只要将问号去掉即可成为一个从句。例如：

(3) What happened at Mary's party?
(4) James knew X.

将 (3) 直接填入 X 的位置，形如：

James knew what happened at Mary's party.（詹姆斯知道在玛丽的聚会上发生了什么。）

由于一般疑问句没有疑问词，例如：

Did I hurt Mary's feeling?

所以若想把一般疑问句改为名词性从句，我们就需要加上从属连接词 whether 或 if，例如：

(5) Did I hurt Mary's feeling?
(6) I doubt X.

去掉问号并且加入 whether 时需要把疑问句的动词还原，即 whether I hurt Mary's feeling。将这个句子放入 (6) 中，则有：

I doubt whether I hurt Mary's feeling.（我怀疑我是否伤害了玛丽的感情。）

从句做什么成分，我们就称其为什么从句。在上文中，所有的从句都是宾语从句。除了宾语从句外，还有表语从句和主语从句，例如：

(7) The question is whether they are able to help me.（问题是他们是否能帮助我。）
(8) That she is still alive is a consolation.（她还活着是一个安慰。）

同位语从句

在名词性从句中有一类较为特殊的从句。在复句中充当同位语的名词性从句称为同位语从句。从句做同位语表示与之同位的名词（短语）的实际内容，它的作用相当于名词。同位语从句本身和名词相等，并不是对名词的修饰。

同位语从句可以由 that、whether、when 等词引导，例如：

(1) We heard the news that our team had won.（我们听说了我们组获胜的消息。）
(2) The question whether we should call in a specialist was answered by the family doctor.（我们是否应该请专家由家庭医生来定。）

由于同位语从句的引导词和定语从句的引导词有四个是相同的 (that、when、where、why)，所以我们需要正确地区分定语从句和同位语从句。两者的区别在于：同位语从句的连接词（例如：that）本身无意义，在同位语从句中不充当任何成分，而定语从句的关系代词或关系副词在从句中一定会充当某种成分。例如：

(3) The fact that he had not said anything surprised everybody.（他没说任何事情这个事实让每个人都很惊讶。）
(4) The fact that you are talking about is important.（你正谈论的这个事实是很重要的。）

(3) 中的先行词 the fact 在从句中不做任何成分，其属于同位语从句；(4) 中的先行词 the fact

015

在从句中做 talk about 的宾语，其属于定语从句。我们会在后文中详细介绍定语从句的相关知识。

另外一种形式的同位语则是用名词对前文出现的词或者句子进行概括，例如：

(5) Mr. Wang, my child's teacher who is a class adviser, will be visiting us on Tuesday.

（王先生——我孩子的老师，是一位课程咨询师，周二他将来拜访我们。）

(6) Barbara McClintock discovered a new class of mutant genes, a discovery that led to greater understanding of cell differentiation.（芭芭拉·麦克林托克发现了突变基因的新序列，这个发现给细胞分化带来了更深层次的理解。）

(5) 中画线部分是 Mr. Wang 的同位语；who 引导的是修饰 teacher 的定语从句。

(6) 中画线部分则是 Barbara McClintock discovered a new class of mutant genes 的同位语；that 引导的是修饰 discovery 的定语从句。

状语从句

状语从句是三种复句（名词性从句、状语从句、定语从句）中最为简单的一种。它的构造和名词性从句基本相同，但是用法不同。名词性从句必须当作名词使用，在句子中必须放在主语、宾语或者补语等名词放置的位置。若删除名词性从句，则会出现语法错误。但是，状语从句则是副词性的，用来修饰主句，是一个可有可无的修饰语，整个删除往往也不会带来语法错误。

和名词性从句相同，状语从句也是由陈述句或疑问句改造而来的，并且两者的改造方式也相同，此处不再赘述。

状语从句和主句之间由连词连接，可以表示时间、条件、结果、原因、让步等。例如：

(1) When I was six, I went to school.（当我六岁的时候，我去上学了。）
(2) As the children walked along, they sang happily.（孩子们一边走一边高兴地唱着。）
(3) If the weather is fine, I will not stay at home.（如果天气很好，我就不会待在家里。）
(4) He did not go to Africa, for the weather is too hot there.（他没有去非洲，因为那里的天气太热了。）
(5) There is so much noise that we can not hear the teacher.（这里如此吵闹以致我们听不见老师讲话了。）

(6) Although he was tired, he had to stay up for work.（他虽然很累，但是还得坚持工作。）

例句中的画线部分均为状语从句。状语从句和主句实际上可以看成两个完全不同的分句，两个分句之间具有明确的关系。

除了这些比较简单的状语从句外，还有一种以 -ever 作为连接词的状语从句，例如：

Wherever you go, I will follow.（无论你去哪里，我都跟着。）

实际上，wh-ever 可以解释为 No matter wh-，表示让步，例如上面的例句等于：

No matter where you go, I will follow.（无论你去哪里，我都跟着。）

又例如：

Whoever (= No matter who) calls, I won't answer.（无论谁叫，我都不会答应。）
However (= No matter how) cold it is, he's always wearing a shirt only.（无论多冷，他都只穿一件衬衫。）
Whenever (= No matter when) you like, you can call me.（无论何时，你都可以给我打电话。）

定语从句

定语从句较其他形式的定语更为复杂，首先需要搞清楚两个概念：

> 先行词：被定语从句所修饰的词称为先行词。
> 关系词：定语从句的引导词称为关系词。关系词在复句中起到两个作用。一是通过其所指对象使得分句和主句之间产生联系，从而起到连接主从句的作用；二是在定语从句内部充当一定成分。

弄清了这些概念后，我们知道，由于关系词一定在定语从句内部充当成分，所以定语从句内部一定会缺失某些成分。换句话说，定语从句内部缺少哪种成分，那么关系词就会充当哪种成分。关系词几乎可以在定语从句内部充当任何成分。

关系词在从句内部可以充当主语、宾语、定语或表语。例如：

(1) The boy who loves the girl is my friend.（喜欢那个女孩儿的男孩儿是我的朋友。）
(2) The boy whom the girl loves is my friend.（那个女孩儿喜欢的男孩儿是我的朋友。）

(1) 中的 who 在定语从句内部充当 loves 的主语，(2) 中的 whom 在定语从句内部充当 loves 的宾语。

关系词还包括：where、when、why、in which 和 during which 等，其在定语从句内部充当状语。例如：

(3) You will never forget the day <u>when you first stepped into this classroom.</u>（你将永远不会忘记你第一次踏入这间教室的那一天。）

(4) He founded a library <u>in which the written remains of Greek literature could be gathered.</u>（他建立了一座可以收集希腊文学遗稿的图书馆。）

(3)(4) 的画线部分写成简单句为：

You first stepped into this classroom <u>in the day</u>.（就在这一天你第一次踏入这个教室。）
The written remains of Greek literature could be gathered <u>in a library</u>.（希腊文学遗稿能收集在一座图书馆里。）

请注意，"介词 +which（例如：in which / on which)"是定语从句的关系词，其只能引导定语从句；when 和 where 等还可以引导状语从句，在一个句子中，其究竟是定语从句还是状语从句需要我们看清其究竟修饰什么成分。若其修饰名词，则是定语；若其修饰动词，则是状语。

1.5.2.3　简化复句

除了最普通的从句外，GMAT 十分喜欢用简化复句的形式写出长难句。什么叫简化复句呢？顾名思义，简化复句是在语法上比正常复句更加简单的句子，也是英语使用者在使用一般复句后的熟练表现。

作为读者，我们需要准确地识别出简化后的从句形式，并且能在脑中迅速将其还原为一般从句，从而掌握句意。

▶ **定语从句省略关系词**

这种省略仅当关系词在定语从句中做宾语时才经常出现，其余情况下则通常不能省略关系词，例如：

简化前：The boy <u>whom the girl liked</u> is my friend.
简化后：The boy <u>the girl liked</u> is my friend.

这种省略在长难句中可谓屡见不鲜，大家请务必熟练识别，例如：

Many recent works by these scholars stress the ways in which differences among Renaissance women — especially in terms of social status and religion — work to complicate the kinds of generalizations <u>both Burckhardt and Kelly made on the basis of their observations about upper-class Italian women.</u>

画横线部分是 generalizations 的定语从句，由于先行词在定语从句中充当 made 的宾语，所以本句省略了 both 前应该有的关系词 that。正常的句子为：

Many recent works by these scholars stress the ways in which differences among Renaissance women — especially in terms of social status and religion — work to complicate the kinds of generalizations that <u>both Burckhardt and Kelly made on the basis of their observations about upper-class Italian women.</u>

简化定语从句

最为典型的简化定语从句的方法是将从句中的关系词去掉并且将动词变为分词，例如：

简化前：People <u>who play games</u> are my friends.
简化后：People <u>playing games</u> are my friends.

若定语从句是被动语态，则我们需要将动词变为过去分词，例如：

简化前：People, <u>who are called Jack,</u> are my friends.
简化后：People, <u>called Jack,</u> are my friends.

由于现在分词和过去分词长得很像是谓语动词的进行时和过去时（尤其是过去分词），所以在阅读长难句时，一定要避免将它们搞混，否则将会严重误读句子的重心，例如：

Circadian rhythms are the biological cycles that recur approximately every 24 hours in synchronization with the cycle of sunlight and darkness <u>caused by the Earth's rotation.</u>

本句的画线部分是一个过去分词短语，其可以看作 sunlight and darkness 的限制性定语从句，还原为正常的定语从句为：

Circadian rhythms are the biological cycles that recur approximately every 24 hours in synchronization with the cycle of sunlight and darkness <u>that are caused by the Earth's rotation.</u>

如果考生们在初次阅读时把 caused 误认为是谓语动词，那么这个句子的重心就会被完全理解歪了。

简化状语从句

简化状语从句的结果有两种：

伴随状语（使用条件：状语从句的主语和主句主语相同）
独立主格（使用条件：状语从句的主语和主句主语不同）

首先，如果状语从句的主语和其主句的主语相同，则其可以用伴随来表示：

简化前：When I sit in front of the door, I watch TV.
简化后：Sitting in front of the door, I watch TV.

简化前：Because the study is based on big data, the study is widely accepted.
简化后：Based on big data, the study is widely accepted.

从这两组例句可以发现，与主句主语相同的状语从句简化为伴随的方式是：去掉连词和从句的主语，之后表主动的变为现在分词，表被动的变为过去分词。

在某些情况下，我们可能会选择保留连词，例如：

简化前：While he was lying on the couch, the boy fell asleep.
简化后：While lying on the couch, the boy fell asleep.

为什么要保留连词 while 呢？这是因为连词除了具有连接的作用外，还有词义的功能，例如：if 和 while 就不同义。连词保留与否完全取决于修辞。

由此可知，如果我们在句首、句末，甚至句中看到由逗号与主句隔开的分词短语（包括前面带有连词的分词短语），则这些内容可能是伴随状语，可以看作普通的状语从句。（在句首和句末的伴随状语也可以不用逗号将其与主句隔开）。

其次，如果状语从句的主语和其主句的主语不相同，则其可以用独立主格来表示，例如：

简化前：Because the weather is fine, we decide to go to the park.
简化后：The weather being fine, we decide to go to the park.

由此例句可以看出，与主句主语不同的状语从句简化为独立主格的方式为：去掉连词后将从句的谓语动词变为分词。

在独立主格前也可以加上 with（只能加 with 这个介词，不能添加诸如 because of、due to 等别的介词），例如：

简化后：With the weather being fine, we decide to go to the park.

由此可知，如果我们在句首、句末，甚至句中看到由逗号与主句隔开的"(with)+ 名词 + 分词"的结构，则这些内容一定是独立主格，可以看作普通的状语从句。（在句首和句末的独立主格也可以不用逗号与其主句隔开）。

请注意，"简化定语从句"和"简化状语从句"这两个称谓其实不甚严谨。分词短语做定语或状语有普通从句表达不了的意义，例如：

A man standing at the window looked outside.

画线部分是 A man 的定语，其表示：在男子看窗外的每时每刻，他都站在窗户前面。

如果用普通的定语从句，无论该定语从句是哪种时态，均无法表达此含义。伴随状语和独立主格与状语从句的关系同理。本书为了描述简便和称谓统一，用了"简化"二字。

1.6 GMAT 长难句典型结构

了解了长难句可能出现的语法结构后，让我们一起来了解一下长难句中经常出现的结构。长难句之所以难，除了长度本身之外，主要集中在对这些结构的理解困难上。

1.6.1 长成分

长成分是长难句之所以长的重要因素之一，也是长难句中最常见的情况。主要表现为某一些成分极长，从而影响了我们对句子主干以及核心意思的把握，下面给出一个简单的例句：

Relational feminists, while agreeing that equal educational and economic opportunities outside the home should be available for all women, continued to emphasize women's special contributions.

例句中的画线部分是一个长达 17 个词的伴随状语，它将主语 Relational feminists 和谓语动词 continued to emphasize 隔开。类似于这样的伴随状语，因为其内容经常会被一前一后两个逗号隔开，所以将主语和谓语动词联系起来还是较容易的。但是，如果这种"明显"的插入语太多，也会让我们心烦不已，例如：

The gravity of a MACHO that had so drifted, astronomers agree, would cause the star's light rays, which would otherwise diverge, to bend together so that, as observed from the Earth, the star would temporarily appear to brighten, a process known as microlensing.

这句话中几乎所有的插入语都被一前一后两个逗号隔开了，但由于插入语过多，显得支离破碎。句子主干为：

The gravity of a MACHO would cause the star's light rays to bend together, so that the star would temporarily appear to brighten.

类似于上述有明显标志的长成分算是比较友好的。由于很多动词的过去分词和其过去式长相相同，现在分词和动名词长相相同，所以以简化定语从句（尤其是限制性定语）方式出现的长成分更加令人讨厌。如果考生稍有不慎，就会将过去分词看作谓语动词，将现在分词看作主语或宾语等主干成分（也就是看成动名词），例如：

The biological cycles recur approximately every 24 hours in synchronization with the cycle of sunlight and darkness caused by the Earth's rotation.

由于谓语动词 recur 是一般现在时，出现的位置又比较靠前，有些读者会"忽略"这个词，直接将后面的过去分词 caused 误认为是谓语动词，从而搞混了句子重心。该例句的主干为：

The biological cycles recur approximately every 24 hours.

又例如：

Like the grassy fields and old pastures that the upland sandpiper needs for feeding and nesting when it returns in May after wintering in the Argentine Pampas, <u>the sandpipers vanishing in the northeastern United States</u> is a result of residential and industrial development and of changes in farming practices.

这个句子中的 vanishing 不是动名词，画线部分的核心词是 the sandpipers，而不是 vanishing。这里的 vanishing 是现在分词，可以看作一个简化的定语从句，修饰 the sandpipers。

要想有效地避开长成分对理解主干句意的干扰，请大家务必学会将句子分层，继而按照层级读懂句子。具体的阅读方法将在 1.7 中详细讨论。

1.6.2 省略

省略在长难句中主要以两种形式出现：平行结构的重复成分省略和定语从句的关系词省略。平行结构的省略例如：

Hardy's weakness derived from his apparent inability to control the comings and goings of these divergent impulses and from his unwillingness to cultivate and sustain the energetic and risky ones.

画线部分其实是合句的后半部分，但是由于这半句中的 Hardy's weakness derived 与前半句相同，所以省略了这部分内容。

较难的平行结构省略如下：

Our current cartographic record relating to Native American tribes and their migrations and cultural features reflects the origins of the data and changes in United States government policy.

例句中有很多个连词 and，它们连接的对象是不同的，如果补全所有省略成分则如下：

Our current cartographic record relating to Native American tribes and relating to their migrations and their cultural features reflects the origins of the data, and our current cartographic record reflects changes in United States government policy.

对于这种省略成分较多且在语法上平行对象很多的句子，我们需要认真理解句意，搞清楚谁和谁是实质平行的。

所谓定语从句的关系词省略，正如前文所述，指的是当先行词在定语从句中充当宾语的时候，经常会省略关系词，例如（由于前文已经详细描述过，此处不再展开）：

Many recent works by these scholars stress the ways in which differences among Renaissance women — especially in terms of social status and religion — work to complicate the kinds of generalizations both Burckhardt and Kelly made on the basis of their observations about upper-class Italian women.

1.6.3 倒装

倒装句可以算得上是长难句中最为复杂难懂的一种结构了。在 GMAT 长难句中，会出现如下四种倒装。大家需牢记这些倒装结构，在阅读长难句时，做到快速识别，第一时间在大脑中勾画出正常语序。当然，这里所说的第一时间在大脑中勾画出正常语序仅仅是对现在的我们来说的。实际上，倒装这种语法现象是为了体现突出重点、美化语言表达等语用功能而出现的。在纯熟掌握概念后，我们会发现倒装就是"正常语序"，就是我们的习惯表达。到了这个时候，你距离征服长难句也就不远了。

1.6.3.1　助动词或 be 前移

第一种倒装方式是把助动词或 be 动词移到主语前面，普通动词不能移动因而无法倒装。这种倒装方式只适用于一种情况：由 if 引导的虚拟语气，可以选择将助动词或 be 动词倒装到主语前面，取代连接词 if。

这种倒装很简单，当条件状语从句中出现助动词或 be 动词时，就可以完成倒装。方法是直接把连接词 if 省略掉，把助动词或 be 动词移动到主语前面来替代连词，例如：

(1) If I were you, I would give Mary a cake.
(2) Were I you, I would give Mary a cake.

句 (1) 和句 (2) 完全相等。句 (2) 属于倒装结构。

长难句中的倒装实例如下：

Low levels of straying are crucial, since the process provides a source of novel genes and a mechanism by which a location can be repopulated should the fish there disappear.

例句中的画线部分是一个倒装的条件状语，还原为正常的复合句则如下：

Low levels of straying are crucial, since the process provides a source of novel genes and a mechanism by which a location can be repopulated, if the fish there should disappear.

1.6.3.2　助动词或 be 前移，普通动词加 do

第二种倒装方式是把助动词或 be 动词移动到主语前面。若只有普通动词，则在前面加助动词 do。这种倒装方式专门用于"否定副词前移 / 地点、范围介词短语前置"的情况，以配合否定句。

> **否定副词前移**

否定副词包括：hardly, in no way, little, scarcely, seldom, never, no more, no longer, not, not only, no sooner, not only … (but also), not until… 等，例如：

(3) I seldom go to work by bus.

(4) <u>Seldom</u> do I go to work by bus.

句 (3) 和句 (4) 完全相等。句 (3) 属于倒装结构。

● 地点、范围介词短语前置

表示地点或范围的介词包括：among，between，in，at，beneath 等，例如：

(5) The rate at which trees grow is believed to be among the surest indications on the Earth of sunspot cycles.

(6) <u>Among</u> the surest indications on the Earth of sunspot cycles is believed to be the rate at which trees grow.

句 (5) 和句 (6) 两个例句完全相等。句 (6) 属于倒装结构。

1.6.3.3　助动词或 be 前移，普通动词以助动词 do 取代，省略宾语

GMAT 考试中这样的倒装通常以比较级的形式出现，纯粹是为了修辞上的需要，没有任何"实际"意义。首先我们来看一个例句：

I eat more apples than you.

这句话是不准确的，因为有歧义的可能（我吃苹果比吃你多）。所以我们应该改成：

I eat more apples than you do.

这样就可以避免歧义。但是，如果 you 有定语修饰，例如：

I eat more apples than you, the president of USA, do.

如此一来，you 和 do 之间又相隔很远了，修辞上"不好看"，所以英语使用者们经常用倒装的结构来规避这个问题，例如：

I eat more apples than <u>do you</u>, the president of USA.

经过倒装，修辞的问题得以很好地解决。

此类倒装的长难句实例为：

Many oculists found that children who played computer games more than eight times a week were about four times more likely to suffer from Myopia than <u>were those who played no computer games at all</u>.

例句中的画线部分是一个倒装结构，正常语序为：

Many oculists found that children who played computer games more than eight times a week were about four times more likely to suffer from Myopia than those who played no computer games at all were.

1.6.3.4 纯粹为了躲避句子过长而倒装

从严格意义上来讲，这种情况不能算作语法的"倒装"。它们只是为了突出重点或者主干而做出的一定的语法妥协。主要分为两种类型："及物动词 + 介词"和"及物动词 + 形容词或副词"。

● 及物动词 + 介词

在某些词组的固定搭配下，会出现这种倒装结构。这些词组是由一个及物动词加一个介词组成的，例如：bring+to。正常语序一般为：bring A to B，但当 A 很长时，为了突出主干，其可能被倒装为 bring to B A 的结构，例如：

Five fledgling sea eagles left their nests in western Scotland this summer, bringing to 34 the number of wild birds successfully raised since transplants from Norway began in 1975.

本例句中的伴随状语部分，由于 the number of wild birds successfully raised since transplants from Norway began in 1975 的长度太长，按照正常语序写的话很可能会令读者忽视 to 34 这个部分，所以其将 to 34 直接放在 bring 的后面，完成倒装。

● 及物动词 + 形容词或副词

这种情况的产生原理与"及物动词 + 介词"一样，依旧是为了突出主干而倒装，例如：

Friedrich Engels predicted that women would be liberated from the "social legal, and economic subordination" of the family by technological developments that made possible the recruitment of "the whole female sex into public industry".

本句的画线部分是定语从句，先行词 technological developments 在该从句中充当主语。正确语序为：technological developments made the recruitment of "the whole female sex into public industry" possible.

另外，有些时候为了达到修辞的效果（例如：避免头重脚轻的情况），也可能会出现直接倒装的情况，例如：

The Achaemenid Empire of Persia brought with it the Aramaic script, <u>from which derive both the northern and the southern Indian alphabets</u>.

例句中的画线部分，合理的语序应该是：

from which both the northern and the southern Indian alphabets derive

综上所述，这种类型的倒装随意性较强，没有什么固定的原理或者现象，请大家在实战中多看，多记，多想。熟悉了自然就习惯了，也就不是阅读障碍了。

1.6.3.5　形式主语或形式宾语 it 引起的倒装

这种情况也是为了避免主语或宾语过长而经常使用的。例如：

It is clear <u>that we are healthy</u>.

例句原本是一个主语从句，由于主语相对于系动词和表语来说太长，所以引入了形式主语 it 来进行倒装，正常语序为：

<u>That we are healthy</u> is clear.

形式主语 it 也可以用于使役动词的后面，例如：

Cherry made <u>it</u> possible to attend the meeting.
Cherry made to attend the meeting possible.
Cherry made possible to attend the meeting.

这三个例句完全相同。

此类倒装的长难句实例为：

It is one of nature's great ironies <u>that the availability of nitrogen in the soil frequently sets an upper limit on plant growth even though the plants' leaves are bathed in a sea of nitrogen gas</u>.

正常语序为：

That the availability of nitrogen in the soil frequently sets an upper limit on plant growth even though the plants' leaves are bathed in a sea of nitrogen gas is one of nature's great ironies.

下面来看几个长难句中的倒装实例。

例句 1

Even a vastly more eco-efficient industrial system could, were it to grow much larger, generate more total waste and destroy more habitat and species than would a smaller, less eco-efficient economy.

分析：本句有两处倒装现象。一处是 were it to grow much larger，这个部分是一个条件句，正常语序为：if it were to grow much larger。另一处是比较中的倒装，正常语序为：...industrial system could ...and destroy more habitat and species than a smaller, less eco-efficient economy would.

译文：相比于一个更小的、生态效益程度不那么高的经济体，即使是一个生态效益程度高很多的工业系统，如果它大很多的话，也会产生更多的垃圾并且破坏更多的栖息地和物种。

例句 2

Thus, not only were decreased protein synthesis and amnesia dissociated, but alternative mechanisms for the amnestic action of puromycin were readily suggested.

分析：本句由于 not only 前置而引起了倒装，正常语序为：Thus, not only decreased protein synthesis and amnesia were dissociated, but alternative mechanisms for the amnestic action of puromycin were readily suggested.

译文：因此，不仅减少的蛋白质合成被证明与健忘症无关，而且有人可能提出了嘌呤霉素导致健忘行为的机制。

例句 3

Although these observations are true, Pessen overestimates their importance by concluding from them that the undoubted progress toward inequality in the late eighteenth century continued in the Jacksonian period and that the United States was a class-ridden, plutocratic society even before industrialization.

- **分析**：本句的倒装出现在 concluding 后面。正常的结构为 A conclude B from C。由于本句中 conclude 的宾语实在太长，所以写为 conclude from C B 的结构，正常语序为：concluding that the undoubted progress toward inequality in the late eighteenth century continued in the Jacksonian period and that the United States was a class-ridden, plutocratic society even before industrialization <u>from them</u>.

- **译文**：虽然这些发现是真实的，但是 Pessen 高估了它们的重要性，他通过这些发现断定，18 世纪晚期向着不平等发展的不容置疑的进程在 Jacksonian 时期仍然继续着，以及美国甚至在工业化之前就是一个受阶级支配的、财阀的社会。

例句 4

These historians, however, have analyzed less fully the development of specifically feminist ideas and activities during the same period.

- **分析**：本句的倒装部分在 analyze 的宾语部分。正常语序为：These historians, however, have analyzed the development of specifically feminist ideas and activities during the same period <u>less fully</u>.

- **译文**：但是这些历史学家对同一时期具体的女权思想和运动分析得较不充分。

例句 5

Noting that the Federal Reserve had raised a key short-term interest rate again last month, analysts said that they expected orders for durable goods to decline soon because rising interest rates make it more expensive to buy on credit.

- **分析**：本句的倒装部分出现在 because 这个从句中。该从句中的 it 是一个形式宾语，正常语序为：rising interest rates make <u>to buy on credit</u> more expensive.

- **译文**：注意到联邦储备系统上个月又上调了关键的短期利率，分析师称他们认为耐用品的订单将会很快下降，这是因为上升的利率使以信贷方式购买东西变得更贵。

1.7 句子读法——分层阅读

本节的标题没有写成"长难句读法"的原因是无论是长难句，还是较短的句子，都应该分层阅读。分层阅读是我们靠近母语阅读者的唯一途径。当然，对于较短的句子来说，分层对阅读理解力以及阅读速度的提升不如长难句那么明显。

什么是分层阅读呢？顾名思义，就是把一个句子分成不同层级来阅读。这里的不同层级表示了一句话中不同分量的成分。第一层的分量最高，是整个句子的主句。主句的从句是第二层信息，从句的从句是第三层信息，以此类推。层级越高，其表达的信息越次级，越可以忽略不计。对于绝大部分的长难句我们只需要掌握到第三层的语义即可，更高层级可以略读甚至不读（第三层就可以略读，更高层级的内容如果时间紧可以干脆放弃不读）。

对于大部分有语法基础的考生来说，如果允许读两遍甚至多遍，正确分层也不是难事。但是，由于考试的时间有限，我们必须在读某一层级的前几个词时就能预知接下来读到的将会是哪层的信息，这是比较难的。

例如：

Relational feminists, while agreeing that equal educational and economic opportunities outside the home should be available for all women, continued to emphasize women's special contributions.

1. 读到第一个词，由于其前面没有连词，所以几乎可以确定这个词应该是主句的主语，即第一层信息。
2. 读到 while agreeing，我们需要有能力迅速反应出它是一个伴随状语，可以看作一个简化的同其主句主语相同的状语从句。由此信息可知，后面要读到的内容均是状语从句（第二层信息）的内容，不是第一层信息，也不如第一层信息重要。大脑中需要时刻记住第一层信息只读了一个主语，还有谓语动词等更多的信息没有出现。
3. 读到 continued to emphasize，发现伴随状语已经结束，进入第一层信息的谓语动词部分，后面也是第一层内容。

正确的分层阅读例句要求我们熟悉伴随状语的"长相"并且知道它的本质。类似地，对于任何句子来说，正确的分层阅读均要求我们对 1.5 节所讲述的语法结构（尤其是简化复句）十分熟悉，并且通过一定量的练习，尽量做到对这些语法结构形成一种"条件反射"。

请注意，这里谈到的分层阅读，不是机械地按照语法结构来分层，而是要一边看意思一边做分层（这就是所谓的按照语法看懂句子）。这是因为，语法本身是用来承载语义的，如果不看语义，很多语法结构会产生歧义（即同样的结构可以有不同的功能），反而不利于阅读。例如，对上文例句稍做改变：

Relational feminists continued to emphasize women's special contributions agreeing that equal educational and economic opportunities outside the home should be available for all women.

从纯粹的语法结构上看，句末出现的 agreeing that 部分既可以做伴随状语（简化状语从句），又可以做 special contributions 的定语（简化定语从句）。只有知道这部分的语义是"同意提供给女性平等的教育和经济机会"，并且它描述的是"关系主义女权主义者(relational feminists)"的行为，我们才可以边读边确定这个部分是伴随状语。

按照这种读法，再多的插入语，再长的句子，相信你都能准确找到主干，并且又快又好地理解句意。

当然，这种读法并非一朝一夕之功，大家需要通过阅读足够多的难句，积攒语法知识和经验才能顺利地完成分层阅读。切记，一开始练习可能有些艰难，但千万不可半途而废。

以下 10 个例句先不要着急练习，请在按照第二章的要求做完长难句练习后再回过头来阅读这些例句。

例句 1

This preference for exogamy, Gutman suggests, may have derived from West African rules governing marriage, which, though they differed from one tribal group to another, all involved some kind of prohibition against unions with close kin.

阅读分析：

1. 由于句首没有连词，可知 preference 是第一层信息的主语。
2. 读到 Gutman suggests，其被一组逗号隔开，是插入语，属于第二层信息。读到此部分时需记住第一层信息还没有读完，该部分的信息相对于主句来说仅是次级信息，尽量把它们放在大脑的次要位置处理。
3. may have derived 是第一层信息的谓语动词。

4. 读到 governing marriage，由于其在语义上修饰的是 rules，所以是简化定语从句（governing 是现在分词），也属于第二层信息；读到此处可知第一层信息已完全结束（A derive from B 已经是一个完整的句子了，除非后面还有合句，否则第一层信息必然已经读完），作为初学者，我们需要在大脑中回顾第一层讲过的全部信息（这个步骤是初学者掌握句意的关键）。第一层给出的信息是：这种与外族通婚的偏好可能是来源于西非的规定。

5. 读到 which，可知其必然引导的是定语从句，理论上就近修饰 marriage，属于第三层信息。

6. though they differed from one tribal group to another 是定语从句内的让步状语，属于第四层信息，看看就行，无须深刻理解。

7. all involved 是定语从句内的谓语动词，后面是其宾语，由于其在逻辑上修饰的是 rules（只有这些 rules 才会有一些禁忌），所以修正步骤 5 的理解，which 引导的定语从句是修饰 rules 的，本句结束。

译文：这种与外族通婚的偏好，Gutman 认为，可能是来源于西非的相关婚姻规定，这些规定虽然在部落间不相同，但是都有一些对近亲结合的禁忌。

请注意，本例句是典型的需要边看语法边看句意的例句。步骤 5，由于定语从句的就近修饰原则，所以理应认为读到的 which 是修饰 marriage 的；步骤 7，读到了谓语，掌握了语义后，则修正 which 的修饰对象，乃至修正层级（修饰 marriage 的是第三层信息，修饰 rules 的则是第二层信息）。

例句 2

In the early 1950's, historians who studied preindustrial Europe (which we may define here as Europe in the period from roughly 1300 to 1800) began, for the first time in large numbers, to investigate more of the preindustrial European population than the 2 or 3 percent who comprised the political and social elite: the kings, generals, judges, nobles, bishops, and local magnates who had hitherto usually filled history books.

阅读分析：

1. 读到 historians，由于其前面没有连词，可以判断为第一层信息的主语。

2. who 引导一个定语从句，就近修饰先行词 historians，属于第二层信息。

3. 括号内的内容显然是在描述 preindustrial Europe，属于第三层信息，可以略读，此时需要记住我们第一层信息的谓语动词还没有出现，不要读着读着就忘了。

4. 读到 began 可知，这是第一层信息的谓语动词。

5. 由于 for the first time in large numbers 由一前一后两个逗号与主句隔开，所以其为插入语，属于第二层信息。

6. 跳过插入语可知，第一层信息的谓语动词为 began to investigate。

7. 读到 who comprised the political and social elite 可知，其为定语从句，就近修饰 the 2 or 3 percent，是第二层信息；读到此处可知第一层内容已完全结束（一般来说，investigate 是一个及物动词，后面只跟一个宾语），第一层给出的信息是：历史学家开始第一次大规模地研究工业化前欧洲的总人口而不是 2%～3% 的人口。

8. 冒号后是解释 the political and social elite 这个名词的内容，本句结束。

译文：在 20 世纪 50 年代早期，研究工业化前的欧洲（我们把工业化前的欧洲定义为 1300—1800 年这段时间内的欧洲）的历史学家开始第一次大规模地研究工业化前欧洲的总人口而不是组成政治和社会精英的 2%～3% 的人口。这些人是国王、将军、法官、贵族、主教，以及地方上的达官显贵，正是这部分人一直以来普遍充斥着历史书。

例句 3

Nitrogen fixation is a process in which certain bacteria use atmospheric nitrogen gas, which green plants cannot directly utilize, to produce ammonia, a nitrogen compound plants can use.

阅读分析：

1. 由于 Nitrogen fixation 前面没有连词，可以判断其为第一层信息的主语。

2. 读到 process 可以发现其后出现了定语从句的关系词 in which，可知第一层信息已经结束（由于谓语动词是系动词 is，process 为表语，表意已经完整）。第一层信息为：固氮是个过程。

3. 从 in which 开始是第二层信息，读到 which green plants cannot directly utilize 可知，其是非限制性定语就近修饰 atmospheric nitrogen gas，属于第三层信息，可以略读，此时需要记住第二层信息还没有讲完。

4. to produce ammonia 是第二层信息的宾语补足语，至此第二层信息结束。

5. a nitrogen compound plants can use 是 ammonia 的同位语从句，属于第三层信息，可以略读。

译文：固氮是个过程，在这个过程中特定的细菌利用大气中的氮气（这是绿色植物不能直接利用的）来产生氨——一种（植物可以利用的）氮的化合物。

例句 4

Perhaps the fact that many of these first studies considered only algae of a size that could be collected in a net (net phytoplankton), a practice that overlooked the smaller phytoplankton (nannoplankton) that we now know grazers are most likely to feed on, led to a de-emphasis of the role of grazers in subsequent research.

阅读分析：

1. 读到 the fact，由于前面没有连词（perhaps 是副词），可以判断其为第一层信息的主语。
2. 读到 that 引导的从句可知，由于其先行词 fact 是抽象名词，所以这个从句是同位语的可能性很大（参照同位语的定义）；再向下读，发现 fact 确实不在从句内部充当成分，所以该从句必为同位语从句，其告诉了读者这个事实究竟是什么。
3. that could be collected 是定语从句，就近修饰先行词 algae of a size，是第二层信息；此时需要记住我们的第一层信息只读了一个主语，还远没有结束。
4. 读到 a practice that 可知其也是一个同位语从句，同位其前面的限制性定语从句 that could be collected。
5. that we now know 是一个第三层定语从句（同位语从句和其先行词或先行句是一个层级的），就近修饰 the smaller phytoplankton，可以略读。
6. 读到 led to，终于可以找到第一层信息的谓语动词了，直接读完本句即可。

译文： 或许这个事实，即很多最初的实验只考虑了能被网捞起来的海藻（净浮游植物）。这种操作忽略了更小的我们现在知道食草动物最有可能食用的浮游植物（微型浮游生物），导致了在后续的研究中对食草浮游动物的角色不够重视。

例句 5

The correlation of carbon dioxide with temperature, of course, does not establish whether changes in atmospheric composition caused the warming and cooling trends or were caused by them.

阅读分析：

1. 由于 correlation 前面没有连词，可以判断其为第一层信息的主语。
2. 读到 whether，由于 establish 后面应该跟宾语，以 whether 开头的肯定是一个从句，可知要读的是宾语从句，属于第二层信息。回顾第一层信息：当然，二氧化碳和温度的相关性并不能确定一件事。

3. 这个宾语从句可以一直读下来，是一个由 or 连接的合句。

译文：当然，二氧化碳和温度的相关性并不能确定是大气构成的变化导致了气候变暖和变冷的趋势，还是由它们引起的。

例句 6

The historian Frederick J. Turner wrote in the 1890's that the agrarian discontent that had been developing steadily in the United States since about 1870 had been precipitated by the closing of the internal frontier—that is, the depletion of available new land needed for further expansion of the American farming system.

阅读分析：

1. 由于 The historian Frederick J. Turner 前面没有连词，可以判断其为第一层信息的主语。
2. 读到 that the agrarian discontent 可知，第一层谓语动词后面是一个从句（宾语从句），即第一层信息已经结束 (write 后面一般只有一个宾语)，其内容为：历史学家 Frederick J. Turner 在 1890's 写了一件事。
3. 读到 that had been developing 可知，该内容是 discontent 的定语从句，属于第三层信息，可以略读，需要记住第二层句子的谓语动词还没有出现，注意不要看漏。
4. had been precipitated 是第二层信息的谓语动词。
5. 破折号表示对前文的某一个词或者某一个句子的解释，通过阅读破折号后面部分的语义，可知其描述的是 the internal frontier 的内容，属于第三层信息，可以略读，至此本句结束。

译文：历史学家 Frederick J. Turner 在 19 世纪 90 年代写到，从大约 1870 年开始就一直在美国稳定发展的农民的不满被内部边界的关闭加剧了。内部边界的关闭是指美国农业系统的进一步扩张所需要的可用新土地的枯竭。

例句 7

What highly creative artistic activity produces is not a new generalization that transcends established limits, but rather an aesthetic particular.

阅读分析：

1. 读到 What 可以知道开端是一个主语从句，由此判断其为第一层信息的主语。

2. 读到 generalization 可以发现它的后面是一个由 that 引导的定语从句，该从句是第二层信息，至此可知第一层信息已经结束，其为：高创造性的艺术活动产出的东西不是一个新范例。

3. 读到 but rather an aesthetic particular，通过语义可知该部分应是由平行结构造成的省略。在逻辑上，A is not B but C 是本句应该有的结构，修正步骤 2 对第一层信息的理解，其为：高创造性的艺术活动产出的东西不是一个新范例，而是一个美学的特例。从逻辑上补全省略部分则有：What highly creative artistic activity produces is not a new generalization, but what highly creative artistic activity produces is rather an aesthetic particular.

译文： 高创造性的艺术活动产出的东西不是一个超越已有限制的新范例，而是一个美学的特例。

例句 8

They were fighting, albeit discreetly, to open the intellectual world to the new science and to liberate intellectual life from ecclesiastical philosophy and envisioned their work as contributing to the growth, not of philosophy, but of research in mathematics and physics.

阅读分析：

1. 由于 They 前面没有连词，可以判断其为第一层信息的主语。

2. 读到 and to liberate intellectual life 可知这里出现了由平行结构产生的省略现象，从逻辑上补全则有：They were fighting to open the intellectual world to the new science and they were fighting to liberate intellectual life from ecclesiastical philosophy.

3. 读到 and envisioned 可知这里又是一个由平行引起省略的现象，从逻辑上补全则有：They were fighting to do A and they envisioned their work as contributing to the growth. 至此，第一层信息结束，其内容为：他们在奋战做两件事并且把他们的工作看作贡献。

4. 在 growth 的定语里还有一个小的插入语 not of philosophy，但是这个比较简单，顺着读下去即可。

译文： 他们在奋战，尽管是谨慎地，打开学术界通向新科学的大门，以及把学术生活从宗教的哲学中解脱出来，并且他们把自己的工作看作是对数学和物理的，而不是对哲学的发展的贡献。

例句 9

Tolstoi's magical simplicity is a product of these tensions; his work is a record of the questions he put to himself and of the answers he found in his search.

阅读分析：

1. 读到分号可知本句由两个分句组成。
2. 读到 he put to himself 处，可以识别出该部分是一个省略了关系词 that 的定语从句（先行词必然在从句中充当宾语），是第二层信息。
3. 由 and 连接的两个部分是由平行结构引起的省略，从逻辑上补全则有：His work is a record of the questions and *his work is a record* of the answers.
4. he found in his search 也是一个省略了关系词 that 的定语从句，是第二层信息。
5. 由于本句较短，并且结构相对比较简单，故而可以直接从头读到尾。

译文：Tolstoi 富有魔力的简明性是这些紧张局势的产物；他的作品是一个充满了对自己提出问题的记录，也是一个在探索中寻找答案的记录。

例句 10

Upwards of a billion stars in our galaxy have burnt up their internal energy sources, and so can no longer produce the heat a star needs to oppose the inward force of gravity.

阅读分析：

1. Upwards of a billion stars in our galaxy 前面没有连词，可以判断其为第一层信息的主语。
2. 读到 and so 可知其后面是一个由平行造成的省略，从逻辑上补全则有：Upwards of a billion stars in our galaxy have burnt up their internal energy sources, and so *upwards of a billion stars in our galaxy* can no longer produce the heat. 第一层的意思是：我们星系中超过 10 亿个星体已经燃尽了它们的内部能源，不再能产生热量。
3. a star needs to oppose the inward force of gravity 前省略了 that，该部分是 the heat 的限制性定语从句，是第二层信息。

译文：我们星系中超过 10 亿个星体已经燃尽了它们的内部能源，不再能产生星体所需要的用来对抗向内引力的热量了。

第二章

长难句详解

仅仅掌握了第一章给出的难句构成原理不足以帮我们战胜长难句，真正征服长难句仍需要辅以一定量的练习。本章的目的就是提供这"一定量的练习"。

建议大家将本章的所有例句从第一句至最后一句阅读至少三遍，方法如下：

第一遍：

顺序阅读本章给出的每一个长难句。读完一个句子，按照第一章讲述的方式给这个句子分层（当然，如果第一遍没看懂，可以再看第二遍，直到看懂并且分层完成为止）。完成分层工作并且读懂语义后，同正确答案及译文对比，检查是否有错误或遗漏。碰到不懂的地方，不要马上寻求译文和解释的帮助，请再多看几遍句子，尽最大努力自己弄懂各层级的功能及语义。如果读了很多遍后依然无法理解，则再去寻求译文和解释的帮助，这会使得你的记忆更加牢固和深刻。

一个句子完成后，不要立刻阅读下一句。要坚持再多看几次这个句子，根据"难点分析"里写的内容，熟悉甚至记忆这个句子中出现的难点及其体现方式，保证下次再看到类似的结构时可以快速识别和联想。是否能读懂句子，尤其是长难句，经验具有决定性的影响。因此，请务必确保阅读每个句子都能积累新的经验。当你感觉到"这个结构怎么又来了，我都看到过很多次了"时，恭喜你，你距离彻底征服长难句已经不远了。

本次阅读完成后，请练习阅读 1.7 中的 10 个例句，检查自己能否在只读一遍的情况下对长难句进行正确分层。

第二遍：

第一遍阅读后，相信大家都会积累下不少经典的长难句结构。第二遍的阅读要求大家在读完每一句后，有能力在阅读遍数尽量少的情况下背诵出该句的第一层和第二层信息。这次阅读主要是训练大家将语法和语义结合的能力，不能本末倒置地只按照语法分层而不读语义（正如第一章所讲，语法是为了承载语义的，不读语义很多语法是存在歧义的）。

第三遍：

阅读长难句，应以读意思为主，分析语法为辅。本次阅读要求读者"忘掉"语法，也忘掉"层级"，直接阅读语义。在实际阅读中，没有人会想如何给句子分层（就像我们读中文从来不分层一样）。通过这三次的练习，我们需要将分层的思想融入大脑中，使其成为一种语言的阅读习惯，反复强化后，再读句子时，分层已经不用再刻意为之，而是潜移默化。

通过这三次的阅读训练，理解难句的水平必会产生质变，加油！

本章所有例句的分析格式如下：

方括号 [X] 表示定语、尖括号 <X> 表示状语、圆括号（X）表示同位语/同位语从句、不加括号表示主干成分、变色部分表示上一层出现过的词（一般是定语从句的先行词）或省略的成分。难度系数从 C 至 A 依次上升 (A 类中还有一些 S 级的句子，那些是更为难懂的句子）。

为了方便大家由易到难地阅读，所有的长难句均按难度进行分类。

C 组

01

Scientists long believed that two nerve clusters in the human hypothalamus, called suprachiasmatic nuclei (SCNs), were what controlled our circadian rhythms.

难度系数：C-

语句结构及读法：

第一层：Scientists long believed X.

第二层：X = that two nerve clusters in the human hypothalamus, [Y$_1$], were Y$_2$

第三层：Y$_1$ = two nerve clusters in the human hypothalamus is called suprachiasmatic nuclei (SCNs)

Y$_2$ = what controlled our circadian rhythms

译　文：科学家们一直认为两个在人体下丘脑内的神经丛（它们被称为 SCN）是那些控制我们昼夜节律的东西。

难点分析：

本句只有一个难点，即 Y$_1$ 是一个简化的定语从句，其使得宾语从句中的主语 two nerve clusters 和系动词 were 相隔较远。

02

Circadian rhythms are the biological cycles that recur approximately every 24 hours in synchronization with the cycle of sunlight and darkness caused by the Earth's rotation.

难度系数：C

语句结构及读法：

第一层：Circadian rhythms are the biological cycles [X].

第二层：X = the biological cycles recur approximately every 24 hours in synchronization with the cycle of sunlight and darkness [Y]

第三层：Y = the cycle of sunlight and darkness is caused by the Earth's rotation

译　文：昼夜节律是一个与阳光和黑暗循环（这个循环是由地球自转所引起的）同步的大概每 24 小时重现一次的生物循环。

难点分析：

　　X 中的谓语动词 recur 不常见，加之 Y 是一个被动语态的"简化定语从句"（可以看作 that is caused by the Earth's rotation），过去分词 caused 和其过去式长相完全相同，因此初学者可能会把 recur 理解为名词，把 caused 理解为 X 这一定语从句中的谓语动词，从而无法准确理解句子的重心及语义。

03

While the most abundant and dominant species within a particular ecosystem is often crucial in perpetuating the ecosystem, a "keystone" species, here defined as one whose effects are much larger than would be predicted from its abundance, can also play a vital role.

难度系数：C

语句结构及读法：

第一层：<X₁>, a "keystone" species, [X₂], can also play a vital role.

第二层：X₁ = While the most abundant and dominant species [within a particular ecosystem] is often crucial in perpetuating the ecosystem

　　　　X₂ = a "keystone" species is defined as one [Y]

第三层：Y = one's effects are much larger than would be predicted from its abundance

译　文：虽然大部分在一个特定的生态系统中丰富且具有统治性的物种经常在保持生态系统方面非常重要，但是 keystone（这个物种产生的影响远大于根据其丰富程度预估的影响）也能扮演一个重要的角色。

难点分析：

主句中藏着的非限制性定语 X_2 是本句的一大难点。

首先，考生需要识别出它是一个简化的定语从句，可以看作：

A "keystone" species, which here is defined as one whose effects are much larger than would be predicted from its abundance, can also play a vital role.

其次，由于这个非限制性定语很长，使得主句主语 a "keystone" species 和谓语动词 play 相隔较远，不易厘清主干。

04

Many environmentalists, and some economists, say that free trade encourages industry to relocate to countries with ineffective or poorly enforced antipollution laws, mostly in the developing world, and that, in order to maintain competitiveness, rich nations have joined this downward slide toward more lax attitudes about pollution.

难度系数：C+

语句结构及读法：

第一层：Many environmentalists, and some economists, say X_1 and X_2.

第二层：X_1 = free trade encourages industry to relocate to countries [with ineffective or poorly enforced antipollution laws], [mostly in the developing world]

X_2 = <in order to maintain competitiveness> rich nations have joined this downward slide [toward more lax attitudes about pollution]

译　　文：很多环境学家和一些经济学家说："自由贸易鼓励工厂把厂房安置在那些反污染法较为薄弱的国家，当然这些国家大部分是发展中国家。并且，为了保持竞争力，发达（富裕）国家也加入到了这种对污染更加漠视的态度中。"

难点分析：

第一层是一个由 and 连接的合句，由于前半句很长，有些初学者可能读到第二个宾语从句的 that (and that, in order to maintain competitiveness) 时就已经不知道这个 that 是干什么的了，从而误解了后半句的重要性。

05

Our first studies sought to determine whether the increase in serotonin observed in rats given a large injection of the amino acid tryptophan might also occur after rats ate meals that change tryptophan levels in the blood.

难度系数：C

语句结构及读法：

第一层：Our first studies sought to determine X.

第二层：X = whether the increase in serotonin [Y_1] might also occur <Y_2>

第三层：Y_1 = the increase in serotonin is observed in rats [Z_1]

Y_2 = after rats ate meals [Z_2]

第四层：Z_1 = rats are given a large injection of the amino acid tryptophan

Z_2 = meals change tryptophan levels in the blood

译　　文：我们的初步研究试图去确定被注射了大量氨基酸色氨酸的老鼠体内的 5- 羟色胺上升是否也可能在老鼠吃了改变血液中的色氨酸含量的食物之后发生。

难点分析：

典型的修饰套修饰的长句，很难一口气读到尾。除"长"外，Y_1 和 Z_1 均是简化定语从句，其中识别 Y_1 部分较难，因为 observe 的过去式和过去分词都是 observed，容易被误认为是第二层信息中的谓语动词。

06

This declaration, which was echoed in the text of *the Fourteenth Amendment*, was designed primarily to counter the Supreme Court's ruling in *Dred Scott v. Sandford* that black people in the United States could be denied citizenship.

难度系数：C

语句结构及读法：

第一层：This declaration, [X_1], was designed primarily to counter the Supreme Court's ruling in *Dred Scott v. Sandford* (X_2).

第二层：X_1 = this declaration was echoed in the text of *the Fourteenth Amendment*

X_2 = that black people in the United States could be denied citizenship

译　　文：这项声明被写入《第十四条修正案》中，主要旨在反对最高法院对德雷德·斯科特诉桑福德案的裁决（这个裁决是：生活在美国的黑人可以被剥夺公民权）。

难点分析：

第一，X_1 这个定语从句使主语 declaration 和谓语 was designed 相隔较远，不容易读懂。

第二，X_2 是一个同位语从句，它并非修饰最近的 *Dred Scott v. Sandford* 这个专有名词，而是修饰 ruling 的。这是因为只有国会的裁决才能规定生活在美国的黑人是否可以被剥夺公民权（从语法的角度来说，同位语从句的先行词也必须是抽象名词）。英语句子会尽量避免这种"跳跃修饰"，但由于某些句法难以改变，这样的情况也偶有发生，这要求大家一定不能只看语法结构，要融合语法和语义，让它们共同作用。

07

Opponents of white-tiger breeding programs argue that white tigers are merely Indian tigers—a subspecies well represented in both zoos and the wild—and that zoos should focus their tiger management efforts on preserving subspecies whose existence is threatened, thus preventing the Chinese and Indochinese tiger subspecies from joining the Javan, Balinese, and Caspian subspecies in extinction.

难度系数：C

语句结构及读法：

第一层：Opponents of white-tiger breeding programs argue X_1 and X_2.

第二层：X_1 = that white tigers are merely Indian tigers — (Y_1)

X_2 = that zoos should focus their tiger management efforts on preserving subspecies [Y_2], <Y_3>

第三层：Y_1 = a subspecies (that is) well represented in both zoos and the wild

Y_2 = preserving subspecies' existence is threatened

Y_3 = zoos thus prevent the Chinese and Indochinese tiger subspecies from joining the Javan, Balinese, and Caspian subspecies in extinction

译　　文：反对施行养殖白虎项目的人认为：白虎仅仅是印度虎——一个在动物园和野外均存在的亚种，并且动物园应该把它们管理老虎的重点集中于保存那些栖息地受到威胁的亚种中，由此可以保护中国和印度支那虎亚种不与爪哇、巴厘岛和里海亚种一起受到灭绝的威胁。

难点分析：

本句的难点主要在于长度较长，尤其是 argue 的两个宾语从句 (X_1 和 X_2)，一口气不容易读下来。第三层的 Y_3 是一个简化状语从句（伴随状语），可以看作主语与主句相同的状语从句。

08

Through 1840, simple enumeration by household mirrored a home-based agricultural economy and hierarchical social order: the head of the household (presumed male or absent) was specified by name, whereas other household members were only indicated by the total number of persons counted in various categories, including occupational categories.

难度系数： C

语句结构及读法：

第 一 层：Through 1840, simple enumeration by household mirrored a home-based agricultural economy and hierarchical social order: (X).

第 二 层：X = the head of the household (presumed male or absent) was specified by name, <Y>

第 三 层：Y = whereas other household members were only indicated by the total number of persons [Z_1], [Z_2]

第 四 层：Z_1 = the total number of persons is counted in various categories

Z_2 = including occupational categories

译　　文： 1840年按家庭所做的简单的统计是一个以家庭为基础的农业经济和等级社会秩序的真实写照：户主（一般被认为是男性或者没有）是具体到姓名的，而其他家庭成员仅仅被表示为按各种类别（包括职业类别）计算的总人数。

难点分析：

第一，冒号后面出现的内容通常是解释说明前面的某个名词或者句子，因此可以归到同位语这个成分中。

第二，including 这个词比较特殊，本身是介词性质，加名词构成介词短语，做定语。

09

Because women were seen as belonging to the private rather than to the public sphere, the discovery of documents about them, or by them, did not, by itself, produce history acknowledging the contributions of women.

难度系数： C-

语句结构及读法：

第一层：<X_1>, the discovery of documents [X_2] did not, by itself, produce history [X_3].

第二层：X₁ = Because women were seen as belonging to the private rather than to the public sphere

X₂ = documents about them or documents by them

X₃ = history acknowledged the contributions of women

译　文：因为女性被看作属于私人领域而不是公共领域，所以发现的那些关于她们的文档或者她们写的文档不能提供承认女性贡献的历史。

难点分析：

本句在"长难句"中应该算是短句了，它的难度主要在于主句中的插入成分非常多，在第一次看的时候容易被这些插入成分迷惑从而无法弄清句子的主干信息。其次，大家需要识别出 X₃ 部分是简化定语从句，是次级信息。

10

Advanced technology is being transferred ever more speedily across borders, but even with the latest technology, productivity and wages in developing countries will remain lower than in developed countries for many years because developed countries have better infrastructure and better-educated workers.

难度系数：C-

语句结构及读法：

第一层：X₁ but X₂.

第二层：X₁ = Advanced technology is being transferred ever more speedily across borders

X₂ = even with the latest technology, productivity and wages in developing countries will remain lower than in developed countries for many years, <Y>

第三层：Y = because developed countries have better infrastructure and better-educated workers

译　文：先进的技术正在世界范围内更快速地传播，但是就算是使用最新的技术，发展中国家的产量和工资依然低于发达国家很多年，这是因为发达国家拥有更好的基础设施和受到更高等教育的工人。

难点分析：

虽然有 40 多个词，但是本句其实比较简单。由于句中没有插入的修饰成分，所以稍有经验的读者就可以在几乎没有任何阻碍的情况下从头读到尾。

11

The explanation they consider most plausible is behavioral differences between extinct and present-day carnivores — in particular, more contact between the teeth of predators and the bones of prey due to more thorough consumption of carcasses by the extinct species.

难度系数：C+

语句结构及读法：

第一层：The explanation [X_1] is behavioral differences between extinct and present-day carnivores — (X_2).

第二层：X_1 = they consider the explanation most plausible

X_2 = in particular, more contact [between the teeth of predators and the bones of prey] [due to more thorough consumption of carcasses by the extinct species]

译　文：他们认为最有道理的解释是已灭绝的食肉动物和现存的食肉动物习性不同——特别是：已灭绝的食肉动物由于吃猎物吃得更加彻底，所以它们的牙齿和猎物的骨骼有更多的接触。

难点分析：

第一，they consider most plausible 是一个定语从句，由于先行词 the explanation 做 consider 的宾语，所以此处省略了关系词 that。

第二，破折号后出现了同位语 more contact，解释说明前面的名词 behavioral differences；contact 后面又出现两个修饰 contact 的定语。

12

Traditional social science models of class groups in the United States are based on economic status and assume that women's economic status derives from association with men, typically fathers or husbands, and that women therefore have more compelling common interest with men of their own economic class than with women outside it.

难度系数：C

语句结构及读法：

第一层：X_1 and X_2.

第二层：X_1 = Traditional social science models of class groups in the United States are based on economic status

X_2 = traditional social science models of class groups in the United States assume Y_1 and Y_2

第三层：Y_1 = that women's economic status derives from association with men, (typically fathers or husbands)

Y_2 = that women therefore have more compelling common interest with men of their own economic class than with women outside it

译　文：美国阶层的传统社会科学模型是基于经济状况的，并且，它假设了两件事，一是女性的经济状况来自于和男性（比如：父亲或者丈夫）的联系，二是女性因此与同经济阶层的男性比与不同经济阶层的女性具有更加令人信服的共同兴趣。

难点分析：

本句的难点主要在于两个很长的宾语从句。读者们需要了解 Y_1 和 Y_2 是合句，均是 assume 的宾语，分量相同。

13

Social historian Mary Ryan, for example, has argued that in early-nineteenth-century America the identical legal status of working-class and middle-class free women outweighed the differences between women of these two classes: married women, regardless of their family's wealth, did essentially the same unpaid domestic work, and none could own property or vote.

难度系数：C-

语句结构及读法：

第一层：Social historian Mary Ryan, for example, has argued X.

第二层：X = that in early-nineteenth-century America the identical legal status of working-class and middle-class free women outweighed the differences between women of these two classes：(Y)

第三层：Y = Z_1 and Z_2

第四层：Z_1 = married women, regardless of their family's wealth, did essentially the same unpaid domestic work

Z_2 = none could own property or vote

译　文：举例来说，社会历史学家 Mary Ryan 争辩说："在 19 世纪早期的美国，工人阶级和中层阶级自由女性同等的法律状态盖过了两个阶级女性的不同：已婚女性，无论她们的家庭财富如何，都做着本质上一样无报酬的家务劳动，并且不可以拥有财产和投票权。

难点分析：

第一个难点在 X 句中，状语 in early-nineteenth-century America 和其主句之间没有逗号，初学者可能会认为它们都是主语。第二个难点依然在 X 句，X 句是一个简单的 SVO 结构，但是主语和宾语较长，需要准确理解此句主干为：identical legal status outweighed the differences。

14

Although northeasters are perceived to be less destructive than other storms, the high waves associated with strong northeasters can cause damage comparable to that of a hurricane, because they can affect stretches of coast more than 1,500 kilometers long, whereas hurricanes typically threaten a relatively small ribbon of coastline — roughly 100 to 150 kilometers.

难度系数：C

语句结构及读法：

第一层：<X_1>, the high waves [X_2] can cause damage comparable to that of a hurricane, <X_3>.

第二层：X_1 = Although northeasters are perceived to be less destructive than other storms

　　　　X_2 = the high waves are associated with strong northeasters

　　　　X_3 = because they can affect stretches of coast more than 1,500 kilometers long, <Y>

第三层：Y = whereas hurricanes typically threaten a relatively small ribbon of coastline—roughly 100 to 150 kilometers

译　文：虽然东北风被认为比其他暴风雨的破坏性更弱，但是由强东北风带来的高波可以产生等同于飓风的破坏，因为它们可以影响超过 1 500 千米长的海岸线，而飓风一般会威胁相对更窄的海岸线——100 ~ 150 千米。

难点分析：

本句的从句较多，但实际难度不算大。当然，这么长的句子本身就是一个难点，因为我们的大脑无法短时间记住这么多信息，读到最后可能就忘了主句是什么了。这样类似的句子对我们的分层能力要求较高，在阅读过程中需要我们知道现在读的是哪层信息，是否重要，该不该深刻记忆。除了长之外，唯一的难点就

是 X_2，这是一个简化的被动语态的定语从句，可以看作：the high waves <u>that are</u> associated with strong northeasters。

15

While there is no blueprint for transforming a largely government-controlled economy into a free one, the experience of the United Kingdom since 1979 clearly shows one approach that works: privatization, in which state-owned industries are sold to private companies.

难度系数：C+

语句结构及读法：

第一层：<X_1>, the experience of the United Kingdom since 1979 clearly shows one approach [X_2].

第二层：X_1 = While there is no blueprint for transforming a largely government-controlled economy into a free one

X_2 = one approach works: (Y)

第三层：Y = privatization, [Z]

第四层：Z = state-owned industries are sold to private companies in privatization

译　文：虽然没有计划从政府控制的经济转变成自由经济，但是英国自从 1979 年的经验表明有一个有效的方法：私有化（就是把政府拥有的产业卖给私人公司）。

难点分析：

while 引导的状语从句较长，在 blueprint 的定语部分存在一个 SVOO 的结构，即 blueprint transforms <u>economy</u> into <u>a free one</u>。

16

These staff members believe their point of view is closer to the original philosophy of MESBIC and they concerned that, unless a more prudent course is followed, MESBIC directors may revert to policies to the disappointing results of the original SBA approach.

难度系数：C

语句结构及读法：

第一层：X_1 and X_2.

第二层：X_1 = These staff members believe Y_1

X_2 = they concerned Y_2

第三层：Y_1 = that their point of view is closer to the original philosophy of MESBIC

Y_2 = that, <Z_1>, MESBIC directors may revert to policies to the disappointing results of the original SBA approach

第四层： Z_1 = unless a more prudent course is followed

译　　文： 这些员工相信他们的观点更加接近于 MESBIC 的原始理念，并且他们关心的是：除非有一个更加严谨的做法，否则 MESBIC 的经理们可能会把政策恢复到原 SBA 方法产生的那些令人失望的结果中去。

难点分析：

本句的难点主要在于 Y_2 的理解。Y_2 是一个 SVOO 句型，即 directors revert to policies to results。画线部分是 revert to 这个及物动词短语的两个宾语。很多考生可能由于对 revert to 这个词组不熟悉而看 policies 后面的 to results 十分别扭，无法理解句意。实际上，revert to 的意思是：恢复。本句的意思是：把政策恢复到结果上。

17

It appears that in areas where weak currents and weak tidal energies allow the accumulation of sediments, mangroves will follow land formation and accelerate the rate of soil accretion; succession will proceed according to Davis' scheme.

难度系数： C+

语句结构及读法：

第一层： It appears X.

第二层： X = that in areas [Y], mangroves will follow land formation and accelerate the rate of soil accretion; succession will proceed according to Davis' scheme.

第三层： Y = weak currents and weak tidal energies allow the accumulation of sediments in areas

译　　文： 在那些弱水流和弱潮汐允许沉淀物积累的地方，红树林似乎会随着土地的构成来生长并且将会加速土壤的堆积；根据 Davis 的构想，更替将会继续进行。

难点分析：

第一层是一个倒装句，读者们需要识别出 it 是形式主语，它是为了避免主语从句过长而产生，正常语序为：X appears。第二个难点在于 areas 的定语部分很长，让 X 中真正的主干出现的时间较晚，不容易弄清楚主干。

18

According to Davis' scheme, the shoreline is being extended in a seaward direction because of the "land building" role of mangroves, which, by trapping sediments over time, extend the shore.

难度系数：C-

语句结构及读法：

第一层：According to Davis' scheme, the shoreline is being extended in a seaward direction, <X>.

第二层：X = because of the "land building" role of mangroves [Y]

第三层：Y = mangroves, by trapping sediments over time, extend the shore

译　文：根据 Davis 的构想，由于红树林（它是通过长时间的固化沉淀物来扩张海岸的）建造土地的角色，海岸线正在沿着朝海的方向扩张。

难点分析：

本句难点主要在于 Y 这个定语从句中有一个方式状语 by trapping sediments over time。这个插入语使得先行词和定语从句中的谓语动词相隔较远。

19

In current historiography, the picture of a consistent, unequivocal decline in women's status with the advent of capitalism and industrialization is giving way to an analysis that not only emphasizes both change (whether improvement or decline) and continuity but also accounts for geographical and occupational variation.

难度系数：C

语句结构及读法：

第一层：In current historiography, the picture [X_1] is giving way to an analysis [X_2].

第二层：X_1 = of a consistent, unequivocal decline in women's status with the advent of capitalism and industrialization

X_2 = not only Y_1 but also Y_2

第三层：Y_1 = an analysis emphasizes both change (whether improvement or decline) and continuity

Y_2 = an analysis accounts for geographical and occupational variation

053

译　　文： 在当前的史学界，伴随着资本主义和工业化的到来而一贯明确的女性地位下降的现象让位于一种分析，这种分析不仅同时强调了变化（提升还是下降）和连续性并且也说明是地域和职业变化的原因。

难点分析：

第一层的主语长达 17 个词，令我们很难找准其中的核心词 picture；第三层信息是 an analysis 的定语从句，该从句本身也是一个复句，由 not only…but also 这个连词引导，长度也很可观，一口气很难读下来。

20

In her influential *Women Workers and the Industrial Revolution* (1930), Pinchbeck argued that the agricultural revolution of the eighteenth and early nineteenth centuries, with its attendant specialization and enlarged scale of operation, curtailed women's participation in the business of cheese production.

难度系数： C

语句结构及读法：

第一层： In her influential *Women Workers and the Industrial Revolution* (1930), Pinchbeck argued X.

第二层： X = that the agricultural revolution of the eighteenth and early nineteenth centuries, <Y>, curtailed women's participation in the business of cheese production

第三层： Y = with its attendant specialization and enlarged scale of operation

译　　文： 在她有影响力的《女工与工业革命》（1930 年）中，Pinchbeck 辩论说："18 世纪和 19 世纪早期的农业革命，随着其专业化和操作领域的扩大，削减了女性对奶酪生产业的参与度。"

难点分析：

插入语 Y 是一个介词短语，做状语修饰 curtail。它的存在使得 X 中的主语 revolution 和谓语动词 curtail 相隔较远。当然，curtail（削减，缩短）这个词的词义理解与否也会左右对本句语义的理解。在阅读理解考题中，类似于这种长得像认识的，但是仔细一想又不知道什么意思的词汇非常影响对句意的掌握，请大家在背单词的过程中一定要格外留心对这些词词义的记忆。

21

In the case of cheese, the rise of factors may have compromised women's ability to market cheese at fairs, but merely selling the cheese did not necessarily imply access to the money: Davidoff cites the case of an Essex man who appropriated all but a fraction of the money from his wife's cheese sales.

难度系数：C+

语句结构及读法：

第一层：X_1 but X_2.

第二层：X_1 = In the case of cheese, the rise of factors may have compromised women's ability to market cheese at fairs

X_2 = merely selling the cheese did not necessarily imply access to the money: (Y)

第三层：Y = Davidoff cites the case of an Essex man [Z]

第四层：Z = an Essex man appropriated all but a fraction of the money from his wife's cheese sales

译　文：在奶酪这个事例中，因素的增加可能损害了女性在市场上售卖奶酪的能力，但是仅仅是卖奶酪并不意味着和"钱"有联系：Davidoff 列举了一个埃塞克斯男人的例子，他从妻子卖奶酪的收入中挪用了大部分钱。

难点分析：

第一，X_2 和 X_1 的关系是合句关系，其主语 merely selling the cheese 是一个动名词短语。由于该动名词短语和现在分词短语长相相同，有些读者读到这里可能以为其是一个伴随状语，进而错误理解层级，直到读至谓语动词 did not imply 才恍然大悟，然后重新理解。

第二，Z 中的谓语动词 appropriate 的意思不好理解。大家都很熟悉它的形容词意义（适当的），但是基本没见过以动词出现的这个词。其做动词的意义为"侵吞；占用；拨（专款等）"。appropriate A from B 这个句型的意思是：从 B 中挪用 A。

22

The very techniques these historians used to uncover mass political behavior in the nineteenth century United States — quantitative analyses of election returns, for example — were useless in analyzing the political activities of women, who were denied the vote until 1920.

难度系数：C+

语句结构及读法：

第一层：The very techniques [X_1] were useless in analyzing the political activities of women, [X_2].

第二层：X₁ =these historians used the very techniques to uncover mass political behavior in the nineteenth century United States—(quantitative analyses of election returns), for example X₂ =women were denied the vote until 1920

译　　文：这些历史学家用来揭示19世纪美国众多政治行为的技术（比如，大部分针对选举结果的定量分析）在分析女性的政治活动方面是没有用处的（女性直到1920年还没有投票权）。

难点分析：

第一，X₁是省略了关系词的定语从句。由于先行词the very techniques 在 X₁中做 use 的宾语，所以省略了关系词that，正常结构为：The very techniques that these historians used to uncover mass political behavior were useless.

第二，由于X₁这个定语从句很长，所以被隔开的主句主语the very techniques 和谓语动词 were useless 也影响了读者的理解。

23

Du Bois's wartime position reflected not a change in his long-term goals but rather a pragmatic response in the face of social pressures: government officials had threatened African American journalists with censorship if they continued to voice grievances.

难度系数： C

语句结构及读法：

第一层：Du Bois's wartime position reflected not a change in his long-term goals but rather a pragmatic response in the face of social pressures: (X).

第二层：X = government officials had threatened African American journalists with censorship, <Y>

第三层：Y = if they continued to voice grievances

译　　文：Du Bois 在战争时期的观点并不是对他长期目标的改变，而是对社会压力的一种实际的反应：政府官员曾用审查来威胁非洲裔美国记者，如果他们继续发牢骚的话。

难点分析：

通常状语从句和其主句之间会由逗号隔开，但是本句中Y和其主句之间没有逗号。请注意，在英语中，状语从句和主句之间可以有逗号，也可以没有逗号，两者完全相等，不改变语义。

24

If a company is already effectively on a par with its competitors because it provides service that avoids a damaging reputation and keeps customers from leaving at an unacceptable rate, then investment in higher service levels may be wasted, since service is a deciding factor for customers only in extreme situations.

难度系数：C

语句结构及读法：

第一层：<X_1>, then investment in higher service levels may be wasted, <X_2>.

第二层：X_1 = If a company is already effectively on a par with its competitors <Y>

X_2 = since service is a deciding factor for customers only in extreme situations

第三层：Y = because it provides service [Z_1 and Z_2]

第四层：Z_1 = service avoids a damaging reputation

Z_2 = service keeps customers from leaving at an unacceptable rate

译　文：如果一家公司已经很有效地与它的竞争对手相提并论了（因为它提供的服务避免了毁坏声誉，并且阻止客户以一个不可接受的比率流失），那么对更高的服务等级的投资可能是一种浪费，因为仅仅在极端情况下，服务对于客户来说才是一个决定因素。

难点分析：

本句最难的部分在于理解词组 on a par with 的意思。这个词组的意思是"相提并论"。另外，本句的从句数量较多，并且开头的这个条件状语的长度惊人，令我们不容易找到主句，难以判断句子重心。

25

Apparently these low-surface-brightness galaxies, as they are called, take much longer than conventional galaxies to condense their primordial gas and convert it to stars—that is, they evolve much more slowly.

难度系数：C-

语句结构及读法：

第一层：X_1—X_2. (X_2 在解释 X_1)

第二层：X₁ = Apparently these low-surface-brightness galaxies, <Y>, take much longer than conventional galaxies to condense their primordial gas and to convert it to stars

X₂ = that is, they evolve much more slowly

Y = as they are called

译　　文：很明显，这些表面亮度低的星系，正如它们被称作的那样，要比传统的星系花费更长的时间来凝聚它们的原始气体并且将其转化为恒星——这个意思是，它们进化得更慢。

难点分析：

由于原句中省略了 convert 前的 to，所以我们需要通过逻辑判断这个 convert 究竟是和 take 平行，还是和 condense 平行。显然，convert 应该和 condense 平行。

26

That many terrestrial snakes in similar spatial orientations do not experience this kind of circulatory failure suggests that certain adaptations enable them to regulate blood pressure more effectively in those orientations.

难度系数：C

语句结构及读法：

第一层：X₁ suggests X₂.

第二层：X₁ = That many terrestrial snakes in similar spatial orientations do not experience this kind of circulatory failure

X₂ = that certain adaptations enable them to regulate blood pressure more effectively in those orientations

译　　文：许多位于相似空间位置的陆生蛇不会面临血液循环方面的问题，这表明某些适应性能使它们在那些空间位置上更有效地调节血压。

难点分析：

本句的主语和宾语均是较长的从句，它们的存在使得谓语动词 suggests 很不明显，令初学者难以抓住这个核心动词。

27

This view may be correct: it has the advantage that the currents are driven by temperature differences that themselves depend on the position of the continents.

难度系数：C-

语句结构及读法：

第一层：This view may be correct: (X).

第二层：X = it has the advantage (Y)

第三层：Y = that the currents are driven by temperature differences [Z]

第四层：Z = temperature differences themselves depend on the position of the continents

译　文：这种观点可能正确：它具备这样的优点，即涌流由温度差异驱动，这些温度差异本身又依赖于大陆板块的位置。

难点分析：

本句中的 it 所指代的对象容易让人产生误解。在语法上，它既可以指代前面出现过的 this view，也可以是一个形式主语，指代 the advantage 后面的从句。我们必须通过本句的语义来判断它真正的指代对象。显然，拥有优势的肯定是 this view，可以通过前半句 this view may be correct 推断出来。Y 是 advantage 的同位语从句，该同位语从句中还套上了 Z 这个 differences 的定语从句。

28

Anthropologists studying the Hopi people of the southwestern United States often characterize Hopi society between 1680 and 1880 as surprisingly stable, considering that it was a period of diminution in population and pressure from contact with outside groups, factors that might be expected to cause significant changes in Hopi social arrangements.

难度系数：C

语句结构及读法：

第 一 层：Anthropologists [X_1] often characterize Hopi society between 1680 and 1880 as surprisingly stable, <X_2>.

第二层：X_1 = anthropologists study the Hopi people of the southwestern United States

　　　　X_2 = anthropologists consider [Y]

第三层：Y = that it was a period of diminution in population and pressure from contact with outside groups, (Z)

第四层：Z = factors that might be expected to cause significant changes in Hopi social arrangements（diminution 和 pressure 的同位语）

译　　文：研究美国西南部霍皮人的人类学家经常把在 1680 年和 1880 年之间的霍皮人社会描述为令人惊讶的稳定，他们认为这是一个人口减少、面临与外部群体接触的压力（人口减少、面临与外部群体接触的压力是一些被认为会引起霍皮人社会安排发生重大变化的因素）的时期。

难点分析：

整个主句是一个很长的 SVOC 结构，X$_1$ 是混入该结构中的简化定语从句，可以看作：anthropologists <u>who</u> study the Hopi people。第一层信息的主干为：Anthropologists characterize Hopi society as surprisingly stable. X$_2$ 是一个简化状语从句。另外，本句出现的从句较多，因此层级也较多，会让初学者有一种怎么读也读不完的感觉。

29

The new school of political history that emerged in the 1960's and 1970's sought to go beyond the traditional focus of political historians on leaders and government institutions by examining directly the political practices of ordinary citizens.

难度系数：C

语句结构及读法：

第一层：The new school of political history [X$_1$] sought to go beyond the traditional focus of political historians on leaders and government institutions <X$_2$>.

第二层：X$_1$ = the new school of political history emerged in the 1960's and 1970's

X$_2$ = by examining directly the political practices of ordinary citizens（X$_2$ 其实不是一个从句，此处单独列出仅仅是因为这个方式状语太长，影响我们对主干的理解。）

译　　文：出现于 20 世纪 60 年代和 20 世纪 70 年代的政治史的新流派力求通过直接考察普通公民的政治实践行为来超越政治历史学家的传统关注点（这个关注点是在领导层和政府机构上的）。

难点分析：

主句的宾语部分包含了 11 个词，增大了找准宾语核心词的难度。宾语的核心词为 focus，整个宾语的意思是：政治史的新流派在领导层和政府机构上的传统关注点。

30

Other experiments revealed slight variations in the size, number, arrangement, and interconnection of the nerve cells, but as far as psychal neural correlations were concerned, the obvious similarities of these sensory fields to each other seemed much more remarkable than any of the minute differences.

难度系数：C

语句结构及读法：

第一层：X_1 but X_2.

第二层：X_1 = Other experiments revealed slight variations in the size, number, arrangement, and interconnection of the nerve cells

X_2 = <Y>, the obvious similarities of these sensory fields to each other seemed much more remarkable than any of the minute differences

第三层：Y = as far as psychal neural correlations were concerned

译　文：尽管其他实验显示神经细胞的大小、数量、排列和相互连接有微小的差异，但是，就心理和神经的关系来说，这些感官区域彼此间明显的相似性看起来要远比它们之间的细微差异更加引人注目。

难点分析：

本句的难点主要在于插入语的加入使得句子主干被肢解。Y 是一个状语，隔开了合句 X_1 和 X_2。另外，X_2 句中的比较对象由于相隔成分较多也会令初学者感到困惑，真正的比较对象为 similarities 和 differences。

31

With respect to their reasons for immigrating, Cressy does not deny the frequently noted fact that some of the immigrants of the 1630's, most notably the organizers and clergy, advanced religious explanations for departure, but he finds that such explanations usually assumed primacy only in retrospect.

难度系数：C+

语句结构及读法：

第一层：X_1 but X_2.

第二层：X_1 = <With respect to their reasons for immigrating>, Cressy does not deny the frequently noted fact (Y)

X_2 = he finds that such explanations usually assumed primacy only in retrospect

第三层：Y = that some of the immigrants of the 1630's, most notably the organizers and clergy, advanced religious explanations for departure

译　文：关于他们移民的理由，Cressy 并没有否认一个经常提到的事实：一些 17 世纪 30 年代的移民者，最突出的是组织者和神职人员，提出宗教理由来解释这种离境活动，但是他发现，这样的解释通常只有在事后回顾时才占据主导地位。

难点分析：

本句的难点主要集中在 Y 这样一个很长的同位语从句中。这个同位语从句使得合句 X_1 和 X_2 的距离相隔较远。在 Y 中，immigrants 的同位语 the organizers and clergy 同样把其主句 immigrants 和谓语动词 advanced 隔开，造成了一定的理解难度。

32

Japanese immigrants, on the other hand, were less constrained, made the transition from sojourners to settlers within the first two decades of immigration, and left low-wage labor to establish small businesses based on a household mode of production.

难度系数： C

语句结构及读法：

第一层：X_1, X_2, and X_3.

第二层：X_1=Japanese immigrants, on the other hand, were less constrained

X_2=Japanese immigrants made the transition from sojourners to settlers within the first two decades of immigration

X_3=Japanese immigrants left low-wage labor to establish small businesses [Y]

第三层：Y=small businesses is based on a household mode of production

译　文：另一方面，日本移民受到的限制相对较小，在移民的前 20 年内从暂居者转变为定居者，并且不再从事薪水低的工作，开始从事以家庭作坊为基础的小本生意。

难点分析：

第一层信息是三者并列的并列句。由于各个成分较长，让人有种一口气怎么读也读不完的感觉。另外，在句末出现了一个简化定语从句 (Y)，based 是过去分词，不可误以为是动词的过去式。

33

In the periods of peak zooplankton abundance, that is, in the late spring and in the summer, Haney recorded maximum daily community grazing rates, for nutrient-poor lakes and bog lakes, respectively, of 6.6 percent and 114 percent of daily phytoplankton production.

难度系数：C+

语句结构及读法：

第一层： In the periods of peak zooplankton abundance, (X), Haney recorded maximum daily community grazing rates, for nutrient-poor lakes and bog lakes, respectively, of 6.6 percent and 114 percent of daily phytoplankton production.

第二层： X = that is, in the late spring and in the summer

译　文： 在浮游动物数量的高峰期，也就是晚春和夏天，Haney 记录了贫养湖和沼泽湖每日群体捕食的最大速率，分别是浮游植物日产量的 6.6% 和 114%。

难点分析：

本句层级不多，也不算长，但是插入语较多，影响了句子语义的连贯性。X 可以算是一个非限制性定语从句，只不过这里的用法不太"标准"，最为标准的用法是：In the periods of peak zooplankton abundance, which is in the late spring and in the summer...另外，community grazing rates 和其定语 of 6.6 percent 被插入语 for nutrient-poor lakes and bog lakes, respectively 隔开，增加了句意的理解难度。

34

Historians such as Le Roy Ladurie have used the documents to extract case histories, which have illuminated the attitudes of different social groups (these attitudes include, but are not confines to, attitudes toward crime and the law) and have revealed how the authorities administered justice.

难度系数：C

语句结构及读法：

第一层：Historians such as Le Roy Ladurie have used the documents to extract case histories, [X].

第二层：X＝Y_1 and Y_2

第三层：Y_1＝case histories have illuminated the attitudes of different social groups (these attitudes include, but are not confines to, attitudes toward crime and the law)

Y_2＝case histories have revealed how the authorities administered justice

译　　文：像 Le Roy Ladurie 这样的历史学家们使用这些记录来提出个案史，这些个案说明了不同社会团体的态度（这些态度包括但不仅限于对犯罪和法律的态度），并且揭示了当权者是如何管理司法的。

难点分析：

本句主要的难点是平行结构的省略。第二层中，Y_2 由于和 Y_1 的主语相同，因而出现了省略的现象。另外，different social groups 后面有一个插入语，割裂了原本连贯的句意，但由于该插入语两端有括号作为提示，所以较为简单。

35

Indeed, one indication of the movement's strength is the fact that its most distinguished critic, Richard A. Posner, paradoxically ends up expressing qualified support for the movement in a recent study in which he systematically refutes the writings of its leading legal scholars and cooperating literary critics.

难度系数：C+

语句结构及读法：

第一层：Indeed, one indication of the movement's strength is the fact (X).

第二层：X = that its most distinguished critic, Richard A. Posner, paradoxically ends up expressing qualified support for the movement in a recent study [Y]

第三层：Y = he systematically refutes the writings of its leading legal scholars and cooperating literary critics in a recent study

译　　文：确实，一个能反映这场运动强烈程度的事实是：这场运动中最杰出的评论人

064

Richard A. Posner，最终矛盾地在最近的一项研究中表达了自己对这场运动有条件的支持，在这项研究中他系统地反驳了这场运动中领军的法律学者和协同的文学评论家的著作。

难点分析：

本句的难点不在于有多少长成分，而是句中这些抽象名词对于一些不熟悉法律或对社会学完全没有感觉的读者来说简直是一个灾难。另外，end up doing sth. 并不是一个常见的词组，它的意思是"最终做了……"。这句话的主要意思落在了一个矛盾上，即在一个反驳某观点的报告中支持了这个观点。

36

Most striking among the many asymmetries evident in an adult flatfish is eye placement: before maturity one eye migrates, so that in an adult flatfish both eyes are on the same side of the head.

难度系数： C+

语句结构及读法：

第一层：Most striking among the many asymmetries evident in an adult flatfish is eye placement: X.

第二层：X = before maturity one eye migrates, \<Y\>

第三层：Y = so that in an adult flatfish both eyes are on the same side of the head

译　　文：在成年比目鱼所展现出的很多不对称中，眼睛的位置是最引人注目的：在成熟以前，一个眼睛迁移了，以致在一条成年比目鱼的身上，两只眼睛在脑袋的同一侧。

难点分析：

本句的难点主要在于倒装。本质上，正如我们在上一章中所述的，当形容词放在句首时，主语和谓语发生倒装。所以本句的正常语序为：Eye placement is most striking among the many asymmetries evident in an adult flatfish. 倒装后形容词部分很长，在一定程度上增加了阅读的困难。

37

Monopoly power is the ability of a firm to raise its prices above the competitive level—that is, above the level that would exist naturally if several firms had to compete—without driving away so many customers as to make the price increase unprofitable.

难度系数：C

语句结构及读法：

第一层：Monopoly power is the ability of a firm to raise its prices above the competitive level —(X)— without driving away so many customers as to make the price increase unprofitable.

第二层：X = that is, above the level [Y]

第三层：Y = the level would exist naturally <Z>

第四层：Z = if several firms had to compete

译　文：垄断权力是指一家公司将其商品价格抬高到竞争水平之上的能力——如果几家公司不得不竞争，那么价格就会自然提高——而不会流失大量的顾客使得价格增长毫无利润可图。

难点分析：

本句中破折号之间的插入成分极长，在一定程度上影响了第一层信息的连贯性。第一层信息实际上仅仅是：Monopoly power is the ability. 这个垄断权力是什么能力？必然是 a firm to raise its prices above the competitive level without driving away so many customers 的能力。由此可知，without 部分是 raise 的状语。

38

In *The Weary Blues*, Hughes chose to modify the traditions that decreed that African American literature must promote racial acceptance and integration, and that, in order to do so, it must reflect an understanding and mastery of Western European literary techniques and styles.

难度系数：C+

语句结构及读法：

第一层：In *The Weary Blues*, Hughes chose to modify the traditions [X].

第二层：X = Y_1 and Y_2

第三层：Y_1 = the traditions decreed that African American literature must promote racial acceptance and integration

　　　　Y_2 = the traditions decreed that, in order to do so, it must reflect an understanding and mastery of Western European literary techniques and styles

译　文：在《萎靡的布鲁斯》这部著作中，Hughes 选择改变某些传统：这些传统规定非裔美国人的文学必须促进种族之间的接纳和融合，并且，为了达到这个目的，它们还规定非裔美国人的文学必须反映自身对西欧文学技巧和风格的了解与掌握。

难点分析：

本句的难度在于平行结构的省略。Y_1 和 Y_2 是 decree 的两个宾语从句，即传统分别规定了两件事。此外，本句中还出现了一些较为生僻和抽象的词汇，增加了阅读句子的难度。

39

They are called virtual particles in order to distinguish them from real particles, whose lifetimes are not constrained in the same way, and which can be detected.

难度系数：C+

语句结构及读法：

第一层：They are called virtual particles in order to distinguish them from real particles, [X].

第二层：X = Y_1, and Y_2

第三层：Y_1 = real particles' lifetimes are not constrained in the same way

　　　　　Y_2 = real particles can be detected

译　文：为了和实粒子区分开，它们被称为"虚粒子"；实粒子的生命期受到制约的方式不同，并且可以被探测到。

难点分析：

本句的难点主要在于第二层有些奇怪的语法结构。由 whose 和 which 引导的两个句子均是定语从句，都修饰先行词 real particles，理论上两者之间直接添加 and 即可，无须在 and 前再添加逗号，本句偏偏添加了逗号，令人很不习惯。

40

In order for the far-ranging benefits of individual ownership to be achieved by owners, companies, and countries, employees and other individuals must make their own decisions to buy, and they must commit some of their own resources to the choice.

067

难度系数：C

语句结构及读法：

第一层：X_1 and X_2.

第二层：X_1 = In order for the far-ranging benefits of individual ownership to be achieved by owners, companies, and countries, employees and other individuals must make their own decisions to buy

X_2 = they must commit some of their own resources to the choice

译　文：为了使个人所有权的深远益处被所有者、公司和国家获得，雇员和其他人必须做出自己的购买决定，而且他们必须为其抉择付出自己的财富。

难点分析：

本句有两处难点。第一处出现在句首状语的部分。实际上，如果这个部分出现在某些大家熟悉的结构中，是不难理解的，例如：It is possible <u>for Mary to help James</u>. 该例句的画线部分在功能上相当于一个从句，即：<u>That Mary helps James</u> is possible. 类比于本句，其状语部分相当于：in order <u>that the far-ranging benefits of individual ownership are achieved by owners</u>。

第二处是 X_2 中的 commit A to B 这一词组的意思不好理解。该词组的意思是"为了某目的 B 而付出某代价 A"。

41

Other theorists propose that the Moon was ripped out of the Earth's rocky mantle by the Earth's collision with another large celestial body after much of the Earth's iron fell to its core.

难度系数：C+

语句结构及读法：

第一层：Other theorists propose X.

第二层：X = that the Moon was ripped out of the Earth's rocky mantle by the Earth's collision with another large celestial body <Y>

第三层：Y = after much of the Earth's iron fell to its core

译　文：其他的理论学家认为：在地球上的大部分铁落入地核后，地球同其他大型天体的撞击把月球从地球的岩石状地幔中撕裂出来了。

难点分析：

> 本句的难点主要在于判断 Y 这个"时间状语"真正的修饰对象。它究竟是修饰名物化后的事件 collision 的，还是修饰动词 was ripped 的呢？做出正确判断要求我们不能只看语法，必须要边读边理解本句的逻辑意思。这里按时间顺序来看，Y 这个时间状语应该修饰 collision：铁落入地核→地球和其他天体相撞击→月球被撕裂出来。

42

Such philosophical concerns as the mind-body problem or, more generally, the nature of human knowledge they believe, are basic human questions whose tentative philosophical solutions have served as the necessary foundations on which all other intellectual speculation has rested.

难度系数：C+

语句结构及读法：

第一层：Such philosophical concerns as the mind-body problem or, more generally, the nature of human knowledge [X_1], are basic human questions [X_2].

第二层：X_1 = they believe the nature of human knowledge

　　　　X_2 = human questions' tentative philosophical solutions have served as the necessary foundations [Y]

第三层：Y = all other intellectual speculation has rested on the necessary foundations

译　文：这些哲学关注的问题，例如：意识和物质的问题，或者更广泛地，他们所认为的人类知识的本质，是某些基本的人类问题，这些问题的实验性哲学解释是其他所有理性思考所基于的必要基础。

难点分析：

本句从句较多，让人感觉一口气很难读下来。

第一，X_1 是一个简化定语从句，正常的定语从句为：the nature of human knowledge that they believe。另外，这个定语从句修饰的并不是离其最近的词 knowledge，而是 nature，这要求我们以理解语义为第一标准，不要拘泥于语法中所谓的就近修饰原则。

第二，主语 philosophical concerns 和其系表结构 are basic human questions 相隔较远，不易联系起来。

43

The isotopic composition of lead often varies from one source of common copper-ore to another, with variations exceeding the measurement error; and preliminary studies indicate virtually uniform isotopic composition of the lead from a single copper-ore source.

难度系数： C

语句结构及读法：

第一层： X_1; X_2.

第二层： X_1 = The isotopic composition of lead often varies from one source of common copper-ore to another, <with variations exceeding the measurement error>

X_2 = and preliminary studies indicate virtually uniform isotopic composition of the lead from a single copper-ore source

译　文： 铅的同位素构成在常见的铜矿之间经常各不相同，这种不同超过了测量误差；而且初步的研究显示，从同一个铜矿源中得到的铅的同位素构成一致。

难点分析：

本句结构比较简单，是一个由分号连接的合句。难点主要在于抽象名词太多，又基本都是科学类的，所以短时间内不容易理解。另外，X_1 中最后部分 with variations exceeding the measurement error 是独立主格结构，可以看作主语与主句不同的普通状语从句的简化。

44

Inheritors of some of the viewpoints of early twentieth-century Progressive historians such as Beard and Becker, these recent historians have put forward arguments that deserve evaluation.

难度系数： C

语句结构及读法：

第一层： (Inheritors of some of the viewpoints of early twentieth-century Progressive historians such as Beard and Becker), these recent historians have put forward arguments [X].

第二层： X = arguments deserve evaluation

译　文： 作为像 Beard 和 Becker 这样的 20 世纪早期的进步派历史学家某些观点的后继者，这些近来的历史学家们提出了一些值得我们评价的观点。

难点分析：

在 GMAT 的长难句中，大部分的同位语都是以后置的方式出现。本句则截然相反，同位语 inheritors 前置于其修饰的对象 these recent historians，并且这个同位语的长度还很长，增加了理解的难度。意思是：这些近来的历史学家们是 Beard 和 Becker 的后继者 (inheritors)。

45

Despite these difficulties, there has been important new work that suggests that this symbiotic association can be harnessed to achieve more economical use of costly superphosphate fertilizer and to permit better exploitation of cheaper, less soluble rock phosphate.

难度系数： C+

语句结构及读法：

第一层：Despite these difficulties, there has been important new work [X].

第二层：X＝new work suggests Y

第三层：Y＝Z_1 and Z_2

第四层：Z_1＝this symbiotic association can be harnessed to achieve more economical use of costly superphosphate fertilizer

Z_2＝this symbiotic association can be harnessed to permit better exploitation of cheaper, less soluble rock phosphate

译 文： 虽然有这些困难，但还是有些重要的新研究。这些新研究显示这种共生结合可以被用来实现昂贵的过磷酸钙肥料更大的经济用途，并且允许更好地利用更便宜而且较不可溶的磷酸岩。

难点分析：

本句的难点主要集中在平行结构的省略上。平行的两者 to achieve more economical use of costly superphosphate fertilizer 和 to permit better exploitation of cheaper, less soluble rock phosphate 相隔较远。另外，本句中出现的词汇较为专业，也增加了理解的难度。

46

It is frequently assumed that the mechanization of work has a revolutionary effect on the lives of the people who operate the new machines and on the society into which the machines have been introduced.

难度系数：C

语句结构及读法：

第一层：It is frequently assumed X.

第二层：X = Y_1 and Y_2

第三层：Y_1 = the mechanization of work has a revolutionary effect on the lives of the people [Z_1]

Y_2 = the mechanization of work has a revolutionary effect on the society [Z_2]

第四层：Z_1 = people operate the new machines

Z_2 = the machines have been introduced into the society

译　文：据经常假设，工作的机械化对那些操作新机器的人们的生活以及引入机器的社会有着革命性的影响。

难点分析：

第一，it 是一个形式主语，是由于原本的主语太长而引起的倒装现象，正常语序为：That the mechanization of work has a revolutionary effect on the lives of the people and on the society is frequently assumed.

第二，在 X 中出现了一个平行结构的省略现象。平行对象为 on the lives of the people 和 on the society, on the society 前省略了 the mechanization of work has a revolutionary effect。

47

Mores, which embodied each culture's ideal principles for governing every citizen, were developed in the belief that the foundation of a community lies in the cultivation of individual powers to be placed in service to the community.

难度系数：C+

语句结构及读法：

第一层：Mores, [X_1], were developed in the belief (X_2).

第二层：X₁ = mores embodied each culture's ideal principles for governing every citizen

X₂ = the foundation of a community lies in the cultivation of individual powers [Y]

第三层：Y = individual powers are placed in service to the community

译　文：道德——体现了每种文化管辖每个公民的理想原则——是发展于某种信念之下的，这种信念是：一个社会的基础在于培养那些被定位为这个社会服务的个人力量。

难点分析：

本句的难点主要体现在出现了许多语义较为抽象的名词以及长成分较多。X₁ 的出现使得第一层信息的主语 mores 和其谓语动词 were developed 相隔较远。另外，Y 原本是一个动词不定式，这个动词不定式做 individual powers 的后置定语。

48

In the waters between the United States and Japan, the starry flounder populations vary from about 50 percent left-eyed off the United States West Coast, through about 70 percent left-eyed halfway between the United States and Japan, to nearly 100 percent left-eyed off the Japanese coast.

难度系数： C+

语句结构及读法：

第一层：In the waters between the United States and Japan, the starry flounder populations vary from X₁, through X₂, to X₃.

第二层：X₁ = about 50 percent left-eyed off the United States West Coast

X₂ = about 70 percent left-eyed halfway between the United States and Japan

X₃ = nearly 100 percent left-eyed off the Japanese coast

译　文：在美国和日本之间的水域里，星鲽的种群是不同的。在美国西海岸大约 50% 的星鲽眼睛在左边，在美国和日本之间的中部水域大约 70% 的星鲽眼睛在左边，在日本海岸几乎 100% 的星鲽眼睛都在左边。

难点分析：

一般来说，大家都很熟悉短语 vary from A to B（从 A 变到 B）。但是，由于本句中的 A 和 B 都很长，并且中间还插入了一个 through X₂，这让一个简单的短语变成了一个复杂的结构，读到最后已经忘了前面的内容。

073

49

That theory maintains that a density wave of spiral form sweeps through the central plane of a galaxy, compressing clouds of gas and dust, which collapse into stars that form a spiral pattern.

难度系数：C

语句结构及读法：

第一层：That theory maintains X.

第二层：X = that a density wave of spiral form sweeps through the central plane of a galaxy, <Y>

第三层：Y = a density wave of spiral form compresses clouds of gas and dust, [Z]

第四层：Z = clouds of gas and dust collapse into stars that form a spiral pattern

译　文：那个理论坚持认为：一个螺旋式的密度波从一个星系的中心面掠过，压缩气体和尘土构成了云状物，这些云状物的崩塌形成了螺旋形态的恒星。

难点分析：

句首出现的 that 很容易让人以为是一个主语从句。很多人可能直到把句子整个读完才反应过来这个 that 是一个代词，指"那个原理"。另外，Y 是一个伴随状语，可以看作一个主语与其主句主语相同的状语从句的简化。

50

However, none of these high-technology methods are of any value if the sites to which they are applied have never mineralized, and to maximize the chances of discovery the explorer must therefore pay particular attention to selecting the ground formations most likely to be mineralized.

难度系数：C+

语句结构及读法：

第一层：X_1 and X_2.

第二层：X_1 = However, none of these high-technology methods are of any value <Y_1>

$X_2 =$ <to maximize the chances of discovery> the explorer must therefore pay particular attention to selecting the ground formations [Y_2]

第三层：$Y_1 =$ if the sites [Z] have never mineralized

　　　　$Y_2 =$ the ground formations are mineralized

第四层：$Z =$ they are applied to the sites

译　文：然而，如果应用高科技的地点从未被矿化，那么这些高科技方法没有任何价值；为了最大限度地提升发现的机会，探矿者必须特别注意选择最有可能被矿化的地形构成。

难点分析：

英文习惯把条件状语放在开头，主句放在后面。本句反其道而行之，将主句放在最前面，条件状语放在后面，并且之间没有逗号，让人很不适应。另外，X_2 中的目的状语 to maximize the chances of discovery 和其主句之间也没有逗号，初学者可能不容易看出这个动词不定式的作用（这个动词不定式是目的状语）。

51

More remarkable than the origin has been the persistence of such sex segregation in twentieth-century industry.

难度系数：C-

语句结构及读法：

本句只有一层。

译　文：比最初的情况更为引人注目的是这种性别歧视在 20 世纪的工业中仍然持续。

难点分析：

我们很少见到以 more...than... 开头的句子。实际上，我们可以把本句看成一个倒装句，原句为：The persistence of such sex segregation in twentieth-century industry has been more remarkable than the origin. 当然，看作倒装仅仅是为了更容易理解。其实两句话的意思是不同的，本句强调的是 more remarkable than the origin 这种状态，而不是"性别歧视"。

52

These techniques have strongly suggested that although the true bacteria indeed form a large coherent group, certain other bacteria, the archaebacterial, which are also prokaryotes and which resemble true bacteria, represent a distinct evolutionary branch that far antedates the common ancestor of all true bacteria.

难度系数：C+

语句结构及读法：

第一层：These techniques have strongly suggested X.

第二层：X = that <Y_1>, certain other bacteria, (the archaebacterial), [Y_2], represent a distinct evolutionary branch [Y_3]

第三层：Y_1 = although the true bacteria indeed form a large coherent group

Y_2 = Z_1 and Z_2

Y_3 = a distinct evolutionary branch far antedates the common ancestor of all true bacteria

第四层：Z_1 = the archaebacterial are also prokaryotes

Z_2 = the archaebacterial resemble true bacteria

译　文：这些技术强烈表明：虽然真菌确实形成了一个大而一致的种群，但是特定的其他细菌，即原始细菌（也是原核生物，并且很像真菌），代表着一个独特的进化分支，该分支远远早于所有真菌的共同祖先。

难点分析：

本句的结构虽然比较复杂，但是算比较清晰的。从第 6 个词开始一直到句末都是宾语从句，长度很吓人，令读者一眼望不到头。另外，在这个宾语从句中，由于 Y_2 的存在，主语 certain other bacteria 和其谓语动词 represent 相隔较远，不易理解。

53

While perhaps true of those officers who joined Black units for promotion or other self-serving motives, this statement misrepresents the attitudes of the many abolitionists who became officers in Black regiments.

难度系数：C-

语句结构及读法：

第一层：<X₁>, this statement misrepresents the attitudes of the many abolitionists [X₂].

第二层：X₁ = While perhaps this statement is true of those officers [Y]

X₂ = the many abolitionists became officers in Black regiments

第三层：Y = those officers joined Black units for promotion or other self-serving motives

译　文：尽管这个陈述对于那些为了升职或其他个人动机而参加黑人部队的军官来说可能是真的，但是它却曲解了许多成为黑人部队军官的废奴主义者的态度。

难点分析：

本句最大的难点在于 X₁。理论上，这个让步状语从句应该写为：While perhaps being true of those officers...正如这句话所写，X₁ 本质上是一个伴随状语，可以看作一个主语与其主句主语相同的普通状语从句的简化。应有的 be 动词应该变为分词 being，但是由于这个动词是 be 动词，本身并不表达实际的意义（这是"系动词"和"实义动词"最大的区别），所以其可以被直接省略。

54

Automakers could schedule the production of different components or models on single machines, thereby eliminating the need to store the buffer stocks of extra components that result when specialized equipment and workers are kept constantly active.

难度系数：C

语句结构及读法：

第一层：Automakers could schedule the production of different components or models on single machines, <X>.

第二层：X = automakers thereby eliminate the need to store the buffer stocks of extra components [Y]

第三层：Y = extra components result <Z>

第四层：Z = when specialized equipment and workers are kept constantly active

077

译　文： 汽车制造商们能够在一台机器上安排制造不同部件或不同型号的零件，因此不需要储存专业设备和专业工人不停运作时所导致的多余零件缓冲库存。

难点分析：

本句的难点主要在于 X。X 是一个伴随状语，是主语与其主句主语相同的普通状语从句的简化。在这个伴随状语中蕴含了很多个从句，Y 是 extra components 的定语从句，在 Y 的谓语动词 result 出现后马上就出现了一个较为复杂的状语从句，并且这个状语从句还是一个合句。总之，从句数量较多是本句最大的难点。

55

If a cell degrades both a rapidly and a slowly synthesized mRNA slowly, both mRNA's will accumulate to high levels.

难度系数： C-

语句结构及读法：

第一层： <X>, both mRNA's will accumulate to high levels.
第二层： X = If a cell degrades both a rapidly and a slowly synthesized mRNA slowly

译　文： 如果一个细胞缓慢地同时降解一个快速合成的和一个缓慢合成的 mRNA 的话，那么两种 mRNA 都会积累到很高的水平。

难点分析：

第一，虽然 degrade 经常以不及物动词的形式出现，但它既可以是及物动词也可以是不及物动词。有些读者可能会因为认定它是不及物动词而不知道其后面的 both a rapidly and a slowly synthesized mRNA 在句中充当什么成分。

第二，条件状语从句 X 中的省略现象很容易让初学者理解错误。将省略部分补全则有：If a cell <u>slowly</u> degrades both a rapidly <u>synthesized mRNA</u> and a slowly synthesized mRNA… 注意，该句中的 slowly 紧挨着 degrades，如果像原句一样放在最后也容易令人不确定其修饰的对象，引起理解困难。

B 组

01

Allen's work is a rather extreme example of the "country community" school of seventeenth-century English history whose intemperate excesses in removing all national issues from the history of that period have been exposed by Professor Clive Holmes.

难度系数：B-

语句结构及读法：

第一层：Allen's work is a rather extreme example of the "country community" school of seventeenth-century English history [X].

第二层：X = the "country community" school's intemperate excesses in removing all national issues from the history of that period have been exposed by Professor Clive Holmes

译　文：阿伦的工作是 17 世纪英国历史的"国家社区"流派的一个极端的例子，这个流派无节制地把所有国家事件移除出那个时期，已经被教授 Clive Holmes 揭发了。

难点分析：

X 的主语和谓语动词相隔较远，中间出现了一个很长的插入成分 in removing all national issues from the history of that period。如果说仅仅是主语和谓语动词距离远，也不是什么特殊的难点，在谓语动词 have been exposed 前面还有一个 that period，初学者如果不注意，很有可能把这个 that 理解为定语从句的关系词，进而误认为 of that period have been exposed by Professor Clive Holmes 是修饰 history 的。实际上，这里的 that 是一个代词，指代前文出现过的一个 period，have been exposed 的主语是 excesses，即只有 that period 这两个词是 history 的定语。

02

Four critical genes governing circadian cycles have been found to be active in every tissue, however, not just the SCNs, of flies, mice, and humans.

难度系数：B

语句结构及读法：

第一层：Four critical genes [X_1] have been found to be active in every tissue, <X_2>, of flies, mice, and humans.

第二层：X₁＝four critical genes govern circadian cycles

X₂＝however, four critical genes have been found to be active in not just the SCNs of flies, mice, and humans

译　　文：四种控制昼夜循环的基因不仅仅被发现活跃于苍蝇、老鼠和人类的 SCNs 中，也被发现活跃于它们的每一个组织中。

难点分析：

首先，X₁ 是一个简化定语从句，修饰 four critical genes。其次，这个句子最难的部分是在 tissue 后面出现了一个讨厌的插入语 "however, not just the SCNs"，这让本来连接得好好的 tissue 和 "of flies, mice, and humans" 被隔开了，有些初学者的注意力可能直接就被这个插入语给带跑了，无法将 tissue 和 "of flies, mice, and humans" 联系到一起。

03

Many recent works by these scholars stress the ways in which differences among Renaissance women—especially in terms of social status and religion—work to complicate the kinds of generalizations both Burckhardt and Kelly made on the basis of their observations about upper-class Italian women.

难度系数： B+

语句结构及读法：

第一层：Many recent works [by these scholars] stress the ways [X].

第二层：X＝differences among Renaissance women—[especially in terms of social status and religion]—work to complicate the kinds of generalizations [Y] in the ways

第三层：Y＝both Burckhardt and Kelly made generalizations on the basis of their observations about upper-class Italian women

译　　文：这些学者很多最近的作品强调了文艺复兴时期女性的不同——尤其是依据社会地位和宗教来区分——使得 Burckhardt 和 Kelly 基于对意大利上流社会女性的观察所做出的那些概括更加复杂化。

难点分析：

考生需要有能力在第三层中看出其是第二层的名词 generalizations 的一个限制性

定语从句。由于先行词 generalizations 在从句中做 made 的宾语，所以省略了关系词 that。本来这种省略非常常见，但是在这么一个长句中出现还是会令一些考生不知所措。其次，X 中的谓语动词 work to complicate 也是一个难点。如果我们强行把 work 翻译为"工作"，则很难搞清楚 X 的意思。实际上，可以把 work to 理解为一个助动词，只翻译 complicate。

04

It is an odd but indisputable fact that the seventeenth-century English women who are generally regarded as among the forerunners of modern feminism are almost all identified with the Royalist side in the conflict between Royalists and Parliamentarians known as the English Civil Wars.

难度系数：B

语句结构及读法：

第一层：[X] is an odd but indisputable fact.（原文中的 X 是一个形式主语 it，指代 fact 后面的从句）

第二层：X = the seventeenth-century English women [Y₁] are almost all identified with the Royalist side in the conflict between Royalists and Parliamentarians [Y₂]

第三层：Y₁ = the seventeenth-century English women are generally regarded as among the forerunners of modern feminism

　　　　Y₂ = the conflict is known as the English Civil Wars

译　　文：一个奇特但不可否认的事实是：那些一般被认为是现代女权主义先驱者的 17 世纪的英国女性在保皇党和议员的斗争（即英国内战）中几乎全部都被认为是保皇党。

难点分析：

第一，由于第一层的 fact 是抽象名词，所以语法基础好的考生可能会把它后面的 that 从句看成 fact 的同位语从句，把 it 看成真正的代词，继而在前文中到处找 it 的指代对象。实际上，这里的 it 是一个形式主语，指代 fact 后面的主语从句。

第二，X 是一个很长的句子，读到 in the conflict between Royalists and Parliamentarians 时前面的内容可能就忘得差不多了，更别说去读懂最后修饰 conflict 的简化定语从句（Y₂）了。in the conflict 是 identify 的状语，读者需要理解它的分量。

05

Five fledgling sea eagles left their nests in western Scotland this summer, bringing to 34 the number of wild birds successfully raised since transplants from Norway began in 1975.

难度系数： B

语句结构及读法：

第一层： Five fledgling sea eagles left their nests in western Scotland this summer, <X>.
第二层： X = five fledgling sea eagles bring to 34 the number of wild birds [Y]
第三层： Y = wild birds are successfully raised <Z>
第四层： Z = since transplants from Norway began in 1975

译　　文： 五只雏鹰在今年夏天离开了它们在西苏格兰岛的巢穴，这五只雏鹰将于1975年开始从挪威迁移并成功养大的野生鸟类的数量提升到了34只。

难点分析：

　　本句的难点主要在于伴随状语中的倒装。由于the number of 后面的内容太长，所以为了让读者认清主干，本句将to 34倒装在了the number of wild birds successfully raised since transplants from Norway began in 1975 前面，本来是为了让句子的重点更为突出，但是这种现象可能会让初学者反而难以快速理解本句的含义。

06

That sex ratio will be favored which maximizes the number of descendants an individual will have and hence the number of gene copies transmitted.

难度系数： B+

语句结构及读法：

第一层： That sex ratio will be favored [X].
第二层： X = Y_1 and Y_2
第三层： Y_1 = that sex ratio maximizes the number of descendants [Z_1]
　　　　　Y_2 = that sex ratio hence maximizes the number of gene copies [Z_2]
第四层： Z_1 = an individual will have descendants
　　　　　Z_2 = gene copies are transmitted

译　　文： 那种性别比率有利于将一个个体所拥有的后代数量最大化，从而可以将遗传的基因份数最大化。

082

难点分析：

本句难点颇多，没给 A 等级主要是因为长度只有 24 个词。

第一，第一层是一个倒装句，谓语动词 will be favored 被提前。这是因为 That sex ratio 的定语部分实在太长，若放在最后，读者读下来很可能就会错失这个谓语动词，正确语序为：That sex ratio which maximizes the number of descendants an individual will have and hence the number of gene copies transmitted will be favored.

第二，Z_1 是一个省略了关系词的定语从句（先行词在从句中做宾语，可以省略关系词 that），还原为正常的定语从句则有：descendants that an individual will have。另外，在最后的 transmitted 是一个简化的定语从句。

07

Among the myths taken as fact by the environmental managers of most corporations is the belief that environmental regulations affect all competitors in a given industry uniformly.

难度系数： B-

语句结构及读法：

第一层： Among the myths [X_1] is the belief (X_2). （此句为倒装结构，正常的语序为：The belief is among the myths.）

第二层： X_1=the myths are taken as fact by environmental managers of most corporations

X_2=environmental regulations affect all competitors in a given industry uniformly

难点分析：

本句先写难点分析是因为其难点主要不在于"长"，而在于"难"上。由于汉语的倒装并不如英语这么普遍，所以大部分的初学者都对倒装句很不熟悉。本句是一个由 among 前置引起的完全倒装结构，正常语序为：The belief that environmental regulations affect all competitors in a given industry uniformly is among the myths taken as fact by the environmental managers of most corporations.

译　文： 环境法规会统一影响一个产业中的所有竞争者，这个信条是大部分公司的环保经理所相信的谣言之一。

08

Sixteenth- and seventeenth-century chartered trading companies, despite the international scope of their activities, are usually considered irrelevant to this discussion: the volume of their transactions is assumed to have been too low and the communications and transport of their day too primitive to make comparisons with modern multinationals interesting.

难度系数：B+

语句结构及读法：

第一层：Sixteenth- and seventeenth-century chartered trading companies, <X_1>, are usually considered irrelevant to this discussion: (X_2).

第二层：X_1 = despite the international scope of their activities

X_2 = the volume of their transactions is assumed to have been too low to make comparisons with modern multinationals interesting and the communications and transport of their day is assumed to have been too primitive to make comparisons with modern multinationals interesting

译　文：尽管有国际性的贸易活动，但是 16、17 世纪的贸易公司经常被认为不在这个讨论的范围内：它们的交易量被认为太小并且它们那个时代的通讯和交通被认为太原始，以至人们没有把它们和现代有吸引力的跨国公司进行比较。

难点分析：

本句的难点主要在于第二层句子的省略现象。第二层中的变色部分均为原文省略的内容，由此可以看出，两个合句均有省略部分。在长难句中，一般的省略都是在合句中的某一个小句中出现的，这种两个句子各省略一部分的情况并不多见，实为难句。

09

Years before the advent of plate tectonics—the widely accepted theory, developed in the mid-1960s, that holds that the major features of the Earth's surface are created by the horizontal motions of the Earth's outer shell, or lithosphere—a similar theory was rejected by the geological community.

难度系数：B

语句结构及读法：

第一层：Years before the advent of plate tectonics (X), a similar theory was rejected by the geological community.

第二层：X = the widely accepted theory, [Y_1], [Y_2]

第三层：Y_1 = the widely accepted theory is developed in the mid-1960s

Y_2 = the widely accepted theory holds [Z]

第四层：Z = that the major features of the Earth's surface are created by the horizontal motions of the Earth's outer shell, or lithosphere

译　　文：在板块构造学说（这个学说是一个被广泛接受的 20 世纪 60 年代中期发展起来的学说，它表明：地球表面的主要特征是由地球外层岩石圈的水平移动所造成的）出现的多年之前，一个相似的理论被地质学界所排斥。

难点分析：

第一，本句中出现了一个很长的由破折号隔开的部分，该部分是 plate tectonics 的同位语。在英语中，破折号是一个很神奇的符号，可以连接任意的两个部分。

第二，Y_1 是一个被动语态的简化定语从句，它的存在将先行词 the widely accepted theory 和其定语 Y_2 隔开了，使得语义不够连贯。

第三，由于破折号中的部分很长，加之 years 可以用作名词，所以初学者看到句首的两个词就可能把它们误认为是主句的主语，在他们读到真正的主语 a similar theory 时反而不知所措了。实际上，years before the advent of plate tectonics 是状语，真正的主句是：A similar theory was rejected by the geological community.

10

Now we must also examine the culture as we Mexican Americans have experienced it, passing from a sovereign people to compatriots with newly arriving settlers to, finally, a conquered people—a charter minority on our own land.

难度系数：B

语句结构及读法：

第一层：Now we must also examine the culture <X>.
第二层：X = as we Mexican Americans have experienced it, <Y>
第三层：Y = we pass from a sovereign people to compatriots with newly arriving settlers to, finally, a conquered people — a charter minority on our own land

译　　文：现在，我们必须也按照我们墨西哥裔美国人的经历审视这种文化，我们的经历是从一个主权的民族变成新定居者的同胞，最终再沦落为一个被征服的民族——在自己的土地上被规定为少数民族。

难点分析：

本句的难点集中在 Y 部分。首先，这个部分是伴随状语，可以看作一个普通的状语从句。其次，在 Y 结构内部，出现了 from... to... to... 的结构。绝大部分人熟悉 from... to...

085

结构，但是没见过 from… to… to… 结构，甚至认为最后一个 to 是定语。这里的 to 还是和 from 搭配的，from A to B to C 的意思是"从 A 到 B 再从 B 到 C"。

11

Federal efforts to aid minority businesses began in the 1960's when the Small Business Administration (SBA) began making federally guaranteed loans and government-sponsored management and technical assistance available to minority business enterprises.

难度系数：B

语句结构及读法：

第一层：Federal efforts to aid minority businesses began in the 1960's <X>.

第二层：X = Y_1 and Y_2

第三层：Y_1 = when the Small Business Administration (SBA) began making federally guaranteed loans available to minority business enterprises

Y_2 = when the Small Business Administration (SBA) began making government-sponsored management and technical assistance available to minority business enterprises

译　　文：从 20 世纪 60 年代起，联邦政府开始致力于帮扶少数民族企业，那时美国联邦中小企业管理局（简称 SBA）开始为少数民族企业提供联邦担保的贷款、政府资助的管理和技术支持。

难点分析：

　　本句的难点有两处，一处是 X 中出现的平行，另一处是 Y_2 最后出现的倒装。观察原句的 X 部分可以发现有两个 and，读者需要搞清楚它们连接的三者的平行关系，即 federally guaranteed loans, government-sponsored management 和 technical assistance 是并列的。

　　在 Y_2 部分，make 的宾语部分出现了倒装现象，正确语序为：Small Business Administration (SBA) began making federally guaranteed loans and government-sponsored management and technical assistance to minority business enterprises available.

12

Acquisitions may well have the desirable effect of channeling a nation's resources efficiently from less to more efficient sectors of its economy, but the individual acquisitions executives arranging these deals must see them as advancing either their own or their companies' private economic interests.

难度系数：B-

语句结构及读法：

第一层：X$_1$ but X$_2$.

第二层：X$_1$ = Acquisitions may well have the desirable effect of channeling a nation's resources efficiently from less to more efficient sectors of its economy

X$_2$ = the individual acquisitions executives [Y] must see them as advancing either their own or their companies' private economic interests

第三层：Y = the individual acquisitions executives arrange these deals

译　文：收购可能在将国家资源从无效的经济领域引到更加有效的经济领域方面具有理想的效果，但是安排这些交易的个人收购高管们必须把它们看作是在推进自己或公司的私人经济利益。

难点分析：

理解 X$_1$ 是本句的一个难点。这个句子的主干为：Acquisitions may well have the desirable effect. effect 后面的所有内容均为其定语（所有格），在这个定语中含有一个 SVOC 结构，即 channel resources from less to more efficient sectors。画线部分是宾语补足语，翻译成中文为：将国家资源从无效的经济领域引到更加有效的经济领域中。另外，Y 是一个简化定语从句。

13

Current feminist theory, in validating women's own stories of their experience, has encouraged scholars of women's history to view the use of women's oral narratives as the methodology, next to the use of women's written autobiography, that brings historians closest to the "reality" of women's lives.

难度系数：B

语句结构及读法：

第一层：Current feminist theory, <X$_1$>, has encouraged scholars of women's history to view the use of women's oral narratives as the methodology, [X$_2$], [X$_3$].

第二层：X$_1$ = current feminist theory validates women's own stories of their experience

X₂ = scholars of women's history to view the use of women's written autobiography as the methodology

X₃ = the methodology brings historians closest to the "reality" of women's lives

译　　文：如今的男女平等理论，在证实女性自己经历的故事时，鼓励研究女性历史的学者们除了用女性的自传外，还可以用女性的口述信息作为方法，这个方法可以让历史学家更加接近女性的真实生活情况。

难点分析：

本句最大的难点在于中间的插入语 next to the use of women's written autobiography。首先，这个插入语的加入使得原本紧挨在一起的先行词 the methodology 和其后置的限制性定语 that brings historians closest to the "reality" of women's lives 相隔得很远，对定语从句的相关用法不熟的考生可能会将这个定语从句认为是 autobiography 的定语，因此误解句意。

其次，这个插入语还有一个省略现象，注意观察 X₂，它其实是一个和主句平行的句子：Current feminist theory has encouraged scholars of women's history to view the use of women's oral narratives as the methodology, and current feminist theory has encouraged scholars of women's history to view the use of women's written autobiography as the methodology. 画线部分均为原句省略内容。

14

Population growth—which could not have occurred in the absence of successful household economy, in which women's work was essential—made possible the large-scale development of labor-intensive chinampa (ridged-field) agriculture in the southern valley of Mexico which, in turn, supported urbanization and political centralization in the Aztec capital.

难度系数：B-

语句结构及读法：

第一层：Population growth [X₁] made possible the large-scale development of labor-intensive chinampa (ridged-field) agriculture in the southern valley of Mexico [X₂].

第二层：X₁ = population growth could not have occurred in the absence of successful household economy, [Y]

X₂ = the large-scale development of labor-intensive chinampa (ridged-field) agriculture in turn supported urbanization and political centralization in the Aztec capital

Y = women's work was essential in household economy

译　文：人口的增长——不能脱离成功的家庭经济（女性的工作在家庭经济中是必要的）而独立存在——它让墨西哥南部山谷的劳动密集型畦田农业的大规模发展成为可能，这种大规模的发展反过来支持了阿兹特克首都的城市化和政治集中化。

难点分析：

阅读了之前那么多句子，相信大家对从句套从句这种难句结构已经不陌生了。本句除了从句套从句外，在第一层中还出现了一个倒装，正确语序为：Population growth made the large-scale development of labor-intensive chinampa (ridged-field) agriculture in the southern valley of Mexico possible.

15

According to P. F. Drucker, the management philosophy known as Total Quality Management (TQM), which is designed to be adopted consistently throughout an organization and to improve customer service by using sampling theory to reduce the variability of a product's quality, can work successfully in conjunction with two older management systems.

难度系数：B-

语句结构及读法：

第一层：According to P. F. Drucker, the management philosophy [X] can work successfully in conjunction with two older management systems.

第二层：X = the management philosophy is known as Total Quality Management (TQM), [Y]

第三层：Y = Z_1 and Z_2

第四层：Z_1 = TQM is designed to be adopted consistently throughout an organization

Z_2 = TQM is designed to improve customer service by using sampling theory to reduce the variability of a product's quality

译　文：根据 P. F. Drucker，被称作 TQM 的经营理念可以和两个较老的管理系统一起运用。（TQM 旨在一直在一家公司中运用，并且通过抽样原理来减少一个产品质量的不确定性从而提高服务质量。）

难点分析：

本句难点在于第一层的主语和谓语动词相隔得实在太远了。主语 the management philosophy 后面有一个简化定语从句，在这个定语从句中的专有名词 TQM 后面又有一个非限制性定语从句，并且这个从句还是个合句，进一步加长了主语和谓语动词之间的距离。

16

Faue stresses the importance of women's contributions to the development of unions at the community level, contributions that made women's ultimate fate within the city's labor movement all the more poignant: as unions reached the peak of their strength in the 1940s, the community base that had made their success possible and to which women's contributions were so vital became increasingly irrelevant to unions' institutional life.

难度系数：B

语句结构及读法：

第一层：Faue stresses the importance of women's contributions to the development of unions at the community level, (X_1).

第二层：X = contributions [that made women's ultimate fate within the city's labor movement all the more poignant]：(Y)

第三层：Y = <Z_1>, the community base [Z_2] became increasingly irrelevant to unions' institutional life

第四层：Z_1 = as unions reached the peak of their strength in the 1940s

Z_2 = M_1 and M_2

第五层：M_1 = the community base had made their success possible

M_2 = women's contributions were so vital to the community base

译　　文：Faue 强调了女性在社区这个层级对于工会发展所做贡献的重要性，这是一种使得女性在城市劳工运动中的最终命运更加凄凉的贡献：当工会在 20 世纪 40 年代达到顶峰时，那些使工会的成功成为可能并且女性的贡献最明显的社区基础与工会的体制生活越来越无关了。

难点分析：

长达 66 个词的句子从来都不会是简单句，难点主要有三处。

第一，本句中有一些含义较为抽象的名词，例如：poignant（凄美的）。很多抽象名词表明作者的态度，不认识这些词可能会对理解句意（尤其是写作方向）产生严重影响。

第二，由于主句的谓语动词 stress 的名词和动词形式相同，且主语 Faue 又不太像一个人名，所以有些人可能会以为整个主句是一个名词词组，直到读完整个句子也没找到谓语动词，直接放弃了对本句的理解。要想克服这样的问题，大家务必边看句子边理解句意，不能只是一味地寻找语法标志。

第三，Z_2 中的两个定语从句的关系词不同，但是在逻辑上 that had made their success possible 和 to which women's contributions were so vital 是平行的，均做先行词 the community base 的限制性定语。实际上，and 连接的对象仅要求功能上的平行（比如：这两者皆为定语），不要求形式上的对称。

17

Many critics of Emily Bronte's novel *Wuthering Heights* see its second part as a counterpoint that comments on, if it does not reverse, the first part, where a "romantic" reading receives more confirmation.

难度系数：B

语句结构及读法：

第一层：Many critics of Emily Bronte's novel *Wuthering Heights* see its second part as a counterpoint [X].

第二层：X = a counterpoint comments on, <Y_1>, the first part, [Y_2]

第三层：Y_1 = if it does not reverse

Y_2 = a "romantic" reading receives more confirmation in the first part

译　文：很多针对 Emily Bronte 的小说《呼啸山庄》的评论家把小说的第二部分看作评论小说第一部分（这个部分中一种浪漫主义的解读得到了更多确认）的一个对应物，如果不反对第一部分的话。

难点分析：

第一，插入语 Y_1 很讨厌，它把本来连接在一起的 comments on the first part 隔开了，增加了阅读难度。

第二，关于 counterpoint 的理解很是关键。很多人因为这个词的构造而把它理解为"对立观点"的意思，这样的理解令插入语 Y_1 变得十分尴尬，会引起我们反复的思考：什么叫"如果不是反对的对立观点"？对立观点本身不就是用来反对的吗？实际上，counterpoint 是"对应物"的意思，这个词来自于音乐，指的是"两种东西和谐一致地对应"。在本句中，我们甚至可以将这个词理解得十分中性，意思近似于 thing 或 part，即：Many critics of Emily Bronte's novel *Wuthering Heights* see its second part as a part. 从而把其表意的功能完全推给它后面的定语从句。如果能理解 counterpoint 在这里没什么特殊意思，那么自然也就能理解插入语 Y₁ 的作用。X 的完整意思为：如果不反对小说第一部分的话，那么第二部分就是在评论第一部分。

18

Although this treaty did not mention water rights, the Court ruled that the federal government, when it created the reservation, intended to deal fairly with American Indians by reserving for them the waters without which their lands would have been useless.

难度系数： B-

语句结构及读法：

第一层： <X₁>, the Court ruled X₂.

第二层： X₁ = Although this treaty did not mention water rights

X₂ = the federal government, <Y₁>, intended to deal fairly with American Indians by reserving for them the waters [Y₂]

第三层： Y₁ = when it created the reservation

Y₂ = their lands would have been useless *without the waters*

译　文： 虽然这个条约并没有提到水权，但是法院裁定：当联邦政府建立保留地时，它的意图就是通过为美国印第安人保留水域（没有这些水域，他们的土地就是完全没用的）来公平对待美国印第安人。

难点分析：

第一，Y₁ 这个时间状语加在了 X₂ 的主语 federal government 和谓语 intended 之间，使得语义被割裂，难以联系起来。

第二，X₂ 中的方式状语是倒装结构，正常语序为：Federal government intended to deal fairly with American Indians by reserving the waters [Y₂] *for them*.

19

Thirty-six years later, historian George Coulton agreed but, paradoxically, attributed a silver lining to the Black Death: prosperity engendered by diminished competition for food, shelter, and work led survivors of the epidemic into the Renaissance and subsequent rise of modern Europe.

难度系数： B

语句结构及读法：

第一层：X_1 but X_2.

第二层：X_1 = Thirty-six years later, historian George Coulton agreed

X_2 = historian George Coulton paradoxically, attributed a silver lining to the Black Death：(Y)

第三层：Y = prosperity [Z] led survivors of the epidemic into the Renaissance and into subsequent rise of modern Europe

第四层：Z = prosperity is engendered by diminished competition for food, shelter, and work

译　文： 36 年之后，历史学家 George Coulton 虽然同意黑死病是件不幸的事，但矛盾的是，他又认为黑死病有一点好处：由于对食物、住所和工作的竞争减少而产生了繁荣，所以黑死病的幸存者经历了文艺复兴并且之后经历了现代欧洲的兴起。

难点分析：

本句的难点有两个。一是关于名词 a silver lining 的理解：很多人可能不认识这个词，这个词的意思是"一丝光亮"。在本句中的引申意义是"一线希望"。也就是说，George Coulton 虽然同意黑死病是坏事，但是还是认为它有一点点好处。二是 Z 是简化定语从句。原句中的 engendered 是过去分词，不能误读为谓语动词。

20

Our current cartographic record relating to Native American tribes and their migrations and cultural features, as well as territoriality and contemporary trust lands, reflects the origins of the data and changes both in United States government policy and in non-Native Americans' attitudes toward an understanding of Native Americans.

难度系数： B

语句结构及读法：

第一层：Our current cartographic record [X_1] reflects X_2 and X_3.

第二层： X₁ = our current cartographic record relates to Native American tribes and their migrations and cultural features, as well as territoriality and contemporary trust lands

X₂ = the origins of the data

X₃ = changes both in United States government policy and in non-Native Americans' attitudes toward an understanding of Native Americans

译　　文： 我们现有的关于美洲原住民部落与他们的迁徙和文化特征，以及属地和现代信托土地的制图记录反映了这个数据的来源，并且反映了美国政府政策的变化和非美洲原住民对于理解美洲原住民态度上的变化。

难点分析：

本句其实就是一个普通的合句。难度主要在于主语实在太长，并且 and 后出现了省略主语和谓语的情况。另外，relating to Native American tribes and their migrations and cultural features, as well as territoriality and contemporary trust lands 是一个简化的定语从句，修饰主语 our current cartographic record。

21

The gravity of a MACHO that had so drifted, astronomers agree, would cause the star's light rays, which would otherwise diverge, to bend together so that, as observed from the Earth, the star would temporarily appear to brighten, a process known as microlensing.

难度系数： B-

语句结构及读法：

第 一 层： The gravity of a MACHO [X₁], X₂, would cause the star's light rays, [X₃], to bend together <X₄>.

第二层： X₁ = a MACHO had so drifted

X₂ = astronomers agree

X₃ = the star's light rays would otherwise diverge

X₄ = <Y₁>, the star would temporarily appear to brighten, (Y₂)

第三层： Y₁ = as observed from the Earth

Y₂ = a process [known as microlensing]

译　　文： 天文学家同意：那个漂浮的 MACHO 的重力将会使恒星的光线折射到一起，（否则光线就会偏离），由此，正如在地球上所观测到的，恒星将会暂时发光，这个过程叫作"微引力透镜"。

难点分析：

本句的主干被"一群"从句切割得支离破碎，造成了很大的阅读难度。本句真正的主干为：The gravity of a MACHO would cause the star's light rays to bend together, so that the star would temporarily appear to brighten. 主干是一个非常简单的复句，中间穿插了同位语从句、定语从句和状语从句。

22

The traditional view supposes that the upper mantle of the Earth behaves as a liquid when it is subjected to small forces for long periods and that differences in temperature under oceans and continents are sufficient to produce convection in the mantle of the Earth with rising convection currents under the mid-ocean ridges and sinking currents under the continents.

难度系数： B-

语句结构及读法：

第一层： The traditional view supposes X_1 and X_2.

第二层： X_1 = that the upper mantle of the Earth behaves as a liquid, <Y_1>

X_2 = that differences in temperature under oceans and continents are sufficient to produce convection in the mantle of the Earth, <Y_2 and Y_3>

第三层： Y_1 = when it is subjected to small forces for long periods

Y_2 = with rising convection currents under the mid-ocean ridges

Y_3 = with sinking currents under the continents

译　文： 传统观点认为：当长期受到较小压力的时候，地球的上层地幔就会像液体一样。并且，海洋和大陆下方地幔温度的不同足以让地幔产生对流——在中部海脊下方产生上升的气流，在陆地下方产生下降的气流。

难点分析：

这是一个长度接近 60 个词的句子。第一层有两个并列的宾语从句，这两个句子相隔的距离较远。第二个宾语从句中含有两个并列的方式状语，它们的存在也使得这个句子结构更加复杂。

23

In their day-by-day tactical maneuvers, these senior executives rely on what is vaguely termed "intuition" to manage a network of interrelated problems that require them to deal with ambiguity, inconsistency, novelty, and surprise; and to integrate action into the process of thinking.

难度系数： B

语句结构及读法：

第一层： In their day-by-day tactical maneuvers, these senior executives rely on X.
第二层： X = what is vaguely termed "intuition" to manage a network of interrelated problems [Y]
第三层： Y = problems require them Z_1 and Z_2
第四层： Z_1 = to deal with ambiguity, inconsistency, novelty, and surprise
　　　　Z_2 = to integrate action into the process of thinking

译　文： 在一天接着一天的战术演练中，这些高级管理人员依靠那些依稀被表示为"直觉"的东西来管理一些相互关联的问题网。这些问题要求他们去处理模糊性、矛盾性、新颖性和惊喜，并且要求他们把行动整合到思考过程中。

难点分析：

　　　　本句中的从句较多，因此层级也较多。最难的地方出现在第四层中。我们常见的合句是用逗号连接的，分号一般是连接两个相对独立的句子。但本句却利用了分号来连接合句的两个部分，我们需要适应这种表达方式。实际上，分号是一个非常灵活的符号，可以连接任何两个部分，并不是一定要连接两个独立的分句。

24

To buttress their case that caffeine acts instead by preventing adenosine binding, Snyder et al. compared the stimulatory effects of a series of caffeine derivatives with their ability to dislodge adenosine from its receptors in the brains of mice.

难度系数： B+

语句结构及读法：

第一层： To buttress their case (X), Snyder et al. compared the stimulatory effects of a series of caffeine derivatives with their ability to dislodge adenosine from its receptors in the brains of mice

第二层：X = that caffeine acts instead by preventing adenosine binding

译　文：为了支持他们所说的情况，即咖啡因是通过防止腺苷的结合而生效的，Snyder 等人将一系列咖啡因衍生物在老鼠大脑中产生的刺激性效果和去除老鼠大脑中的腺苷接收器后这些咖啡因衍生物的能力做了比较。

难点分析：

第一层主句比较长，大家需要对词组 compare... with... 比较熟悉才能找出比较对象。但是，由于没有上下文，所以这句话的比较对象显得有些"奇怪"。在表面意思上，本句的比较对象是："一系列咖啡因衍生物的刺激性效果"和"它们去除老鼠大脑中腺苷接收器的能力"。这两者显然是不可比的。实际上，这句话所论述的内容是：咖啡因是依靠阻止大脑接收腺苷来实现提神效果的。如果我们能从文中读出这个信息，那么自然可以理解作者在类比什么，即"把咖啡因注射进老鼠身体后的效果（理论上可以阻止腺苷的接收）"和"去掉老鼠的腺苷接收器（不能再接收腺苷）后咖啡因的效果"。

25

Relational feminists, while agreeing that equal educational and economic opportunities outside the home should be available for all women, continued to emphasize women's special contributions to society as homemakers and mothers; they demanded special treatment for women, including protective legislation for women workers, state-sponsored maternity benefits, and paid compensation for housework.

难度系数：B

语句结构及读法：

第一层：X_1 ; X_2.

第二层：X_1 = Relational feminists, <Y_1>, continued to emphasize women's special contributions to society as homemakers and mothers

　　　　X_2 = they demanded special treatment for women [Y_2]

第三层：Y_1 = while relational feminists agree Z

　　　　Y_2 = special treatment for women includes protective legislation for women workers, state-sponsored maternity benefits, and paid compensation for housework

第四层：Z = equal educational and economic opportunities outside the home should be available for all women

译　文：关系女权主义者，在同意应该在家庭以外给所有女性提供同等的教育和经济机会的同时，继续强调了女性作为家庭主妇和母亲对社会做出的特殊贡献；她们要求给女性提供特殊的待遇，包括针对女性工作者的保护法令、国家资助的生育津贴和对家务的补偿金。

难点分析：

Y_1 是伴随状语，可以看作一个普通状语从句的简化。它的存在使得主语 relational feminists 和谓语 continued to emphasize 相隔较远，不易认清主干。另外，X_2 中的平行也是一个难点。在语法上，"国家资助的生育津贴 (state-sponsored maternity benefits)" 和 "对家务的补偿金 (paid compensation for housework)" 既可以和 "针对女性工作者的保护法令 (protective legislation for women workers)" 平行，也可以和 "给女性的特殊待遇 (protective legislation for women workers)" 平行。在逻辑上，由于津贴和补偿金都是女性特殊待遇的子集，所以两者平行的对象应该是 "针对女性工作者的保护法令"。

26

The individualist approach, by attacking gender roles, denying the significance of physiological difference, and condemning existing familial institutions as hopelessly patriarchal, has often simply treated as irrelevant the family roles important to many women.

难度系数：B

语句结构及读法：

第一层：The individualist approach, <X_1, X_2, and X_3>, has often simply treated as irrelevant the family roles important to many women.

第二层：X_1 = the individualist approach attacks gender roles

X_2 = the individualist approach denies the significance of physiological difference

X_3 = the individualist approach condemns existing familial institutions as hopelessly patriarchal

译　文：个人主义的方法，通过攻击性别角色、否认生理区别的重要性、谴责现有的家族制度重男轻女，经常简单地把对许多女性很重要的家庭角色看作是无关紧要的。

难点分析：

第一，主句主语 the individualist approach 和谓语 has often simply treated 由于插

入了 X₁, X₂, X₃ 这三个方式状语而相隔很远。初学者可能一下子不容易将主语和谓语动词联系起来。

第二，主句的宾语和宾补部分出现了一个倒装结构，正常语序为：The individualist approach has often simply treated <u>the family roles important to many women as irrelevant</u>.

27

As a result of such contradictory evidence, it is uncertain whether those suffering seriously as a result of labor market problems number in the hundreds of thousands or the tens of millions, and, hence, whether high levels of joblessness can be tolerated or must be countered by job creation and economic stimulus.

难度系数：B

语句结构及读法：

第一层：<X₁>, it is uncertain X₂ and X₃.

第二层：X₁ = As a result of such contradictory evidence
X₂ = whether those [Y₁] number in the hundreds of thousands or the tens of millions
X₃ = whether Y₂ or Y₃

第三层：Y₁ = those suffer seriously as a result of labor market problems
Y₂ = high levels of joblessness can be tolerated
Y₃ = high levels of joblessness must be countered by job creation and economic stimulus

译 文：这种矛盾证据的结果是：有两个问题是不确定的，一是那些由于劳动力市场问题而遭受严重伤害的人是否是数以千万计的；二是高失业率是否可以忍受或者是否一定要通过创造新工作和刺激经济来应对。

难点分析：

本句的第一个难点在于一个较为明显的倒装句。由于 X₂ 和 X₃ 的长度吓人，所以在第一层主句中，两者被形式主语 it 所替代，由此构成了一种常见的倒装结构，还原为正常语序则为：X₂ and X₃ is uncertain. 对于这种结构，大家一定要尽快习惯，它们在 GMAT 考试的各个部分中都经常出现。

第二个难点在于 X₂ 的谓语动词是 number。由于 number 的动词形式和名词形式相同，初学者在 X₂ 中可能一下子找不到谓语动词。另外，Y₁ 为简化定语从句。

28

Managers under pressure to maximize cost-cutting will resist innovation because they know that more fundamental changes in processes or systems will wreak havoc with the results on which they are measured.

难度系数： B-

语句结构及读法：

第一层： Managers under pressure to maximize cost-cutting will resist innovation <X>.
第二层： X = because they know Y
第三层： Y = that more fundamental changes in processes or systems will wreak havoc with the results [Z]
第四层： Z = they are measured on the results

译　　文： 面临需要最大程度降低成本的压力的管理者会抵制创新，这是因为他们知道在工艺流程或体系方面产生的更加根本的变化将会对被用来考核他们业绩的结果造成巨大灾难。

难点分析：

本句主要的难点在于对词组 wreak havoc with 的理解。有些同学不知道 wreak 是"造成"的意思，有些同学以为 with the results on which they are measured 是一个独立主格或者普通状语。这两种情况都会造成不理解本句意思。实际上，wreak havoc with 可以一起看作一个动词，意思是：对某件事造成巨大灾难。如果能理解到这层意思，那么 Y 将很容易看懂。

29

Defining "politics" as "any action taken to affect the course of behavior of government or of the community", Baker concludes that, while voting and holding office were restricted to men, women in the nineteenth century organized themselves into societies committed to social issues such as temperance and poverty.

难度系数： B

语句结构及读法：

第一层： <X_1>, Baker concludes X_2.
第二层： X_1 = Baker defines "politics" as "any action taken to affect the course of behavior of government or of the community"

$X_2 = <Y_1>$, women in the nineteenth century organized themselves into societies [Y_2]

第三层： Y_1 = while voting and holding office were restricted to men

Y_2 = societies are committed to social issues such as temperance and poverty

译　文： 把"政治"定义为"任意能影响政府或者社区行为过程的行动"，Baker 下了一个结论：虽然投票和担任职位都被限制于男性，但是 19 世纪的女性自己组成了一个社会，这个社会致力于解决像禁酒和贫穷这样的社会问题。

难点分析：

第一，在 Y_1 中，语法基础较好的同学可能一看 while 后面出现了 doing 就直接向伴随的方向想，但是这里的 voting 和 holding 其实是动名词，是这个状语从句中的主语。

第二，Y_2 是一个简化定语从句，可以看作一个被动语态的普通定语从句，注意不要将 committed 误认为是谓语动词。

30

In other words, Baker contends, women activists were early practitioners of nonpartisan, issue-oriented politics and thus were more interested in enlisting lawmakers, regardless of their party affiliation, on behalf of certain issues than in ensuring that one party or another won an election.

难度系数： B

语句结构及读法：

第一层： In other words, X_1, X_2 and X_3.

第二层： X_1 = Baker contends

X_2 = women activists were early practitioners of nonpartisan, issue-oriented politics

X_3 = women activists thus were more interested in enlisting lawmakers, regardless of their party affiliation, on behalf of certain issues than in ensuring Y

第三层： Y = that one party or another won an election

译　文： 换句话说，Baker 主张：女性活动家是早期的无党派和以问题为导向的政治的早期实践者，并且她们因此在某些特定的事情上对笼络国会议员们更感兴趣（无论是否是她们的党派），而不是保证某一个党派赢得选举。

难点分析：

> 第一，插入语 Baker contends 才应该被看成是真正的主句，现在的主句可以被看作是其宾语从句，即：Baker contends that women activists were early practitioners of nonpartisan, issue-oriented politics.
>
> 第二，在 X_3 中出现的比较结构由于插入语以及比较对象本身的长度，比较对象被相隔得较远，真正的比较对象为：Women activists were more interested in enlisting lawmakers than in ensuring.

31

Baryons—subatomic particles that are generally protons or neutrons—are the source of stellar, and therefore galactic, luminosity, and so their numbers can be estimated based on how luminous galaxies are.

难度系数： B

语句结构及读法：

第一层：X_1 and so X_2.

第二层：X_1 = Baryons—(Y)—are the source of stellar, and therefore galactic, luminosity

　　　　X_2 = their numbers can be estimated based on how luminous galaxies are

第三层：Y = subatomic particles that are generally protons or neutrons

译　　文： 重子——一般是质子或中子的亚原子粒子——是恒星和银河亮光的来源，所以它们的数量可以基于星系的亮度来估算。

难点分析：

> 第一，在 X_1 中出现了两个名词的平行，即 stellar luminosity 和 galactic luminosity。由于原句在 galactic 前面加了副词 therefore，所以有些人会认为这里开启了新的一个句子，从而认为 galactic 是新句子的主语。
>
> 第二，由于 and 和 so 都是连词，所以在语法上它们通常不一起使用，而本句中却出现了 and 和 so 的连用。在阅读句子时，请不要太注重这些"语法错误"，要以读懂句子为第一标准。
>
> 第三，本句中出现了一些关于天文的专有名词，加大了理解的难度。

32

His conclusion that australopithecines were frugivores (fruit eaters) is based upon his observation that the tooth micro-wear characteristics of east African australopithecine specimens are indistinguishable from those of chimpanzees and orangutans, which are commonly assumed to be frugivorous primates.

难度系数：B-

语句结构及读法：

第一层：His conclusion (X_1) is based upon his observation (X_2).

第二层：X_1 = that australopithecines were frugivores (fruit eaters)

X_2 = that the tooth micro-wear characteristics of east African australopithecine specimens are indistinguishable from those of chimpanzees and orangutans, [Y]

第三层：Y = *chimpanzees and orangutans* are commonly assumed to be frugivorous primates

译　文：他的结论，即南方古猿是吃水果的动物，是基于他的观察的，即东非南方古猿标本的齿微磨损特性和黑猩猩以及红毛猩猩的是无法区分的（黑猩猩以及红毛猩猩通常被认为是吃水果的灵长类动物）。

难点分析：

X_2 虽然结构简单，但是词汇难度较大，尤其是主语部分的核心词不太明显，容易让我们产生厌烦的情绪，其核心内容为：Characteristics are indistinguishable from those of chimpanzees and orangutans.

33

Black Fiction surveys a wide variety of novels, bringing to our attention in the process some fascinating and little-known works like James Weldon Johnson's *Autobiography of an Ex-Colored Man*.

难度系数：B

语句结构及读法：

第一层：*Black Fiction* surveys a wide variety of novels <X>.

第二层：X = *Black Fiction* brings to our attention in the process some fascinating and little-known works like James Weldon Johnson's *Autobiography of an Ex-Colored Man*

译　　文：《黑人小说》调查了各种各样的小说，在这个过程中我们的注意力被引向了一些迷人的、鲜为人知的作品，比如 James Weldon Johnson 的《一位前黑奴的自传》。

难点分析：

本句首先出现了一个 GMAT 考试中常见的倒装句，由于 bring 的第一个宾语太长，所以为了方便阅读，把第二个宾语 our attention 倒装到了第一个宾语前面。正常语序为：

Black Fiction brings some fascinating and little-known works like James Weldon Johnson's *Autobiography of an Ex-Colored Man* to our attention.

第二个难点是关于 in the process 的作用问题。在语法上，它既可以当 our attention 的定语，又可以做 bring 这个句子的状语，大家需要根据上下文的文意来判断其真正的作用。在本句中它做 bring 的状语。

34

Nevertheless, researchers of the Pleistocene epoch have developed all sorts of more or less fanciful model schemes of how they would have arranged the Ice Age had they been in charge of events.

难度系数： B-

语句结构及读法：

第一层： Nevertheless, researchers of the Pleistocene epoch have developed all sorts of more or less fanciful model schemes [X].

第二层： X = of how they would have arranged the Ice Age <Y>

第三层： Y = had they been in charge of events

译　　文： 但是，更新世时期的研究者已经建立了各种各样的或多或少有些奇思妙想的模型，这些模型展示了如果由研究者来决定地质事件的话，他们会如何排布冰河世纪。

难点分析：

本句的难点主要在于最后的倒装句（Y 部分）。这种倒装的模式在 GMAT 考题里十分常见，即条件状语可以通过去掉 if 并且将助动词提前来完成倒装。Y 的正常语序为：if they had been in charge of events。

35

According to a recent theory, Archean-age gold-quartz vein systems were formed over two billion years ago from magmatic fluids that originated from molten granite-like bodies deep beneath the surface of the Earth.

难度系数： B-

语句结构及读法：

第一层： According to a recent theory, Archean-age gold-quartz vein systems were formed over two billion years ago from magmatic fluids [X].

第二层： X = magmatic fluids originated from molten granite-like bodies deep beneath the surface of the Earth

译　文： 根据一个最近的理论，来源于岩浆流的太古代的金－石英矿脉系统形成于20多亿年前，这些岩浆流来自地球表面下方深处熔融的花岗岩状体。

难点分析：

本句有两个难点。一是主句中的谓语动词 were formed from 被状语 over two billion years ago 隔开了，给阅读增加了一些难度。二是在 X 末尾的 deep beneath the surface of the Earth 是 molten granite-like bodies 的限制性定语，这里出现了一个省略的现象，可以还原为：granite-like bodies <u>that is</u> deep beneath the surface of the Earth，画线部分为省略部分。

36

For example, the spiral arrangement of scale-bract complexes on ovule-bearing pine cones, where the female reproductive organs of conifers are located, is important to the production of airflow patterns that spiral over the cone's surfaces, thereby passing airborne pollen from one scale to the next.

难度系数： B-

语句结构及读法：

第一层： For example, the spiral arrangement of scale-bract complexes on ovule-bearing pine cones, [X_1], is important to the production of airflow patterns [X_2].

第二层： X_1 = the female reproductive organs of conifers are located in ovule-bearing pine cones

> X_2 = airflow patterns spiral over the cone's surfaces, <Y>
>
> 第三层：Y = airflow patterns thereby pass airborne pollen from one scale to the next
>
> 译　　文：例如，在带有胚珠的松球上的鳞苞综合体的螺旋状排列（这些松球是针叶树的雌性繁殖器官所在的地方）对于产生一种气流模式很重要，这种气流模式在松球表面螺旋式上升，因此把空气中的花粉传到一个又一个的鳞苞上。
>
> **难点分析：**
>
> 　　　　主句的主语十分长，而且其中有许多专有名词，很多考生在考试中可能看完这个主语就崩溃了。这个主语的核心词是 arrangement，简单来讲其意思是：一种螺旋状排列对于产生一种气流是很重要的。Y 是一个伴随状语，可以近似看作和其主句主语相同的普通状语从句。

37

New data from United States Forest Service ecologists show that for every dollar spent on controlled small scale burning, forest thinning, and the training of fire-management personnel, seven dollars are saved that would have been spent on extinguishing big fires.

难度系数： B+

语句结构及读法：

第一层：New data from United States Forest Service ecologists show X.

第二层：X = <Y_1>, seven dollars are saved [Y_2]

第三层：Y_1 = for every dollar [Z]

　　　　Y_2 = seven dollars would have been spent on extinguishing big fires

第四层：Z = every dollar is spent on controlled small scale burning, forest thinning, and the training of fire-management personnel

译　　文：来自 USFS 的生态学者的新数据显示：在控制小规模燃烧、森林抚育间伐和训练消防人员上每花费一美元，就会节省可能会花在扑灭森林大火上的七美元。

难点分析：

　　　　第一，Y_1 是一个很长的状语，其由核心词 every dollar 和一个简化定语从句 Z 构成。也正是由于这个状语的长度很长，可能会让初学者无法分清第二层信息内部的主干结构。for 本身既可以做介词，表示"对于"；也可以做连词，表示"因为"。如果看不清句意，则很有可能误认为 Y₁ 是一个"原因状语从句"，从而产生理解偏差。

第二，Y₂ 是一个定语从句，由于这个从句相较于主干谓语 are saved 来说也很长，所以其被倒装于谓语动词后面，正常语序为：<u>Seven dollars that would have been spent on extinguishing big fires</u> are saved.

38

Although the June insurrection of 1848 and the Paris Commune of 1871 would be considered watersheds of nineteenth-century French history by any standard, they also present the social historian with a signal advantage: these failed insurrections created a mass of invaluable documentation as a by-product of authorities' efforts to search out and punish the rebels.

难度系数：B+

语句结构及读法：

第一层：<X₁>, they also present the social historian with a signal advantage: (X₂).

第二层：X₁ = Although the June insurrection of 1848 and the Paris Commune of 1871 would be considered watersheds of nineteenth-century French history by any standard

X₂ = these failed insurrections created a mass of invaluable documentation as a by-product of authorities' efforts to search out and punish the rebels

译　文：虽然 1848 年 6 月起义和 1871 年巴黎公社无论从何种标准来看都可以被认为是 19 世纪法国历史的分水岭，但同时，它们也给社会历史学者带来一个显著的优势：作为当局在努力搜寻和惩罚反叛者时所带来的副产品，这些失败的起义创造了大量非常宝贵的档案。

难点分析：

本句的修饰成分不多，仅从语法概念上看算不上什么难句。但是，本句中有很多抽象名词以及较难掌握的词汇，它们给这个句子添加了许多额外的难度。watershed：分水岭；signal advantage：显著优势（这里的 signal 是形容词，不是"信号"的意思）；insurrection：起义；rebel：叛军。

39

This succession was based primarily on a series of deposits and events not directly related to glacial and interglacial periods, rather than on the more usual modern method of studying biological remains found in interglacial beds themselves interstratified within glacial deposits.

难度系数：B

语句结构及读法：

第一层：This succession was based primarily on a series of deposits and events [X_1], rather than on the more usual modern method of studying biological remains [X_2].

第二层：X_1 = deposits and events are not directly related to glacial and interglacial periods
X_2 = biological remains are found in interglacial beds [Y]

第三层：Y = interglacial beds are themselves interstratified within glacial deposits

译　文：这个排序主要建立在一系列与冰川期和间冰期没有直接联系的沉积物和事件之上，而不是建立在更常用的研究生物残骸的现代方法之上。这些生物残骸被发现夹杂在冰川期沉积物之间的间冰期的底层。

难点分析：

本句包含很多简化定语从句：X_1 是简化定语从句，修饰 deposits and events；X_2 是简化定语从句，修饰 biological remains；Y 是简化定语从句，修饰 interglacial beds。另外，第一层中由 rather than 连接的两个平行对象较长，初学者不易将两者联系起来，即 on a series of deposits and events 和 on the more usual modern method 平行。

40

Most senior executives are familiar with the formal decision analysis models and tools, and those who use such systematic methods for reaching decisions are occasionally leery of solutions suggested by these methods which run counter to their sense of the correct course of action.

难度系数：B

语句结构及读法：

第一层：X_1 and X_2.
第二层：X_1 = Most senior executives are familiar with the formal decision analysis models and tools

第三层：X_2 = those [Y_1] are occasionally leery of solutions [Y_2]
　　　　Y_1 = those use such systematic methods for reaching decisions
　　　　Y_2 = solutions are suggested by these methods [Z]

第四层：Z = these methods run counter to their sense of the correct course of action

译　文：大多数高级管理者熟悉那些正式的决策分析模型和工具，而且，使用这些系统的方法来做出决策的高级管理者会偶尔对这些方法所建议的解决方案心怀疑虑，因为这些方法与他们对行动的正确路径的感觉相反。

难点分析：

主干由合句构成。X_2 具有一个很长的定语从句 who use such systematic methods for reaching decisions，它使得主语和谓语相隔较远。Z 是一个简化定语从句，来自于一个普通的被动语态定语从句。由于这个 suggest 是过去分词，很像谓语动词，由此容易导致错判句子重心。

41

Though these maps incorporate some information gleaned directly from Native Americans, rarely has Native American cartography contributed to this official record, which has been compiled, surveyed, and authenticated by non-Native Americans.

难度系数：B-

语句结构及读法：

第一层：<X_1>, rarely has Native American cartography contributed to this official record, [X_2].

第二层：X_1 = though these maps incorporate some information [Y]
　　　　X_2 = this official record has been compiled, surveyed, and authenticated by non-Native Americans

第三层：Y = some information is gleaned directly from Native American

译　文：虽然这些地图包含了一些直接从美洲原住民那里搜集来的信息，但是美洲原住民的地图很少能对官方记录有用。这些官方记录是由非美洲原住民编辑、调查和认证的。

难点分析：

由于把否定副词 rarely 提前，所以第一层句子中出现了一个倒装结构，还原为正常语序则有：Native American cartography rarely has contributed to this official record.

42

Even as the number of females processed through juvenile courts climbs steadily, an implicit consensus remains among scholars in criminal justice that male adolescents define the delinquency problem in the United States.

难度系数： B

语句结构及读法：

第一层： <X₁>, an implicit consensus remains among scholars, <X₂>.

第二层： X₁ = Even as the number of females [Y] climbs steadily

X₂ = in criminal justice that male adolescents define the delinquency problem in the United States

第三层： Y = females are processed through juvenile courts

译　文： 即使被青少年法庭审理的女性的人数稳定增加，但是在刑事司法中，男性青少年是美国青少年犯罪问题的重点，这个没有明说的共识仍然在学者中存在。

难点分析：

第一，Y 是一个简化定语从句，来自于被动语态的定语从句。由于在 X₁ 中有很多名词并非"熟脸"，所以初学者可能会把过去分词 processed 误看作谓语动词，从而弄错句意。

第二，X₂ 中的 that male adolescents define the delinquency problem in the United States 是 consensus 的同位语从句，解释此"共识"的具体内容。其中一些不常见的名词（诸如：adolescents、delinquency 等）增加了读者的理解难度。

43

Low levels of straying are crucial, since the process provides a source of novel genes and a mechanism by which a location can be repopulated should the fish there disappear.

难度系数： B

语句结构及读法：

第一层： Low levels of straying are crucial, <X₁ and X₂>.

第二层： X₁ = since the process provides a source of novel genes

　　　　　　X₂ = since the process provides a mechanism [Y]

第三层：Y = a location can be repopulated by a mechanism, <Z>

第四层：Z = should the fish there disappear

译　文：低等级的走失是重要的，因为这个过程提供了一个新基因的来源和一种机制。通过这种机制一个地方可以有新的鱼入驻，如果当地的鱼消失了的话。

难点分析：

首先需要看出 a source of novel genes 和 a mechanism 是平行的，它们都是 provide 的宾语。其次，在句子的末尾，should the fish there disappear 是一个倒装结构，还原为正常语序为：if the fish there should disappear。

44

Evolutionary psychology holds that the human mind is not a "blank slate" but instead comprises specialized mental mechanisms that were developed to solve specific problems human ancestors faced millions of years ago.

难度系数： B-

语句结构及读法：

第一层：Evolutionary psychology holds X.

第二层：X = that the human mind is Y₁ but Y₂

第三层：Y₁ = not a "blank slate"

　　　　Y₂ = the human mind instead comprises specialized mental mechanisms [Z]

第四层：Z = mental mechanisms were developed to solve specific problems [M]

第五层：M = (that) human ancestors faced specific problems millions of years ago

译　文：进化心理学认为人类的大脑不是一块"空白石板"，而是包含为了解决特殊问题而开发的专门的心理机制，这些问题是人类祖先在几百万年以前就面对的。

难点分析：

本句层级较多。第一个难点是由 not... but... 引导的 but 后面的主语 human mind 的省略；第二个难点在最后出现，由于先行词 specific problems 在其后面的定语从句中充当 face 的宾语，所以此处省略了关系词 that（见第五层括号内）。对定

111

语从句的省略不熟悉的考生可能会误判 face 句的层级以致读错句子重心或无法理解句意。

45

With the conclusion of a burst of activity, the lactic acid level is high in the body fluids, leaving the large animal vulnerable to attack until the acid is reconverted, via oxidative metabolism, by the liver into glucose, which is then sent (in part) back to the muscles for glycogen resynthesis.

难度系数： B+

语句结构及读法：

第一层： <With the conclusion of a burst of activity>, the lactic acid level is high in the body fluids, <X>.

第二层： X = the lactic acid level leaves the large animal vulnerable to attack, <Y>

第三层： Y = until the acid is reconverted, via oxidative metabolism, by the liver into glucose, [Z]

第四层： Z = glucose is then sent (in part) back to the muscles for glycogen resynthesis

译　文： 随着爆发出来的运动的结束，体液中的乳酸含量会变得很高，这使得大型动物处于易受攻击的状态一直到乳酸通过有氧新陈代谢的方式被肝脏转化成葡萄糖为止。这些葡萄糖接下来又会为了糖原的重新合成而被（部分地）传送回肌肉中。

难点分析：

本句的修饰语较多，由此构成了"长成分"这一难点。

第一，在第二层中，原句是一个"伴随状语"，是一个主语与其主句相同的普通状语从句的简化，这种简化复合句一直是阅读长难句的难点，请大家务必熟悉简化句的长相以及来源。

第二，词组 reconvert sth. into 被插入语 via oxidative metabolism 和被动语态的逻辑主语 by the liver 隔开了，造成了一定的理解难度。改为主动语态应为：Via oxidative metabolism, the liver reconverted the acid into glucose.

第三，本句中的专有名词比较多。在 GMAT 考试中，虽然绝大部分的专有名词在阅读文章中会被完整地解释，但是能不靠解释就认识这些单词绝对是有好处的。

46

If anatomical similarity in the flippers resulted from similar environmental pressures, as posited by the convergent-evolution theory, one would expect walruses and seals, but not seals and sea lions, to have similar flippers.

难度系数：B

语句结构及读法：

第一层：<X₁>, X₂ but X₃.

第二层：X₁ = If anatomical similarity in the flippers resulted from similar environmental pressures, <Y>

X₂ = one would expect walruses and seals to have similar flippers

X₃ = one would not expect seals and sea lions to have similar flippers

第三层：Y = as posited by the convergent-evolution theory

译　文：如果鳍脚的结构相似是由环境压力相似造成的，正如趋同演化原理所假定的那样，那么我们就会期待海象和海豹，而不是海豹和海狮，有类似的鳍脚。

难点分析：

第一，第一层信息中的合句出现了大量的省略现象，属于平行结构的省略。类似于这样的省略在 GMAT 长难句中屡见不鲜，要求大家能在大脑中还原出正常结构。

第二，as posited by the convergent-evolution theory 是一个状语，在语法上既可以修饰前面的 result 句，又可以修饰后面的 expect 句。读懂它要求考生拥有边看语法边读语义的能力。由于其在意思上讲的是 result 句的内容，所以其是 result 句的状语。

47

Granted that the presence of these elements need not argue for an authorial awareness of novelistic construction comparable to that of Henry James, their presence does encourage attempts to unify the novel's heterogeneous parts.

难度系数：B+

语句结构及读法：

第一层： <X>, their presence does encourage attempts to unify the novel's heterogeneous parts.

第二层： X= Granted that the presence of these elements need not argue for an authorial awareness of novelistic construction [Y]

第三层： Y=novelistic construction is comparable to that of Henry James

译　　文： 即使这些要素的存在不必为作者对小说结构（此小说结构可以与 Henry James 的相媲美）的意识辩护，但是它们的存在的确鼓励人们尝试去统一这部小说里那些成分混杂的部分。

难点分析：

第一，如果我们不认识 granted that，乃至不知道这个词是连词，那么这个句子的难度则会陡然上升。将这个句子评为 B+ 级难度也主要来源于此。granted that 整体是一个连词，是"即使"的意思，与后文（它的主句）之间有一种"让步、转折"的关系。

第二，argue for 这个词组虽然常见，但是也有一定的难度，尤其是和 need not 连在一起的时候。need not argue for 的意思是"不必为……辩护"。

第三，comparable to that of Henry James 是省略了 that is 的定语从句。这是一个不规则的省略。当先行词在定语从句中充当主语时，通常不能省略关系词。但是，本句省略了这个关系词和 be 动词，没有别的办法，必须读懂并且熟悉。正常语句为：novelistic construction (that is) comparable to that of Henry James。

48

His thesis works relatively well when applied to discrimination against Blacks in the United States, but his definition of racial prejudice as "racially-based negative prejudgments against a group generally accepted as a race in any given region of ethnic competition", can be interpreted as also including hostility toward such ethnic groups as the Chinese in California and Jews in medieval Europe.

难度系数： B

语句结构及读法：

第一层： X_1 but X_2.

第二层：X_1 = His thesis works relatively well <Y_1>

X_2 = his definition of racial prejudice as "racially-based negative prejudgments against a group [Y_2]", can be interpreted as also including hostility toward such ethnic groups as the Chinese in California and Jews in medieval Europe

第三层：Y_1 = when his thesis is applied to discrimination against Blacks in the United States
Y_2 = a group is generally accepted as a race in any given region of ethnic competition

译　文：当被应用于针对美国黑人的种族歧视时，他的论点较为有效，但是，他把种族偏见定义为"对于一组人基于种族的负面判断（这组人通常在种族竞争的任意特定区域里被认作一个种族）"，这能够解释为也包括了对诸如加州华人和中世纪欧洲犹太人这样的种族团体的敌意。

难点分析：

由 60 个词构成的句子永远不会是简单的句子。虽然语法结构不是很复杂，但是长成分频繁地插入还是会令本句跻身长难句之列。

第一，Y_1 是一个伴随状语（由"连词 + 分词"构成的从句一定是伴随状语），来自一个与其主句主语相同的简化状语从句，由此可知 applied 的主语为 his thesis。

第二，X_2 的主语极长，这使得真正主语的核心词 definition 与其谓语动词 can be interpreted as 相隔很远。这一长串主语描述的其实是一个事件，即：He defines racial prejudice as "racially-based negative prejudgments against a group". 当然，由于本句的语义逻辑，这个句子被名物化为名词短语。

49

However, recent scholarship has strongly suggested that those aspects of early New England culture that seem to have been most distinctly Puritan, such as the strong religious orientation and the communal impulse, were not even typical of New England as a whole, but were largely confined to the two colonies of Massachusetts and Connecticut.

难度系数：B

语句结构及读法：

第一层： However, recent scholarship has strongly suggested X.

第二层： X = that Y_1 but Y_2

第三层： Y_1 = those aspects of early New England culture [Z], such as the strong religious orientation and the communal impulse, were not even typical of New England as a whole

Y_2 = those aspects of early New England culture were largely confined to the two colonies of Massachusetts and Connecticut

第四层： Z = those aspects of early New England culture seem to have been most distinctly Puritan

译　文： 但是，最近的学术研究强烈表明一个观点：早期新英格兰文化中那些看起来带有非常明确的清教徒风格的方面，比如强烈的宗教意识与社群意识，从整体上来说并不是新英格兰的典型特征，而是大部分被限制在马萨诸塞州和康涅狄格州这两个殖民地中的特征。

难点分析：

第一，定语从句 Z 的出现使得 suggest 宾语从句中的主语 aspects 和其谓语动词 were 相隔较远，形成了"长成分"的难点。

第二，第二层信息中由 but 引导的两个合句出现了平行结构的省略现象。大家需要通过语义判断出 were largely confined to 的平行对象，进而在大脑中补出其主语 aspects。

50

Those of us who hoped, with Kolb, that Kolb's newly published complete edition of Proust's correspondence for 1909 would document the process in greater detail are disappointed.

难度系数： B+

语句结构及读法：

第一层： Those of us [X] are disappointed.

第二层： X = those of us hoped, with Kolb, Y

第三层： Y = that Kolb's newly published complete edition of Proust's correspondence for 1909 would document the process in greater detail

译　文：我们当中的一些人失望了，那些人和 Kolb 都希望 Kolb 新出版的 Proust 1909 年书信的完整版可以更详细地记录这个过程。

难点分析：

虽然本句不长，但难度不小。

第一，第一层信息的主语 those of us 和谓语动词 are disappointed 相隔了 22 个词，很容易让初学者找不到真正的主语，感觉动词堆了好几个，无法分清层级。

第二，第二层信息的谓语动词 hope 和其宾语（从句）之间插入了 with Kolb，需联想到该插入部分为状语，修饰 hope 这个行为。

第三，第三层信息是 hope 的宾语从句。该从句中的主语也很长，并且掺入了过去分词 published。由于 publish 的过去分词和过去式"长相"相同，且真正的谓语动词 document 又和名词长相相同，所以我们很容易看错谓语动词，从而彻底无法理解整个句子。

51

Hank Morgan, the hero of Mark Twain's *A Connecticut Yankee in King Arthur's Court*, is a nineteenth-century master mechanic who, mysteriously awakening in sixth-century Britain, launches what he hopes will be a peaceful revolution to transform Arthurian Britain into an industrialized modern democracy.

难度系数：B+

语句结构及读法：

第一层：Hank Morgan, the hero of Mark Twain's *A Connecticut Yankee in King Arthur's Court*, is a nineteenth-century master mechanic [X].

第二层：X= a nineteenth-century master mechanic, <Y_1>, launches Y_2 to transform Arthurian Britain into an industrialized modern democracy

第三层：Y_1= a nineteenth-century master mechanic mysteriously awakens in sixth-century Britain

Y_2= what he hopes will be a peaceful revolution

译　文：Hank Morgan——Mark Twain 的著作《康州美国佬在亚瑟王朝》的主人公，是 19 世纪一位杰出的机械师。这位机械师在 6 世纪的英国神秘苏醒并且发动了一场他所希望的和平革命，从而把亚瑟英国转变为工业化的现代民主国家。

难点分析：

第一，Y_1 是一个伴随状语，可以近似看作一个主语与其主句主语相同的普通状语从句。它的加入使得定语从句 X 中的主语"机械师"和其谓语动词"发动（launch）"相隔较远。

第二，由于 Y_2 这种不常见的宾语从句的存在，本来十分简单的第二层信息会令很多考生困惑。第二层信息是一个 SVOC 结构，Y_2 充当了宾语。由 what 引导的名词性从句是十分常见的，但是大部分考生熟悉的是 what 在从句中充当主语的情况，例如：What is much more difficult to determine is the number of players. 实际上，what 也可以在其引导的从句内部充当宾语，例如 Y_2 的正常语序为：he hopes what will be a peaceful revolution。

52

Even the requirement that biomaterials processed from these materials be nontoxic to host tissue can be met by techniques derived from studying the reactions of tissue cultures to biomaterials or from short-term implants.

难度系数： B-

语句结构及读法：

第一层： Even the requirement (X_1) can be met by techniques [X_2].

第二层： X_1 = that biomaterials [Y] be nontoxic to host tissue

X_2 = techniques are derived from studying the reactions of tissue cultures to biomaterials or from short-term implants

第三层： Y = biomaterials are processed from these materials

译　文： 即使是这样的要求（即从这些材料中处理得到的生物材料应该对宿主组织无害）也可以由一些技术来满足。这些技术是从研究组织培养对生物材料的反应或从短期植入中得到的。

难点分析：

本句中出现了两次过去分词做定语（即简化定语从句）的现象，分别是 processed

和 derived。另外，X₂ 中存在一个平行结构的省略，正常语序为：Techniques are derived from studying the reactions of tissue cultures to biomaterials or techniques are derived from short-term implants.

53

When, in the seventeenth century, Descartes and Hobbes rejected medieval philosophy, they did not think of themselves, as modern philosophers do, as proposing a new and better philosophy, but rather as furthering "the warfare between science and theology".

难度系数：B-

语句结构及读法：

第一层：<X₁>, X₂ but rather X₃.

第二层：X₁=When, in the seventeenth century, Descartes and Hobbes rejected medieval philosophy

X₂=they did not think of themselves, <Y>, as proposing a new and better philosophy

X₃=they did think of themselves as furthering "the warfare between science and theology"

第三层：Y=as modern philosophers do

译　文：当 Descartes 和 Hobbes 在 17 世纪拒绝接受中世纪的哲学时，他们像现代哲学家那样，没有认为自己能提出一种新的、更好的哲学，而是认为自己在推进"科学与神学之间的战争"。

难点分析：

本句中出现了很多插入语，在一定程度上增加了阅读的障碍。另外，整个主句是一个长长的平行结构的省略（见 X₂ 和 X₃），可能会让初学者误判 but 后面句子的层级。

54

The physicist rightly dreads precise argument, since an argument that is convincing only if it is precise loses all its force if the assumptions on which it is based are slightly changed, whereas an argument that is convincing though imprecise may well be stable under small perturbations of its underlying assumptions.

难度系数： B+

语句结构及读法：

第一层： The physicist rightly dreads precise argument, <X>.

第二层： X=since Y_1, whereas Y_2

第三层： Y_1=an argument [Z_1] loses all its force <Z_2>

Y_2=an argument [Z_3] may well be stable under small perturbations of its underlying assumptions

第四层： Z_1=an argument is convincing <M_1>

Z_2=if the assumptions [M_2] are slightly changed

Z_3=an argument is convincing though imprecise

第五层： M_1=only if it is precise

M_2=it is based on assumptions

译　文： 物理学家不敢做出精确的论证，因为一个仅当精确时才具有说服力的论证在它基于的假设稍微改变的情况下就会失去其全部说服力，而一个尽管不精确但具有说服力的论证在其基于的假设稍有变动时依然可能是很稳定的。

难点分析：

虽然长度"只"有51个词，但是本句的层级却有五层。一个拥有如此多从句的句子必然会涉及"长成分"这一难点，如果不能很好地进行分层的话，则很容易弄错句子重心。更加令人感到头疼的是，一般的句子，如果不读第三层之后的信息对理解文意影响不大，但是本句若是不读细节信息，则很难理解句意。Y_1和Y_2中产生对比的部分全在第四层的信息中，这就要求大家仔细观察每一层的信息，这无疑也加大了句子的难度。

55

As they gained cohesion, the Bluestockings came to regard themselves as a women's group and to possess a sense of female solidarity lacking in the salonnieres, who remained isolated from one another by the primacy each held in her own salon.

难度系数：B-

语句结构及读法：

第一层：X_1 and X_2.

第二层：X_1 = <Y_1>, the Bluestockings came to regard themselves as a women's group

X_2 = the Bluestockings came to possess a sense of female solidarity [Y_2]

第三层：Y_1 = As they gained cohesion

Y_2 = female solidarity lacks in the salonnieres, [Z]

第四层：Z = salonnieres remained isolated from one another by the primacy [M]

第五层：M = each held the primacy in her own salon

译　文：随着她们增加了凝聚力，"蓝袜女们"开始把自己视为一个妇女团体，并且持有一个"沙龙女们"所缺乏的团结意识。这些沙龙女们由于每个人都在自己的沙龙中占据老大地位而彼此间仍然相互不来往。

难点分析：

第一，第一层信息中含有"平行结构省略"这一难点。但是，作者友好地在 possess 前面补出了 to，让本句的难度下降不少。

第二，Y_2 是一个简化定语从句；M 是一个定语从句的省略现象。由于 M 部分（定语从句）的先行词 the primacy 在 M 中做 held 的宾语，所以作者在此处省略了关系词 that，还原成正常的定语从句则有：the primacy that each held in her own salon。

56

A long-held view of the history of the English colonies that became the United States has been that England's policy toward these colonies before 1763 was dictated by commercial interests and that a change to a more imperial policy, dominated by expansionist militarist objectives, generated the tensions that ultimately led to the American Revolution.

难度系数：B

语句结构及读法：

第一层：A long-held view of the history of the English colonies [X_1] has been X_2 and X_3.

第二层：X_1 = the English colonies became the United States

X_2=that England's policy toward these colonies before 1763 was dictated by commercial interests

X_3=a long-held view of the history of the English colonies has been that a change to a more imperial policy, [Y_1], generated the tensions [Y_2]

第三层：Y_1=a more imperial policy is dominated by expansionist militarist objectives

Y_2=the tensions ultimately led to the American Revolution

译　　文： 对于后来成为美国的英国殖民地的历史，长期以来的观点是：英国在1763年以前对这些殖民地的政策是由商业利益决定的，并且一个更趋向于帝国主义政策的改变是被扩张主义军事主义目标所主宰的，这产生了最终导致美国革命的矛盾。

难点分析：

第一，第一层信息的主语长达15个词，而谓语动词只有两个词，表语部分又是一直到句尾的两个合句。因此，本句的主干部分不容易找对，稍有不慎就容易误判句子的重心。

第二，X_3是一个平行结构省略的现象。作者比较友好地补出了连词that来展示其平行对象X_2。

第三，Y_1是一个简化定语从句，可以近似看作：a more imperial policy, which is dominated by expansionist militarist objectives。

57

As my own studies have advanced, I have been increasingly impressed with the functional similarities between insect and vertebrate societies and less so with the structural differences that seem, at first glance, to constitute such as immense gulf between them.

难度系数： B

语句结构及读法：

第一层：X_1 and X_2.

第二层：X_1=<Y_1>, I have been increasingly impressed with the functional similarities between insect and vertebrate societies

X_2=I have been less impressed with the structural differences [Y_2]

第三层：Y₁=As my own studies have advanced

Y₂=the structural differences seem, at first glance, to constitute such as immense gulf between them

译　文：随着我自己的研究不断进展，我越来越深刻地感觉到昆虫社群和脊椎动物社群之间功能上的相似性，并且越来越感觉不到它们之间乍看上去构成类似鸿沟的结构差异。

难点分析：

第一，本句的主要难点是平行结构的省略。在 X₂ 部分，原句中出现了 less so with，一些经验不足的考生可能看不出这里的 so 是干什么的。实际上，英语口语中经常出现 do so 这样的句子，这时 so 指代前面说过的整个句子。同理，本句中的 so 也是指代前面出现的句子，即 I have been impressed。由此可知，X₂ 原本是一个完整的句子，由于其主谓结构和前半句相同，所以用了 so 来代替。

第二，在 Y₂ 这个定语从句中，seem to 被插入语 at first glance 隔开，我们会难以把 seem to constitute 联系在一起。

58

Because the potential hazards pollen grains are subject to as they are transported over long distances are enormous, wind-pollinated plants have, in the view above, compensated for the ensuing loss of pollen through happenstance by virtue of producing an amount of pollen that is one to three orders of magnitude greater than the amount produced by species pollinated by insects.

难度系数： B

语句结构及读法：

第一层：<X₁>, wind-pollinated plants have, in the view above, compensated for the ensuing loss of pollen through happenstance by virtue of producing an amount of pollen [X₂].

第二层：X₁=Because the potential hazards [Y₁] are enormous

X₂=an amount of pollen is one to three orders of magnitude greater than the amount [Y₂]

第三层：Y₁=pollen grains are subject to the potential hazards <Z₁>

Y₂=the amount is produced by species [Z₂]

第四层：Z_1=as they are transported over long distances

Z_2=species are pollinated by insects

译　　文：因为花粉颗粒在长距离传播的过程中所面临的危险十分巨大，所以，按照上述观点，风媒植物为了补偿因为偶然事件所带来的花粉损失，就会产生很多花粉，这个花粉量会比昆虫传粉的物种所产生的花粉量大 1～3 个数量级。

难点分析：

第一，在 X_1 中，the potential hazards 拥有 Y_1 这个定语从句，虽然很多考生可能已经熟悉了定语从句的省略现象，但是在本句中可能依然难以分辨。实际上，Y 是一个省略了关系词的定语从句（先行词在从句中充当宾语），还原为正常的定语从句则有：the potential hazards that pollen grains are subject to。

第二，X_2 是一个被各种从句切割得支离破碎的句子。其中，Y_2 和 Z_2 均是简化定语从句。并且由于两者均是过去分词短语，所以初学者很容易将其误认为是句子的谓语动词。

59

The recent discovery of detailed similarities in the skeletal structure of the flippers in all three groups undermines the attempt to explain superficial resemblance as due to convergent evolution—the independent development of similarities between unrelated groups in response to similar environmental pressures.

难度系数： B

语句结构及读法：

第一层：The recent discovery of detailed similarities in the skeletal structure of the flippers in all three groups undermines the attempt [X].

第二层：X=the attempt explains superficial resemblance as due to convergent evolution—the independent development of similarities between unrelated groups in response to similar environmental pressures

译　　文：最近在所有三个种群的鳍（flipper）的骨骼结构上发现了详细的相似性，这破坏了把表面的相似性解释为趋同进化的尝试。趋同进化是指在相似的环境压力下，不相关的种群独立发展出相似性。

难点分析：

第一，本句的主语长度惊人，很难找到核心词。仔细分析可知，主语的核心词是 discovery，detailed similarities 是该核心词的定语，in the skeletal structure 是 similarities 的定语，of the flippers in all three groups 是 structure 的定语。

第二，我们都熟悉 explain A as B 这个句型，意思是"把 A 解释为 B"，A 和 B 应为名词。在本句中，B 却是一个介词短语，即 due to convergent evolution。有些考生在这里就卡住了，拼命在 as 后面寻找名词，认为只有一个名词才能是"被解释成为"的对象。在阅读句子的过程中，碰上这种"语法错误"一定要以理解意思为第一标准，不要过分纠结（这种情况其实称不上语法错误，只是大家不熟悉罢了）。

60

With regard to this last question, we might note in passing that Thompson, while rightly restoring laboring people to the stage of eighteenth-century English history, has probably exaggerated the opposition of these people to the inroads of capitalist consumerism in general; for example, laboring people in eighteenth-century England readily shifted from home-brewed beer to standardized beer produced by huge, heavily capitalized urban breweries.

难度系数： B+

语句结构及读法：

第一层：X_1 ; X_2.

第二层：X_1 = With regard to this last question, we might note in passing Y_1

X_2 = for example, laboring people in eighteenth-century England readily shifted from home-brewed beer to standardized beer [Y_2]

第三层：Y_1 = that Thompson, <Z>, has probably exaggerated the opposition of these people to the inroads of capitalist consumerism in general

Y_2 = standardized beer is produced by huge, heavily capitalized urban breweries

第四层：Z = while Thompson rightly restores laboring people to the stage of eighteenth-century English history

译　　文：关于这最后一个问题，我们可以顺便指出：虽然 Thompson 正确地把劳动人民恢复到了 18 世纪英国历史的舞台上，但是他可能夸大了这些人对一般资本主义消费主义侵蚀的抵制；例如，在 18 世纪英国的劳动人民已经从家酿的啤酒转向了由巨大的、高度资本化的城市啤酒厂所生产的标准化啤酒。

难点分析：

第一，X_1 的谓语动词是 note，其后的从句是 note 的宾语从句。那么，in passing 是什么呢？这里大家可以把 in passing 处理为一个副词（即状语），是"顺便地"的意思。

第二，Z 是一个伴随状语，是主语与其主句相同的普通状语从句的简化。

第三，句末出现的"produced by huge, heavily capitalized urban breweries"是一个简化定语从句，正常的定语从句为：standardized beer that is produced by huge, heavily capitalized urban breweries。由于此处是过去分词短语，所以初学者可能会以为 produce 是谓语动词，从而错判句子的重心。

61

Achieving necessary matches in physical properties across interfaces between living and non-living matter requires knowledge of which molecules control the bonding of cells to each other — an area that we have not yet explored thoroughly.

难度系数：B-

语句结构及读法：

第一层：Achieving necessary matches in physical properties across interfaces between living and non-living matter requires knowledge of which molecules control the bonding of cells to each other — (X).

第二层：X = an area [that we have not yet explored thoroughly]

译　　文：实现有生命的与无生命的物质之间在物理性质上达到必要的匹配需要了解到底是什么分子在控制细胞的彼此连接——这是我们到目前为止尚未透彻研究的领域。

难点分析：

第一，本句主语较长：主语是 Achieving necessary matches 这样一个动名词（从 in 开始是修饰 matches 的定语）。谓语是 requires，宾语是 knowledge。

第二，最大的难点应该是对 of which 的理解。考生们看到 which 可能就会条件反射地认为这是一个定语从句，从而开始找其先行词，对句子进行分层。但是，本句中的这个 which 偏偏不是定语从句的关系词，而是一个普通的形容词，意思是"哪个，什么"。

62

Some support for his theory can be found in evidence such as that drawn from Herodotus, the Greek "historian" of the fifth century B. C., who speaks of an Amazonian society, the Sauromatae, where the women hunted and fought in wars.

难度系数： B

语句结构及读法：

第一层：Some support for his theory can be found in evidence such as [X].

第二层：X=evidence is drawn from Herodotus,（the Greek "historian" of the fifth century B. C.）, [Y]

第三层：Y=Herodotus speaks of an Amazonian society,（the Sauromatae）, [Z]

第四层：Z=the women hunted and fought in wars in the Sauromatae

译　　文： 对于他的理论的一些支持可以在证据中发现，例如从 Herodotus 处得到的证据。Herodotus 是公元前 5 世纪希腊的"历史学家"，他提到了一个亚马孙社会 Sauromatae，在那里女性捕猎而且在战争中打仗。

难点分析：

第一，such as 后面出现的 that 为限定词，that 后面省略了 evidence，可还原为：such as that（evidence）drawn from Herodotus。

第二，Herodotus 后面出现了许多同位语和定语，由于这些修饰语中含有许多不认识的专有名词，所以我们只能通过分析语法来确定它们各自的修饰对象，进而理解句意。

63

In order to understand the nature of the ecologist's investigation, we may think of the density-dependent effects on growth parameters as the "signal" ecologists are trying to isolate and interpret, one that tends to make the population increase from relatively low values or decrease from relatively high ones, while the density-independent effects act to produce "noise" in the population dynamics.

难度系数：B+

语句结构及读法：

第一层： In order to understand the nature of the ecologist's investigation, we may think of the density-dependent effects on growth parameters as the "signal" [X_1], <X_2>.

第二层： X_1＝ecologists are trying to isolate and interpret the "signal", (Y)

X_2＝while the density-independent effects act to produce "noise" in the population dynamics

第三层： Y＝ one [that tends to make the population increase from relatively low values or decrease from relatively high ones]

译　文： 为了理解生态学家研究的本质，我们可以把对生长参数产生的与密度相关的影响当作生态学家尝试去分离和解释的"信号"。这个信号趋向于使总量从相对较低的值增高或者从相对较高的值降低，而与密度无关的影响会在总量的动态变化中扮演"噪音"的角色。

难点分析：

本句用的暗喻较为抽象。对于本科学习通信的人来说，本句是非常容易理解的，类似于信号、噪音等相关的概念早已不陌生。但是对于没有任何通信经验的考生来说，这种暗喻本身不但没有令人更容易理解，反而增加了理解难度。

第一，X_1是一个定语从句。由于先行词在从句内部充当宾语，所以省略了关系词that，正常的定语从句为：the "signal" that ecologists are trying to isolate and interpret。

第二，在句末出现的状语从句X_2也是本句的难点之一。在语法上，状语从句应该"就近修饰"一个句子，也就是说，本句中理论上X_2应该修饰Y句。但是，正如我们之前谈到过的，语法永远是为了承载意思而存在的，如果只读语法不看意思，那将会误判很多句子，尤其是长难句的语义。例如本句，在逻辑上，"与密度无关的影响会在总量的动态变化中扮演'噪音'的角色"很明显是与第一层信息(即我们可以把对生长参数产生的与密度相关的影响当作"信号")具有"同时(while)"关系的，因此 X_2 必然是第一层信息的状语从句。

64

Although these molecules allow radiation at visible wavelengths, where most of the energy of sunlight is concentrated, to pass through, they absorb some of the longer-wavelength, infrared emissions radiated from the Earth's surface, radiation that would otherwise be transmitted back into space.

难度系数：B-

语句结构及读法：

第一层：<X_1>, they absorb some of the longer-wavelength, infrared emissions radiated from the Earth's surface, (X_2).

第二层：X_1 = Although these molecules allow radiation at visible wavelengths, [Y], to pass through

X_2 = radiation [that would otherwise be transmitted back into space]

第三层：Y = most of the energy of sunlight is concentrated in visible wavelengths

译　文：尽管这些分子允许可见波长的辐射通过，这段波长上集中了大部分太阳光的能量，但是它们吸收了一些从地球表面放散出的波长更长的红外线的辐射，这种辐射如果没有被吸收就会被传回太空。

难点分析：

第一，本句的第一个难点在于"长成分"，X_1 中的定语从句 Y 将其中的宾语 radiation 和宾补 to pass through 隔开，使得句意看起来不够连贯。

第二，类似于 the longer-wavelength 这样由 "the *adj.*+*n.*" 构成的复合词均是形容词词性，也就是说，the longer-wavelength 和 infrared 都是名词 emissions 的定语。如果不小心把 the longer-wavelength 看成一个纯名词去和后面的 emissions 并列，那么这个句子就完全理解歪了。

第三，第一层信息中 emissions 的后面是简化定语从句，正常的定语从句为：emissions that are radiated from the Earth's surface。

65

Just as young children can count numbers in series without grasping the principle of ordination, young adolescents may have in their heads many random bits of political information without a secure understanding of those concepts that would give order and meaning to the information.

难度系数：B-

语句结构及读法：

第一层：<X_1>, young adolescents may have in their heads many random bits of political information without a secure understanding of those concepts [X_2].

第二层：X_1=Just as young children can count numbers in series without grasping the principle of ordination

X_2=those concepts would give order and meaning to the information

译　文：就像小孩子不需要掌握排列的原理就可以数数那样，青少年也可以在大脑里储存很多随机的政治信息，但对赋予这些信息次序和意义的概念没有准确了解。

难点分析：

本句的难点主要在第一层信息中。作者在这一层中用了倒装句，这里用倒装是因为直接宾语太长而使宾语补足语 in their heads 和谓语动词 have 相距太远，不利于读者阅读。正常语序为：Young adolescents may have many random bits of political information in their heads. 类似于这样的倒装在 GMAT 考试语文部分十分常见，请大家务必攒足相关经验，在考场上快速识别。

66

Thus, what in contrast to the Puritan colonies appears to Davis to be peculiarly Southern—acquisitiveness, a strong interest in politics and the law, and a tendency to cultivate metropolitan cultural models —was not only more typically English than the cultural patterns exhibited by Puritan Massachusetts and Connecticut, but also almost certainly characteristic of most other early modern British colonies from Barbados north to Rhode Island and New Hampshire.

难度系数：B+

语句结构及读法：

第 一 层： Thus, X₁ was not only more typically English than the cultural patterns [X₂], but also almost certainly characteristic of most other early modern British colonies from Barbados north to Rhode Island and New Hampshire.

第 二 层： X₁=what in contrast to the Puritan colonies appears to Davis to be peculiarly Southern—acquisitiveness, a strong interest in politics and the law, and a tendency to cultivate metropolitan cultural models

X₂=the cultural patterns are exhibited by Puritan Massachusetts and Connecticut

译　　文： 因此，相对于清教徒殖民地来说，那些在 Davis 看来特别有南方色彩的特征——进取心、对政治和法律的强烈兴趣、培养大都市文化模式的欲望——不但比清教的马萨诸塞州和康涅狄格州所展现出来的文化模式更具有典型的英国特征，而且几乎是大部分其他从巴巴多斯岛以北到罗德岛和新罕布什尔州的早期英国殖民地的典型特征。

难点分析：

本句的难点主要在第一层信息的主语上。X₁是一个相当长的主语从句，其主干为：what appears to be peculiarly Southern。这个主语和其谓语动词 was not only… but also… 由于破折号中间插入语的存在而相隔较远，令人一口气看不到谓语动词。另外，X₂是一个简化定语从句，正常的定语从句为：the cultural patterns that are exhibited by Puritan Massachusetts and Connecticut。

67

Fallois proposed that Proust had tried to begin a novel in 1908, abandoned it for what was to be a long demonstration of Saint-Beuve's blindness to the real nature of great writing, found the essay giving rise to personal memories and fictional developments, and allowed these to take over in a steadily developing novel.

难度系数： B+

语句结构及读法：

第一层： Fallois proposed X₁, X₂, X₃ ,and X₄.

第二层： X₁=that Proust had tried to begin a novel in 1908

X₂=that Proust abandoned it for what was to be a long demonstration of Saint-Beuve's blindness to the real nature of great writing

X_3=that Proust found the essay giving rise to personal memories and fictional developments

X_4=that Proust allowed these to take over in a steadily developing novel

译 文：Fallois（法国学者）认为：1908年Proust（《追忆似水年华》的作者）原想写一部小说，随后放弃这一计划转而试图详尽地论证Saint-Beuve（1804—1869年，法国作家、文艺批评家）对于杰作真正本质的盲目无知，后来发现自己写的这篇论文牵扯出一些个人记忆和虚构情节，于是就让这些东西保留在一本平稳铺开的小说中。

难点分析：

本句的结构还算清晰，但是句意着实让人不容易看懂。原句是四个并列句，都是Proust做的事情，这点不难，难的是需要理解这四件事的关系。前两个事件很好理解，即Proust打算写一部小说，然后出于某种原因放弃了。第三件事和前两件事的关系不易读懂，这里的essay前面加了定冠词the，理论上应该指代前面出现过的essay，只不过本句中的essay并非前文的原词重复，而前文用的词是long demonstration。

68

None of these translations to screen and stage, however, dramatize the anarchy at the conclusion of *A Connecticut Yankee in King Arthur's Court*, which ends with the violent overthrow of Morgan's three-year-old progressive order and his return to the nineteenth century, when he apparently commits suicide after being labeled a lunatic for his incoherent babblings about drawbridges and battlements.

难度系数：B+

语句结构及读法：

第一层：None of these translations to screen and stage, however, dramatize the anarchy at the conclusion of *A Connecticut Yankee* [X].

第二层：X=Y_1 and Y_2

第三层：Y_1=*A Connecticut Yankee in King Arthur's Court* ends with the violent overthrow of Morgan's three-year-old progressive order

Y₂=*A Connecticut Yankee in King Arthur's Court* ends with his return to the nineteenth century, [Z]

第四层：Z=he apparently commits suicide <M> in the nineteenth century

第五层：M=after he was labeled a lunatic for his incoherent babblings about drawbridges and battlements

译　　文：但是，这些搬上荧幕或者舞台的译本都没有戏剧性地表现出《康州美国佬在亚瑟王朝》结尾处的无政府主义。《康州美国佬在亚瑟王朝》的结尾是 Morgan 维持了三年的进步秩序被暴动推翻并且他回到了 19 世纪，在 19 世纪他由于语无伦次地说着吊桥和战役而被认为是疯子，之后自杀了。

难点分析：

本句的主要难点是抽象名词较多，它们占用了我们大量的脑容量，使我们很难再把注意力集中在对原句整体语义的把握上。例如：dramatize、anarchy、overthrow。另外，M 部分是一个伴随状语，可以看作主语与其主句相同的普通状语从句的简化。

69

Not only are liver transplants never rejected, but they even induce a state of donor-specific unresponsiveness in which subsequent transplants of other organs, such as skin, from that donor are accepted permanently.

难度系数：B+

语句结构及读法：

第一层：Not only X₁ but X₂.

第二层：X₁=are liver transplants never rejected

X₂=they even induce a state of donor-specific unresponsiveness [Y]

第三层：Y=subsequent transplants of other organs, such as skin, from that donor are accepted permanently in a state of donor-specific unresponsiveness

译　　文：不仅肝脏移植从未被排斥，并且这些移植还诱导了一种供体特异性无反应状态，在这种状态下从供体后续移植来的像皮肤这样的其他器官会被永久地接受。

难点分析：

第一，not only 前置会引起倒装，还原为正常语序则有：Liver transplants are never rejected. 另外，常见的短语是 not only… but also…，但本句中是 not only… but…，这个 also 去哪里了呢？如果没有 also 是否还依然是"递进"的意思呢？答案是肯定的。实际上，not only＋but 才是"不但……而且……"的意思，also 仅是一个副词，可加可不加，没有对错之分。

第二，a state of donor-specific unresponsiveness 后面的定语从句不是就近修饰 unresponsiveness 的，而是修饰 state 的，这要求考生不能只看语法，而要同时兼顾语义。

第三，Y 这个定语从句的结构有些干扰性。such as skin 的插入使得挨在一起的 subsequent transplants of other organs 和 from 被隔开，割裂了原本的语义。另外，from 后面的 that 是一个限定词，对应前面的那个供体，但是在语法形式上很像是引导了一个从句，即 that donor are accepted permanently。我们如果只看语法而没有同步理解语义，则很容易陷入困惑。

70

As rock interfaces are crossed, the elastic characteristics encountered generally change abruptly, which causes part of the energy to be reflected back to the surface, where it is recorded by seismic instruments.

难度系数： B

语句结构及读法：

第一层： <X_1>, the elastic characteristics [X_2] change abruptly, [X_3].

第二层： X_1 = As rock interfaces are crossed

　　　　　X_2 = the elastic characteristics are encountered generally

　　　　　X_3 = which causes part of the energy to be reflected back to the surface, <Y>

第三层： Y = it is recorded by seismic instrument on the surface

译　文： 当穿过岩石界面时，遇到的弹性性质一般会突然改变，这使得一部分的能量被反射回地面，在地面上这些能量被震波记录仪所记录。

难点分析：

第一，X_2 是一个简化定语从句，可以近似看作：the elastic characteristics that

are encountered generally。这种简化定语从句本来是十分常见的，但是本句中的谓语动词 change 偏偏又和其名词形式相同，因此很多人会以为 encountered 不是过去分词而是动词的过去式，从而错判句子重心，无法理解第一层信息。

第二，从语法上来说，X_3 是一个由 which 引导的定语从句，但通过语义及 causes 的单复数（此处 cause 是第三人称单数形式，但其前面的名词均为复数，所以其主语只能是前面的整个句子了）可知，X_3 修饰整个第一层主句。所以在阅读句子时，我们必须以理解文意为先，不必过于拘泥于语法形式。

71

It is not known how rare this resemblance is, or whether it is most often seen in inclusions of silicates such as garnet, whose crystallography is generally somewhat similar to that of diamond; but when present, the resemblance is regarded as compelling evidence that the diamonds and inclusions are truly cogenetic.

难度系数：B

语句结构及读法：

第一层：X_1; X_2.

第二层：X_1 = It is not known how rare this resemblance is, or whether it is most often seen in inclusions of silicates such as garnet, [Y_1]

X_2 = <Y_2>, the resemblance is regarded as compelling evidence (Y_3)

第三层：Y_1 = garnet's crystallography is generally somewhat similar to that of diamond

Y_2 = when present

Y_3 = that the diamonds and inclusions are truly cogenetic

译　文：还不知道这种相似有多罕见，或者它是否最常出现于像石榴石 (garnet) 之类的硅酸盐的包含物中，这种石榴石的晶体结构一般或多或少地类似于钻石的晶体结构；但是当它出现时，这种相似就被认为是证明钻石和这种包含物同源的有力证据。

难点分析：

第一，X_1 句首是一个形式主语 it，其指代后面的两个从句，即 how rare this

resemblance is 和 whether it is most often seen in inclusions of silicates such as garnet（由于这两个从句比较简单，所以没有单独分为一层）。设置该形式主语的原因是那两个从句过长，容易引起头重脚轻。

第二，Y₂ 是一个出现了省略现象的时间状语从句。正常的状语从句为：when crystallography is present。

72

Apparently most massive stars manage to lose sufficient material that their masses drop below the critical value of 1.4 M before they exhaust their nuclear fuel.

难度系数：B+

语句结构及读法：

第一层：Apparently most massive stars manage to lose sufficient material <X>.
第二层：X=that their masses drop below the critical value of 1.4 M <Y>
第三层：Y=before they exhaust their nuclear fuel

译　　文：显然，大部分巨星能够成功地减少足够多的物质来使得它们在耗尽核燃料之前将质量降到 1.4 M 的临界值以下。

难点分析：

本句的难点在于 material 后面由 that 引导的从句。在语法上，单独由 that 引导的从句可能是名词性从句、定语从句、同位语从句。这三种情况在本句中均不适用。实际上，本句的 that 相当于 so that，即其引导了一个结果状语从句。这种现象在 GMAT 考试中非常罕见，难以理解。不过，如果大家能仔细体会本句语义，相信可以猜出此处 that 的用法，还是那句话，不要拘泥于语法形式。

73

Friedrich Engels, however, predicted that women would be liberated from the "social, legal, and economic subordination" of the family by technological developments that made possible the recruitment of "the whole female sex into public industry".

难度系数：B-

语句结构及读法：

第一层：Friedrich Engels, however, predicted X.

第二层：X=that women would be liberated from the "social, legal, and economic subordination" of the family by technological developments [Y]

第三层：Y=technological developments made possible the recruitment of "the whole female sex into public industry"

译　文：但是，Friedrich Engels 预测：女性会被某些技术发展从家庭的"社会、法律和经济的从属地位"中解放出来，这些技术发展使"整个女性群体进入公共事业"成为可能。

难点分析：

第一，X 中被动语态的逻辑主语 technological developments 和其谓语动词 be liberated 被宾补 from the "social, legal, and economic subordination" of the family 隔开，相距较远，所以我们很难把它们联系到一起。

第二，Y 是一个定语从句。在这个定语从句中出现了倒装现象。正常语序为：Technological developments made the recruitment of "the whole female sex into public industry" possible.

74

If she defines feminist criticism as objective and scientific — a valid, verifiable, intellectual method that anyone, whether man or woman, can perform — the definition not only precludes the critic-as-artist approach, but may also impede accomplishment of the utilitarian political objectives of those who seek to change the academic establishment and its thinking, especially about sex roles.

难度系数：B-

语句结构及读法：

第一层：<X_1> the definition not only precludes the critic-as-artist approach, but may also impede accomplishment of the utilitarian political objectives of those [X_2].

第二层： X₁=If she defines feminist criticism as objective and scientific—(Y)—

X₂=those seek to change the academic establishment and its thinking, especially about sex roles

第三层： Y=a valid, verifiable, intellectual method that anyone, whether man or woman, can perform

译　文： 如果她把女权主义评论定义为客观的、科学的——任何一个人，不管是男是女，都可以实行的有效的、可验证的、理性的方式——那么这个定义不仅排除了评论者作为艺术家的方式，而且有可能阻碍那些想要去改变学术界秩序及其思维（特别是关于性别角色的思维）的人达成功利主义的政治目标。

难点分析：

通常来说，条件状语从句应该和主句用逗号隔开。在本句中，由于破折号的存在（两个破折号间的内容本身是用来进一步解释"客观和科学"的），主句和条件状语从句之间不再有逗号，又由于主句主语 the definition 和条件状语中的谓语动词相同，可能更容易让初学者无法搞清 the definition 的作用，无法辨别主句的位置。

75

The appreciation of traditional oral American Indian literature has been limited, hampered by poor translations and by the difficulty, even in the rare culturally sensitive and aesthetically satisfying translation, of completely conveying the original's verse structure, tone, and syntax.

难度系数： B

语句结构及读法：

第一层： The appreciation of traditional oral American Indian literature has been limited, <X>.

第二层： X=Y₁ and Y₂

第三层： Y₁=the appreciation of traditional oral American Indian literature is hampered by poor translations

Y₂=the appreciation of traditional oral American Indian literature is hampered by the difficulty, even in the rare culturally sensitive and aesthetically satisfying translation, of completely conveying the original's verse structure, tone, and syntax

译　　文： 对美国印第安传统口头文学的欣赏还是有限的，因为这种欣赏被拙劣的翻译和在完全传达原作的韵律结构、语调和句法上遇到的困难所阻碍。即使那些少有的对文化敏感的并且在美学上让人满意的翻译中也存在此类困难。

难点分析：

　　第一，X 是伴随状语，可以看作一个主语与其主句主语相同的状语从句的简化。

　　第二，在 Y_2 中，修饰语 even in the rare culturally sensitive and aesthetically satisfying translation 的插入割裂了名词 the difficulty 和其定语"of completely conveying the original's verse structure, tone, and syntax"，使得语义不连贯，增加了理解句子的难度。

76

They were fighting, albeit discreetly, to open the intellectual world to the new science and to liberate intellectual life from ecclesiastical philosophy and envisioned their work as contributing to the growth, not of philosophy, but of research in mathematics and physics.

难度系数： B+

语句结构及读法：

第一层： X_1 and X_2.

第二层： $X_1 = Y_1$ and Y_2

　　　　　$X_2 =$ they envisioned their work as contributing to the growth, not of philosophy, but of research in mathematics and physics

第三层： $Y_1 =$ They were fighting, albeit discreetly, to open the intellectual world to the new science

　　　　　$Y_2 =$ they were fighting to liberate intellectual life from ecclesiastical philosophy

译　　文： 他们谨慎地战斗着，为了对新科学打开学术界的大门，并且为了把学术生活从宗教哲学中解脱出来；他们把自己的工作看成是为数学和物理学的发展而不是为哲学的发展做出贡献。

难点分析：

　　第一，本句中出现了由两个 and 来连接三个成分的情况，大家需要通过结构和语义来判断平行对象。

第二，X₂中，the growth of 是一个很简单的结构，但是本句中的这个结构被分割成了 "the growth, not of philosophy, but of research in mathematics and physics"，加大了句子的难度。

第三，本句中存在很多抽象名词，这些抽象名词看似不重要，但却会增加大脑的负担。例如：albeit 虽然；discreetly 谨慎地；liberate 解放；ecclesiastical 教会的。

77

Furthermore, the ozone molecule is so unstable that only a tiny fraction of ground-level ozone could survive the long trip to the stratosphere, so the ozone layer will not be replenished to any significant degree by the increasing concentrations of ozone that have been detected in recent years near the Earth's surface.

难度系数：B-

语句结构及读法：

第一层：Furthermore, the ozone molecule is so unstable that only a tiny fraction of ground-level ozone could survive the long trip to the stratosphere, <X>.

第二层：X= so the ozone layer will not be replenished to any significant degree by the increasing concentrations of ozone [Y]

第三层：Y=the increasing concentrations of ozone have been detected in recent years near the Earth's surface

译　文：而且，臭氧分子是如此不稳定以至于只有很小一部分地平面的臭氧可以成功渡过这个漫长的旅途到达平流层(stratosphere)，因此臭氧层不可能被近来在地表附近发现的增加的臭氧浓度大幅补充。

难点分析：

本句的难点主要集中在动词 survive 上。在绝大部分的 GMAT 句子中，survive 均以不及物动词的形式存在，所以本句中其后面直接加上宾语令很多考生十分不习惯，甚至由于看到了句首的 only 而认为这是某种倒装现象，进而完全无法理解 the long trip to the stratosphere 真正的作用。实际上，survive 既可以是不及物动词，又可以是及物动词。它作为及物动词的意思是：经历……之后还存在。

78

It has thus generally been by way of the emphasis on oral literary creativity that these Chicano writers, whose English-language works are sometimes uninspired, developed the powerful and arresting language that characterized their Spanish-language works.

难度系数：B+

语句结构及读法：

第一层：It has thus generally been by way of the emphasis on oral literary creativity X.

第二层：X=that these Chicano writers, [Y₁], developed the powerful and arresting language [Y₂]

第三层：Y₁=these Chicano writers' English-language works are sometimes uninspired

Y₂=the powerful and arresting language characterized their Spanish-language works

译　文：这些墨西哥裔美国作家们的英文作品有时缺乏灵感，由此创作出一些具有他们西班牙语作品特征的有力而引人注目的语言，这件事一般是通过强调口头文学的创造性来实现的。

难点分析：

第一，句首的 it 是一个形式主语，是由于真正的主语太长而引起的一个倒装现象。但是，该形式主语和真正的主语相隔比较远，很难一下子就找到。正常语序为：That these Chicano writers developed the powerful and arresting language has thus generally been by way of the emphasis on oral literary creativity.

第二，Y₁ 这个插入语使得 X 中的主语 these Chicano writers 和谓语动词 developed 被隔开，割裂了句意关系。

第三，在 X 中，and 后面出现了现在分词 arresting，有些有一定经验的读者可能会到前句中去寻找另一个"现在分词"作为平行对象。实际上，这个 arresting 仅仅是一个普通的形容词，和 powerful 形成并列关系。

79

The common belief of some linguists that each language is a perfect vehicle for the thoughts of the nation speaking it is in some ways the exact counterpart of the conviction of the Manchester school of economics that supply and demand will regulate everything for the best.

难度系数： B

语句结构及读法：

第一层：The common belief of some linguists (X_1) is in some ways the exact counterpart of the conviction of the Manchester school of economics (X_2).

第二层：X_1=that each language is a perfect vehicle for the thoughts of the nation [Y]

X_2=that supply and demand will regulate everything for the best

第三层：Y=the nation speaks it

译　文： 一些语言学家的共同看法是每种语言对使用它的民族的思想而言均是完美的工具。在某种程度上这种共同看法是曼彻斯特经济学信念的一个确切的对应物，即供需可以把每一件事调控到最优。

难点分析：

第一，X_1是同位语从句，它将第一层信息的主语belief和其系表结构is in some ways... 隔开，割裂了句子的连贯性。另外，由于主句的谓语动词is又挨着从句中的代词it，更容易让初学者找不到主句。

第二，Y是一个简化定语从句，可以看作：the thoughts of the nation that speaks it。

80

Anthropologists and others are on much firmer ground when they attempt to describe the cultural norms for a small homogeneous tribe or village than when they undertake the formidable task of discovering the norms that exist in a complex modern nation-state composed of many disparate groups.

难度系数：B

语句结构及读法：

第一层：Anthropologists and others are on much firmer ground <X_1> than <X_2>.

第二层：X_1=when they attempt to describe the cultural norms for a small homogeneous tribe or village

X_2=when they undertake the formidable task of discovering the norms [Y]

第三层：Y=the norms exist in a complex modern nation-state [Z]

第四层：Z=a complex modern nation-state is composed of many disparate groups

译　文：人类学家们和其他人在试图描述一个小同族部落或村庄的文化标准时基于的基础要比他们承担艰巨任务去探寻存在于一个由很多不同群体组成的复杂的现代民族国家的行为准则时基于的基础更为坚实。

难点分析：

本句中的比较结构算不上多难，但是比较的对象实在长得可怕。X_1 和 X_2 分别是两个时间状语从句，比较的其实是两个时间。另外，Z 是一个简化定语从句，由于从句中是被动语态，所以这里用了过去分词 composed，容易被初学者误认为是谓语动词。

81

The absence of recorded sunspot activity in the notes kept by European observers in the late seventeenth and early eighteenth centuries has led some scholars to postulate a brief cessation of sunspot activity at that time a period called the Maunder minimum.

难度系数：B-

语句结构及读法：

第一层：The absence of recorded sunspot activity in the notes [X_1] has led some scholars to postulate a brief cessation of sunspot activity at that time (X_2).

第二层：X_1=the notes are kept by European observers in the late seventeenth and early eighteenth centuries

X_2=a period that is called the Maunder minimum

译　　文：在 17 世纪晚期和 18 世纪初期欧洲观察者保存的笔记中没有关于太阳黑子活动的记录，这让一些学者假定在那个时候太阳黑子活动短暂停止，这个时期被称作蒙德极小期。

难点分析：

第一，X_1 和 X_2 均是简化定语从句。由于两者都是被动语态，所以被简化为过去分词短语，容易让人误会成谓语动词，从而错判句子重心。另外，X_1 的插入尤其令人讨厌，它令第一层信息的主语和其谓语动词相隔较远。

第二，X_2 其实是一个同位语从句，但是这个同位语从句和其先行词 that time 之间没有逗号，这种情况在长难句中较为少见。正常语句为：at that time, a period called the Maunder minimum。

82

Unfortunately, emancipation has been less profound than expected, for not even industrial wage labor has escaped continued sex segregation in the workplace.

难度系数：B+

语句结构及读法：

第一层：Unfortunately, emancipation has been less profound than expected, <X>.

第二层：X=for not even industrial wage labor has escaped continued sex segregation in the workplace

译　　文：不幸的是，解放并没有设想的那么深入，因为即使是工业雇佣劳动力也没能逃脱工作场所中持续的性别隔离。

难点分析：

第一，for 通常用作介词，但其也有用作连词的时候。for 用作连词的意思是：因为。因此，但凡是 for 引导句子的情况，都说明此时 for 是连词用法。

第二，X 由于否定词 not 的前置而倒装。正常语序为：Even industrial wage labor has not escaped continued sex segregation in the workplace.

83

Woodward confessed with ironic modesty that the first edition "had begun to suffer under some of the handicaps that might be expected in a history of the America Revolution published in 1776".

难度系数：B-

语句结构及读法：

第一层：Woodward confessed with ironic modesty X.

第二层：X=that the first edition "had begun to suffer under some of the handicaps [Y]"

第三层：Y=some of the handicaps might be expected in a history of the America Revolution [Z]

第四层：Z=a history of the America Revolution was published in 1776

译　　文：Woodward 以一种讽刺的谦虚承认："第一版已经开始受到 1776 年出版的关于美国革命史的书中可能出现的一些不利条件的影响了。"

难点分析：

第一，第一层谓语动词和其宾语（从句）间被插入了一个状语 with ironic modesty，并且由于很多人可能不太认识 confess、ironic、modesty 这三个词，所以很难看出 X 是 confess 的宾语从句。confess：承认；ironic：讽刺的；modesty：谦虚。

第二，Z 是一个简化定语从句，published 是一个过去分词，容易被误认为是动词过去式。

A 组

01

Since Royalist ideology is often associated with the radical patriarchalism of seventeenth century political theorist Robert Filmer — a patriarchalism that equates family and kingdom and asserts the divinely ordained absolute power of the king and, by analogy, of the male head of the household — historians have been understandably puzzled by the fact that Royalist women wrote the earliest extended criticisms of the absolute subordination of women in marriage and the earliest systematic assertions of women's rational and moral equality with men.

难度系数：A-

语句结构及读法：

第一层：<X_1>, historians have been understandably puzzled by the fact (X_2).

第二层：X_1 = Since Royalist ideology is often associated with the radical patriarchalism of seventeenth century political theorist Robert Filmer—(Y)—

X_2 = that Royalist women wrote *the earliest extended criticisms of the absolute subordination of women in marriage* and *the earliest systematic assertions of women's rational and moral equality with men*

第三层：Y = a patriarchalism that equates family and kingdom and asserts the divinely ordained absolute power of the king and, by analogy, of the male head of the household

译　　文：因为保皇党的意识形态经常和 17 世纪政治理论家 Robert Filmer 的激进父权主义联系在一起，这种父权主义将家庭和王国等同了起来，并且声明国王就像家庭中的男性那样拥有神圣的绝对权威，所以历史学家一直被一个事实所困惑。这个事实是保皇党女性最早提出了对于婚姻中女性地位低下的批判，并且最早发表了女性在理性和道德上与男性平等的声明。

难点分析：

这个句子的长度达到了 80 个词，中间的插入语极多，算得上是 GMAT 考试中绝对的长难句了。最为"可气"的是，由于句中的破折号，原本应该在主句和原因状语从句之间的"逗号"消失了。一些不细心的读者可能直接一口气读到最后一个词，然后直接放弃对于这句话的理解。

02

The Hopis' retention of their distinctive sociocultural system has been attributed to the Hopi religious elite's determined efforts to preserve their religion and way of life, and also to a geographical isolation greater than that of many other Native American groups, an isolation that limited both cultural contact and exposure to European diseases, but equally important to Hopi cultural persistence may have been an inherency in their social system that may have allowed preservation of traditions to change.

难度系数： A

语句结构及读法：

第一层： X_1 and X_2.

第二层： X_1 = The Hopis' retention of their distinctive sociocultural system has been attributed to the Hopi religious elite's determined efforts to preserve their religion and way of life

X_2 = the Hopis' retention of their distinctive sociocultural system has been attributed also to a geographical isolation greater than that of many other Native American groups, (Y_1), but Y_2

第三层： Y_1 = (an isolation) [that limited both cultural contact and exposure to European diseases]

Y_2 = equally important to Hopi cultural persistence may have been an inherency in their social system [Z]

第三层： Z = their social system may have allowed preservation of traditions to change

译　文： 霍皮人保留独特的社会文化系统可以归因为霍皮宗教精英对于保存他们宗教和生活方式的坚定努力，也可以归因为其与世隔绝得比许多其他的美洲土著部落更加彻底，这种隔绝会同时限制文化的传播和欧洲疾病的扩散，但是，与保存霍皮文化同等重要的可能是他们那种可以允许改变传统的社会系统的内在属性。

难点分析：

第一层信息中的 X_2 是一个省略句，考生们需要看出其省略的是 X_1 的主语及谓语动词。Y_1 是同位语从句，Y_2 是一个和 X_2 并列的合句。另外，本句长达 78 个词，其中有三个合句，还包含了合句的省略。在阅读这样的句子时，考生们一定不能心急，要一个一个小句地去读，在适当的时候可以稍微用笔记录一下句中的信息。

03

The dominant view in recent decades has been that family hunting territories, like other forms of private landownership, were not found among Algonquians (a group of North American Indian tribes) before contact with Europeans but are the result of changes in Algonquian society brought about by the European-Algonquian fur trade, in combination with other factors such as ecological changes and consequent shifts in wildlife harvesting patterns.

难度系数：A-

语句结构及读法：

第一层：The dominant view in recent decades has been X_1 but X_2.

第二层：X_1 = that family hunting territories, like other forms of private landownership, were not found among Algonquians (a group of North American Indian tribes), $<Y_1>$

X_2 = family hunting territories are the result of changes in Algonquian society [Y_2], $<Y_3>$

第三层：Y_1 = before contact with Europeans

Y_2 = Algonquian society is brought about by the European-Algonquian fur trade

Y_3 = in combination with other factors such as ecological changes and consequent shifts in wildlife harvesting patterns

译　　文：近年来占主流的观点是：家庭捕猎领地像其他模式的私人领土一样，在和欧洲人接触以前并没有在阿尔冈基人（北美印第安部落的一个群体）中被发现，但是这种领地是阿尔冈基社会变化的结果，这种变化是在和欧洲人做皮毛贸易生意后产生的，当然，这种变化也结合了一些诸如生态变化和野生动植物收获模式的变化等其他因素。

难点分析：

本句是 GMAT 考试中典型的长难句。由于修饰成分、并列句较多，所以整句很多时候不得不做出妥协，把状语等附加成分放在最后来写，但这对之前已经看英语看到头大的考生来说可能反而会十分痛苦，还没读到后面的状语就已经崩溃了。这种长句对我们的"分层"阅读要求极强，考生需要利用所学语法知识迅速区分清楚层级，从而有轻有重地阅读本句，只有这样才能顺利读懂这类句子。

04

An impact capable of ejecting a fragment of the Martian surface into an Earth-intersecting orbit is even less probable than such an event on the Moon, in view of the Moon's smaller size and closer proximity to the Earth.

难度系数： A

语句结构及读法：

  本句只有一层。

译　文： 因为月球比火星更小、距地球更近，所以火星表面的碎片喷射到地球轨道上这种事件的概率比在月球上发生类似事件的概率要小。

难点分析：

  本句是长达 38 个单词的"简单句"，只有一套主谓宾结构。但是，尤其在没有上下文参照的情况下，想看懂这个简单句却非常不容易。首先，理解 in view of 的意思很重要，这个词组的意思是：考虑到。其次，就算理解了 in view of，很多考生也没法理解这句话的逻辑。这句话主干部分对比的对象其实是两种类型的事件，而不是 impact 和 event（这正是难点之一；即这句话的语法其实是有问题的，在逻辑上不应该是某种撞击和事件相对比）。哪两种类型的事件呢？第一个事件是：火星某处发生强撞击，以至于撞击产生的碎片"飞"到了地球的轨道上；第二个事件是在月球上发生的类似事件。本句告诉我们，由于月球更小以及距离地球更近，所以前者发生的概率小于后者。读到这里，大部分人会有一个疑问，即为什么"月球更小以及距离地球更近"和"两个事件发生的概率大小"之间有因果关系呢？实际上，这里需要一点常识。在星球表面垂直向上射出一物体，若其初速度小于某个定值，该物体将仅上升一段距离，之后由星球引力产生的加速度最终使其下落（你可以尝试向天上扔一件较重的物体来验证这个说法）。这个定值被称为该星球的逃逸速度。一个星球逃逸速度的大小和这个星球的质量是正相关的。那么，因为月球比火星小且轻，所以月球的逃逸速度肯定比火星小。因此，同等程度的撞击，月球表面的碎片"逃出"月球的重力场的可能性比火星高。又因为月球比火星离地球近，所以月球上的碎片比火星上的碎片由于被其他星球或物体干扰而没到达地球轨道的概率更低。综合这两点，同样的撞击，源自火星的碎片到达地球轨道的概率必然小于源自月球的碎片到达地球轨道的概率。

05

Only when a system possesses natural or artificial boundaries that associate the water within it with the hydrologic cycle may the entire system properly be termed hydrogeologic.

难度系数：A-

语句结构及读法：

第一层：<X> may the entire system properly be termed hydrogeologic.

第二层：X = Only when a system possesses natural or artificial boundaries [Y]

第三层：Y = natural or artificial boundaries associate the water within it with the hydrologic cycle

译　　文：只有当一个系统拥有自然或人工的边界来把它里面的水和水文循环联系起来时，这整个系统才有可能被恰当地称为水文地质。

难点分析：

only 修饰的状语从句前置，引起了主句的倒装，还原为正常语序则有：The entire system may properly be termed hydrogeologic only when a system possesses natural or artificial boundaries.

06

Only in the case of the February Revolution do we lack a useful description of participants that might characterize it in the light of what social history has taught us about the process of revolutionary mobilization.

难度系数：A-

语句结构及读法：

第一层：Only in the case of the February Revolution do we lack a useful description of participants [X].

第二层：X = participants might characterize it, <Y>

第三层：Y = in the light of what social history has taught us about the process of revolutionary mobilization

译　　文：只有就二月革命而言，我们才缺乏对参加者的有用描述，这些描述可能会根据社会历史教给我们的关于这场革命运动的过程来形容这场革命的特点。

难点分析：

> 有了上一句的基础，相信本句看起来会容易很多。首先要看出一个由 only 前置引起的倒装，第一层句子还原为正常语序则有：We lack a useful description of participants only in the case of the February Revolution. 其次，我们需要理解 in the light of 的意思，这个词组的意思是：本着，基于，按照。

07

Just as economists were blind to the numerous cases in which the law of supply and demand left actual wants unsatisfied, so also many linguists are deaf to those instances in which the very nature of a language calls forth misunderstandings in everyday conversation, and in which, consequently, a word has to be modified or defined in order to present the idea intended by the speaker: "He took his stick—no, not John's, but his own."

难度系数： A

语句结构及读法：

第一层： Just as X_1, so X_2.

第二层： X_1 = economists were blind to the numerous cases [Y_1]

X_2 = also many linguists are deaf to those instances [Y_2 and Y_3]

第三层： Y_1 = the law of supply and demand left actual wants unsatisfied in the numerous cases

Y_2 = the very nature of a language calls forth misunderstandings in everyday conversation in those instances

Y_3 = in those instances, consequently, a word has to be modified or defined in order to present the idea [Z]

第四层： Z = the idea is intended by the speaker: "He took his stick—no, not John's, but his own."

译　文： 就像经济学家们对于供需法则使得真正的需求无法得到满足的众多案例视而不见一样，很多语言学家也对一些事例充耳不闻，在那些事例中语言的真正本质在日常对话中引起误解，因此单词必须被修正和定义以表现说话者想要表达的意思，例如："他拿了他的手杖——不，不是约翰的，是他自己的。"

难点分析：

> 识别出"just as A, so B"的意思"就像 A 一样，B 也怎么样"是理解本句的关键。另外，本句的定语从句均较长，其中还夹杂一些诸如 call forth（呼唤）等抽象词汇，更增加了理解难度。

08

Fundamentally, the conditions under which women work have changed little since before the Industrial Revolution: the segregation of occupations by gender, lower pay for women as a group, and jobs that require relatively low levels of skill and offer women little opportunity for advancement all persist, while women's household labor remains demanding.

难度系数：A-

语句结构及读法：

第 一 层：Fundamentally, the conditions [X_1] have changed little since before the Industrial Revolution: (X_2).

第 二 层：X_1 = women work under the conditions

X_2 = the segregation of occupations by gender, lower pay for women as a group, and jobs [Y_1 and Y_2] all persist, <Y_3>

第 三 层：Y_1 = jobs require relatively low levels of skill

Y_2 = jobs offer women little opportunity for advancement

Y_3 = while women's household labor remains demanding

译　　文：归根结底，自从工业革命前以来女性工作的条件一直改变得很少：性别导致职业隔离、女性群体的工资更低，以及提供给女性的工作都是技术要求低并且上升空间较小的工作，这些问题都还存在，与此同时女性的家务劳动却依旧费神。

难点分析：

本句的特点是谓语动词（无论是主句的还是从句的）都不明显，很容易被直接忽略，读到最后才感觉自己好像还没有看到谓语动词，从而不得不重新读一遍。X_1 的谓语动词是 work，X_2 的谓语动词是 persist（存在），Y_3 的谓语动词是 remain。

09

Virginia Woolf's provocative statement about her intentions in writing *Mrs. Dalloway* has regularly been ignored by the critics, since it highlights an aspect of her literary interests very different from the traditional picture of the "poetic" novelist concerned with examining states of reverie and vision and with following the intricate pathways of individual consciousness.

难度系数：A

语句结构及读法：

第一层： Virginia Woolf's provocative statement about her intentions in writing *Mrs. Dalloway* has regularly been ignored by the critics, <X>.

第二层： X = since it highlights an aspect of her literary interests [Y]

第三层： Y = her literary interests (are) very different from the traditional picture of the "poetic" novelist [Z_1 and Z_2]

第四层： Z_1 = the "poetic" novelist (is) concerned with examining states of reverie and vision

Z_2 = the "poetic" novelist (is) concerned with following the intricate pathways of individual consciousness

译　文： Virginia Woolf 对她写《达洛卫夫人》一书的意图发起的挑衅性声明通常被评论家们忽视，因为这个陈述突出了不同于传统的诗性小说家的文学兴趣的一个方面，诗性小说家关心的是审视白日梦和幻想的状态以及追寻个人意识的曲折历程。

难点分析：

除了主语较长外，本句的第一层信息不难。难的是第二层信息（原因状语从句）中有很多省略的语法现象。

第一，her literary interests 的定语从句 (Y) 是一个简化后的定语从句。还原成正常语句为：interests that are different from... 当先行词在定语从句中充当主语时，我们可以对其进行简化：去掉关系词 that，将谓语按照主被动关系改成 doing 或 done，但如果谓语是 be 动词，表主动关系则需要将其改为 being，但 being 常常可以省略，所以只留下了 different。

第二，第三层中 "poetic" novelist 后面的 concerned 是过去分词（简化定语从句），不是谓语动词。有些考生可能不熟悉 be concerned with 这个词组，他们认为小说家应该是主动 concern，而不是被动 concern，由此误以为这个 concern 是谓语动词。实则不然，be concerned with 这个词组就是"关心"的意思，concern 理应是被动。

第三，第四层是一个合句，后半句涉及平行结构的省略现象。不过由于 and 后的介词 with 和前半句的 with 相互呼应，所以判断出来不算十分困难。

10

The increase in the numbers of married women employed outside the home in the twentieth century had less to do with the mechanization of housework and an increase in leisure time for these women than it did with their own economic necessity and with high marriage rates that shrank the available pool of single women workers, previously, in many cases, the only women employers would hire.

难度系数：A

语句结构及读法：

第一层：The increase in the numbers of married women [X_1] had less to do with the mechanization of housework and an increase in leisure time for these women than it did with their own economic necessity and with high marriage rates [X_2]

第二层：X_1 = married women are employed outside the home in the twentieth century

X_2 = high marriage rates shrank the available pool of single women workers [Y]

第三层：Y = previously, in many cases, the only women employers would hire women workers

译　文：20世纪在家庭之外就业的已婚女性数量的增长与家务劳动机械化和这些女性休闲时间的增长关系不大，而与其有关系的是她们自己的经济需要和高结婚率减少了单身女性工人的劳力资源库。这些单身女性，在20世纪以前，多数情况下，只有女性雇主会雇用她们。

难点分析：

这是一个含有66个词的长句。整个主句（第一层信息）是一个比较结构。

第一，X_1是一个简化定语从句，即：married women who are employed outside the home。由于employ的过去式和过去分词长相相同，有些考生可能会误判employ的层级。

第二，本句的比较对象还算清晰，但是动词have less to do 的意思令很多考生较为困惑。have less to do with A than with B 的意思是：和A的关系不如和B的关系大。

第三，最后的 the only women employers would hire 是一个定语从句。这里出现

154

了一个长难句中经典的省略现象，即当先行词 single women workers 在定语从句中充当宾语时，经常省略关系 whom(宾格)。正常的定语从句为：single women workers whom, previously, in many cases, the only women employers would hire。

11

It may come as a shock to mathematicians to learn that the Schrodinger equation for the hydrogen atom is not a literally correct description of this atom, but only an approximation to a somewhat more correct equation taking account of spin, magnetic dipole, and relativistic effects; and that this corrected equation is itself only an imperfect approximation to an infinite set of quantum field-theoretical equations.

难度系数：A+

语句结构及读法：

第一层：X may come as a shock to mathematicians.

第二层：X = It (=to learn Y_1; and Y_2)

第三层：Y_1 = that the Schrodinger equation for the hydrogen atom is not a literally correct description of this atom, but only an approximation to a somewhat more correct equation [Z]

Y_2 = that this corrected equation is itself only an imperfect approximation to an infinite set of quantum field-theoretical equations

第四层：Z = a somewhat more correct equation takes account of spin, magnetic dipole, and relativistic effects

译　文：得知以下两个事件可能令数学家们震惊不已：一是氢原子的薛定谔方程并不真的是对这种原子的正确描述，而是对于在某种程度上更为正确的方程式的一个近似表述，该方程式是描述旋转、磁偶极子和相对论效应的；二是这个正确的方程式也仅是对无限序列的量子场论方程式的一个不完美的近似表述。

难点分析：

本句包含许多数理专业词汇，有些对理科不感兴趣的考生看译文都未必能完全理解。对于大部分考生来说，只要能把这个句子的结构和大概意思看懂即可，因为文章肯定会用一些篇幅用来解释这些复杂的专业名词，无须过分担心。

第一，第一层信息包含了一个主语从句。但是，由于这个主语从句实在太长，影响了整个句子的平衡，所以作者用了形式主语 it。这个 it 实际上指代从 to learn 开始一直到句尾的全部内容。

第二，Y_1 是 learn 的宾语从句，其中包含了一个由 not...but... 引起的合句，涉及平行结构的省略现象。补全则有（为了清晰，此处抛去一些修饰成分）：The Schrodinger equation is not a literally correct description, but the Schrodinger equation is only an approximation. 另外，Z 是一个简化定语从句。

第三，Y_1 和 Y_2 是两个并列的宾语从句，只是不知道为什么，此处本应用逗号隔开的两个部分被作者用"分号"隔开（分号两边一般是两个完整的句子，GMAT 考试偶尔会出现与逗号类似的用法），令人产生困惑。

12

Physicists, looking at the original Schrodinger equation, learn to sense in it the presence of many invisible terms in addition to the differential terms visible, and this sense inspires an entirely appropriate disregard for the purely technical features of the equation.

难度系数：A+

语句结构及读法：

第一层：X_1, and X_2.

第二层：X_1 = Physicists, <Y_1>, learn to sense in it the presence of many invisible terms in addition to the differential terms [Y_2]

　　　　X_2 = this sense inspires an entirely appropriate disregard for the purely technical features of the equation

第三层：Y_1 = physicists look at the original Schrodinger equation

　　　　Y_2 = the differential terms are visible

译　文：物理学家们看着原始的薛定谔方程，学会在其中感知那些除了可见微分项之外的很多不可见的东西，并且，这种感知引发了对这个方程纯技术特性的完全恰当的忽视。

难点分析：

这句话的评级难度之所以为 A+，不是因为本句的结构有多困难，而是理解语义需要我们具有一定的背景知识。本句和上一句是连续的，上一句算是提供了一些背景。在 X_1 中出现的两个 terms 不是一种 terms，薛定谔方程其实是一个二阶偏微分方程，顾名思义，该方程中有许多微分项，这就是原句中谈到的"可见微分项 (the differential terms visible)"。那么什么是不可见的东西呢？其实，薛定谔方程目前来说并非是一个能被证明的方程，而是一种趋近估值，因此，在方程中还有很多不确定性（薛定谔方程是量子力学的基本假设，其对微观领域的重要性与牛顿定律对宏观领域的重要性相当），这也是因为粒子的运动本身就是一种概率。原句中的第一个 terms，即 invisible terms，指的就是这些可能会引发不确定性的东西。综合上述信息可知，这句话讲的就是，物理学家们意识到了薛定谔方程是一个近似的估值，进而就不会特别去苛求这个方程的准确度了。

从语法角度来说，X_1 中出现了倒装现象，正常语序为：Physicists learn to sense the presence of many invisible terms in addition to the differential terms visible in it. 另外，the differential terms visible 是一个省略，正常的定语从句为：the differential terms that are visible。

13

It was possible to demonstrate by other methods refined structural differences among neuron types; however, proof was lacking that the quality of the impulse or its condition was influenced by these differences, which seemed instead to influence the developmental patterning of the neural circuits.

难度系数：A

语句结构及读法：

第一层：X_1 was possible；however, proof was lacking (X_2).

第二层：X_1 = It (= to demonstrate by other methods refined structural differences among neuron types)

X_2 = that the quality of the impulse or its condition was influenced by these differences, [Y]

第三层：Y = these differences seemed instead to influence the developmental patterning of the neural circuits

译　文：用其他方法来说明神经元种类间的细微结构差异是有可能的；但是，缺乏证据。这个证据是：神经冲动的性质或状态是被这些差异影响的，这些差异看起来能影响神经网络的发育模式。

难点分析：

两个倒装结构使本句的难度陡然增大。

第一，句首出现的 it was possible 中的 it 是一个形式主语，由于类似的结构经常出现在报纸甚至是口语中，所以这点对读者来说不难。难的在于真正的主语 X_1。X_1 是一个倒装结构，正常语序为：to demonstrate refined structural differences among neuron types by other methods。由于 refined 可以是动词，也可以是一个过去分词短语做简化定语从句，还可以是一个纯粹的形容词，所以很多考生对于原句中 other methods 后面出现的 refined 十分头疼。如果不小心把它理解成简化定语从句来修饰 other methods，那便会彻底读不懂原句。这里的 refined 是一个纯粹的形容词，是"精炼的，细微的"的意思。

第二，X_2 是 proof 的同位语从句。由于该同位语从句过长，所以为了突出句子主干，同时避免头重脚轻，我们将其直接放在了系表结构后面，正常语序为：Proof (X_2) was lacking.

14

Islam, on the other hand, represented a radical breakaway from the Arab paganism that preceded it; Islamic law is the result of an examination, from a religious angle, of legal subject matter that was far from uniform, comprising as it did the various components of the laws of pre-Islamic Arabia and numerous legal elements taken over from the non-Arab people of the conquered territories.

难度系数：A

语句结构及读法：

第一层：X_1; X_2.

第二层：X_1 = Islam, on the other hand, represented a radical breakaway from the Arab paganism [Y_1]

X_2 = islamic law is the result of an examination, from a religious angle, of legal subject matter [Y_2]

第三层：Y₁ = the Arab paganism preceded it

Y₂ = legal subject matter was far from uniform, <Z>

第四层：Z = legal subject matter comprises <M₁> the various components of the laws of pre-Islamic Arabia and numerous legal elements [M₂]

第五层：M₁ = as it did

M₂ = numerous legal elements are taken over from the non-Arab people of the conquered territories

译　　文：在另一方面，伊斯兰教与它之前的阿拉伯异教决然断裂；从宗教的角度来看，伊斯兰法律是对远算不上统一的法律主体的检验结果，这些法律主体包括伊斯兰教之前的阿拉伯法律的各个组成部分和很多从被征服地区的非阿拉伯人民那里借鉴的法律。

难点分析：

本句是典型的 A 级长难句，成分又多又长，中间还充斥着难懂的词汇。

第一，在 X₂ 中，插入语 from a religious angle 把 an examination 和 of legal subject matter 隔开，令人不容易将两个概念联系起来。

第二，M₁ 也是一个插入语，此处 as 是连词，表示"像……一样"。由于这个插入语两端没有逗号，所以容易将 it did 和 the various components 联系在一起。

第三，Z 句中 and 后面的 numerous legal elements 与其前面的 the various components 平行。该部分在语法上可以与前句的任何部分平行，要判断出真正的平行对象要求我们把握整句的语义。

15

One such novel idea is that of inserting into the chromosomes of plants discrete genes that are not a part of the plants' natural constitution: specifically, the idea of inserting into nonleguminous plants the genes, if they can be identified and isolated, that fit the leguminous plants to be hosts for nitrogen-fixing bacteria.

难度系数：A

语句结构及读法：

第 一 层： One such novel idea is that of inserting into the chromosomes of plants discrete genes [X].

第 二 层： X = discrete genes are not a part of the plants' natural constitution: specifically, the idea of inserting into nonleguminous plants the genes, <Y₁>, [Y₂]

第 三 层： Y₁ = if they can be identified and isolated

Y₂ = the genes fit the leguminous plants to be hosts for nitrogen-fixing bacteria

译　文： 有一个这样的全新想法，把不是植物自然组成部分的不相关基因插入植物的染色体中：具体来说，这是一个把一些基因插入非豆科植物中去的想法。如果这些基因能够被找到并分离出来的话，就会使豆科植物成为固氮菌的寄主。

难点分析：

第一，本句最大的困难在于两个倒装，并且这两个倒装要是能看出来便一起能看出来，看不出来就一起看不出来，十分影响对整句的理解。在第一层信息中，由于 insert 的宾语后面有定语从句，加起来长度太长，所以为了突出主干并且避免头重脚轻，将宾语放到了宾补的后面，形成倒装。正常语序为：One such novel idea is that of inserting discrete genes that are not a part of the plants' natural constitution into the chromosomes of plants. 第二层信息中有一个如出一辙的倒装，正常语序为：the idea of inserting the genes that fit the leguminous plants to be hosts for nitrogen-fixing bacteria into nonleguminous plants。

第二，Y₁ 这个条件状语把先行词 the genes 和它的定语 that fit the leguminous plants 隔开了，让人不容易连贯起来理解。

16

Its subject (to use Maynard Mack's categories) is "life-as-spectacle", for readers, diverted by its various incidents, observe its hero Odysseus primarily from without; the tragic *Iliad*, however, presents "life-as-experience": readers are asked to identify with the mind of Achilles, whose motivations render him a not particularly likable hero.

难度系数： A

语句结构及读法：

第一层： X_1; X_2.

第二层： X_1 = Its subject (to use Maynard Mack's categories) is "life-as-spectacle," <Y_1>

X_2 = the tragic Iliad, however, presents "life-as-experience": Y_2

第三层： Y_1 = for readers, <Z_1>, observe its hero Odysseus primarily from without

Y_2 = readers are asked to identify with the mind of Achilles, [Z_2]

第四层： Z_1 = readers are diverted by its various incidents

Z_2 = Achilles' motivations render him a not particularly likable hero

译　　文： 它的主题（使用 Maynard Mack 的分类法）是"把生活当作景象"，读者由于被它的不同事件转移了注意力，主要从外部来观察主人公 Odysseus；然而，悲剧《伊利亚特》表现的是"把生活当作经历"：读者被要求认同 Achilles 的思想，他的动机令他成为一个不是很讨人喜欢的主人公。

难点分析：

给本句评为 A 级，并不是因为其从句或插入语的数量及难度，而是因为其词汇的难度。当然，不可否认的是，这句话中还有一些诸如 Z_1 的简化状语从句（伴随状语）这类大家早已司空见惯的难点，只是相比词汇上的难度，这些难点已经不算什么了。

第一，一般来说，for 是介词，后面应该直接跟一个名词，表示"对于"的意思。在本句中，如果按照这种方式理解，那么会一直困惑其后面的 observe 究竟属于哪个句子，是什么词性。实际上，for 除了用作介词外，也经常会用作连词。当 for 是连词时，其意思为：因为。理解了这层意思，自然就可以看出 observe 的主语是 readers，其所在的句子是 X_1 的原因状语从句。

第二，理解第三层 Y_1 部分 from 后面的 without 也是关键。可以说，这个词是理解整个句子的关键。without 通常的意思是"没有"，但在本句中显然不是这个意思。我们引申一下，所谓"没有"的东西，无非就是一个圈子之外的东西。由此可知，这里的 without 是"外部"的意思，相当于 outside。

第三，hero 这里是"主人公"的意思，相信很多考生都能通过整句语义猜测出来。另外，原句的倒数第二个词 likable 是"有吸引力的"的意思，类似于 attractive，千万不可望文生义地认为是"喜欢"或者"像"的意思。

17

Some geologists, however, on the basis of observations concerning mantle xenoliths, argue that the mantle is not layered, but that heterogeneity is created by fluids rich in "incompatible elements" (elements tending toward liquid rather than solid state) percolating upward and transforming portions of the upper mantle irregularly, according to the vagaries of the fluids' pathways.

难度系数：A

语句结构及读法：

第一层： Some geologists, however, on the basis of observations concerning mantle xenoliths, argue X.

第二层： X = Y_1 but Y_2

第三层： Y_1 = that the mantle is not layered

Y_2 = that heterogeneity is created by fluids [Z]

第四层： Z = fluids are rich in "incompatible elements" (elements tending toward liquid rather than solid state) [M]

第五层： M = incompatible elements percolate upward and transform portions of the upper mantle irregularly, according to the vagaries of the fluids' pathways.

译　文： 但是，一些地质学家基于对地幔捕虏体的观察认为：地幔不是分层的，而其不同的成分是由某些富含"不相容的成分"（那些趋向于液体而不是固体的成分）的流体所产生的。这些流体向上渗透，并依照这些流体所经过的随机路径不规则地改变地幔上的某些部分。

难点分析：

第一，本句中出现了很多抽象名词和专有名词，很多词看着像认识的，但是总想不起来是什么意思（例如：incompatible 和 percolate）。这样的词汇在阅读中占据我们大脑中很多思维空间。

第二，第一层信息的主语 some geologists 和谓语动词 argue 之间有一个很长的插入语，即"however, on the basis of observations concerning mantle xenoliths"隔开了主语和谓语。

第三，Y_2 中 fluids 的定语从句 Z 中省略了关系词和 be 动词，还原为正常的定语从句则有：fluids that are rich in "incompatible elements"。

第四，Z 中还有定语 M，这是本句最大的难点。M 与其先行词 incompatible elements 间被 (elements tending toward liquid rather than solid state) 隔开，造成难以判断修饰对象。另外，M 还是一个简化定语从句，可以近似看作："incompatible elements" that percolate upward and transform portions of the upper mantle irregularly。

18

For the woman who is a practitioner of feminist literary criticism, the subjectivity versus objectivity, or critic-as-artist-or-scientist, debate has special significance; for her, the question is not only academic, but political as well, and her definition will court special risks whichever side of the issue it favors.

难度系数：A-

语句结构及读法：

第一层：X_1; X_2.

第二层：X_1 = For the woman [Y_1], the subjectivity versus objectivity, or critic-as-artist-or-scientist, debate has special significance

X_2 = Y_2 and Y_3

第三层：Y_1 = the woman is a practitioner of feminist literary criticism

Y_2 = for her, the question is not only academic, but political as well

Y_3 = her definition will court special risks whichever side of the issue [Z]

第四层：Z = it favors the issue

译　文：对于从事女权主义文学批评的女性来说，关于文学评论应该是主观的还是客观的，文学评论家究竟是艺术家还是科学家的讨论具有特殊意义；对于她来说，这不仅仅是一个学术问题，更是一个政治问题，并且她对文学评论的定义无论有利于这一问题的哪一方都会招致特殊的风险。

难点分析：

第一，本句开篇就是一个状语，加之其主句的主语 "the subjectivity versus

objectivity, or critic-as-artist-or-scientist, debate"的长相也不怎么"标准"，所以我们很容易找不到第一层信息的主语。这个主语其实就是一个 debate，the subjectivity versus objectivity 和 critic-as-artist-or-scientist 均是这个 debate 的定语。

第二，在分号后的半句中，我们常见的连词是 not only...but also...，但本句给出的连词是 not only...but...as well。我们需学会变通，两者等价。

第三，Z 是一个定语从句，由于先行词在从句中充当宾语，所以此处省略了 that，正常的定语从句为：the issue that it favors。

19

Open acknowledge of the existence of women's oppression was too radical for the United States in the fifties, and Beauvoir's conclusion, that change in women's economic condition, though insufficient by itself, "remains the basic factor" in improving women's situation, was particularly unacceptable.

难度系数：A+

语句结构及读法：

第一层：X_1 and X_2.

第二层：X_1 = Open acknowledge of the existence of women's oppression was too radical for the United States in the fifties

X_2 = Beauvoir's conclusion, (Y), was particularly unacceptable

第三层：Y = that change in women's economic condition, though insufficient by itself, "remains the basic factor" in improving women's situation

译　　文：公开承认对妇女的压迫对于 50 年代的美国而言有些过分激进，并且，Beauvoir 的结论特别不能让人接受。即妇女经济状况的变化，尽管它本身不是一个充分的因素，但仍然是提高妇女地位的根本因素。

难点分析：

本句是由 and 连接的合句。难点集中在后半句。

第一，X_1 中的主语较长，修饰成分将核心词 acknowledge 和系表结构 was too

radical 隔开。当然，相对于 X_2 的难度来说，X_1 还算"友好"。

第二，X_2 中最令人困惑的当属 Beauvoir's conclusion 后面的同位语从句了。一般来说，"抽象名词 +that"形式的同位语是常见的、容易理解的，但是，本句中抽象名词 conclusion 和其同位语从句 Y 之间加了一个"不符合语法"的逗号，这让很多考生根本看不出 Y 是什么成分。又由于 Y 这个同位语从句的谓语动词在一对引号中间（"remains the basic factor"），初学者可能根本不把 remains 看作谓语，再加上其前面还有一个讨厌的插入语 though insufficient by itself，一切都让人感到绝望。

第三，Y 这个同位语很长，将主语 conclusion 和系表结构 was particularly unacceptable 隔开了，使我们不容易找准主干。

20

Although it has been possible to infer from the goods and services actually produced what manufactures and servicing trades thought their customers wanted, only a study of relevant personal documents written by actual consumers will provide a precise picture of who wanted what.

难度系数：A+

语句结构及读法：

第一层：<X_1>, only a study of relevant personal documents [X_2] will provide a precise picture of who wanted what.

第二层：X_1 = Although it has been possible to infer from the goods and services [Y_1] Y_2

X_2 = relevant personal documents are written by actual consumers

第三层：Y_1 = the goods and services are actually produced

Y_2 = what manufactures and servicing trades thought their customers wanted

译　文：尽管有可能从真正生产的商品和服务中推测出生产商和服务商所认为的他们的顾客想要什么，但是只有对真正顾客所写的相关个人记录的研究才能提供关于谁想要什么的准确描述。

难点分析：

本句最难理解的部分出现在让步状语从句中，produced 后面出现的由 what 引导的从句其实是一个名词性从句（宾语从句）。由于出现了倒装现象，所以 X_1 十分难懂，是分量十足的长难句。

第一，让步状语从句中有一个倒装结构，infer 是一个及物动词，后面应该直接加宾语，构成 infer A from B 的句型。X_1 中的句型是 infer from B A，由此可知，该语句出现了倒装现象，正常语序为：It has been possible to infer what manufactures and servicing trades thought their customers wanted <u>from the goods and services</u>。

第二，这个让步状语从句的主语 it 是一个形式主语，指代后面出现的 to infer sth.。

第三，X_2 是一个简化定语从句，正常的定语从句为：a study of relevant personal documents that are written by actual consumers。

21

It was not the change in office technology, but rather the separation of secretarial work, previously seen as an apprenticeship for beginning managers, from administrative work that in the 1880s created a new class of "dead-end" jobs, thenceforth considered "women's work".

难度系数：A-

语句结构及读法：

第一层：It was not the change in office technology, but rather the separation of secretarial work, [X_1], from administrative work that in the 1880s created a new class of "dead-end" jobs, [X_2].

第二层：X_1 = secretarial work was previously seen as an apprenticeship for beginning managers

X_2 = "dead-end" jobs are thenceforth considered "women's work"

译　文：不是办公室技术的改变，而是秘书工作（秘书工作以前被认为是初级经理的学徒工作）与管理工作的分离在19世纪80年代创造了一种新的"死胡同"式的工作，这种工作后来被认为是"女性的工作"。

难点分析：

本句是一个强调句，难点主要出现在 but 后面，其中包含了许多修饰成分。

第一，X_1 是一个简化定语从句，正常的从句为：secretarial work, <u>which was</u> previously seen as an apprenticeship for beginning managers。

第二，由于 X_1 的加入，本来连接在一起的 the separation of A from B 被隔开，造成了阅读困难。

第三，整句话的主句用了强调句型：It was... that...。正常的句子主干应该为：not the change but the separation created a new class。

第四，有些考生可能不认识 thenceforth（后来），由此看不出 Y 的作用。Y 也是一个简化定语从句，正常的从句为："dead-end" jobs, <u>which are</u> thenceforth considered "women's work"。

22

Under the force of this view, it was perhaps inevitable that the art of rhetoric should pass from the status of being regarded as of questionable worth because although it might be both a source of pleasure and a means to urge people to take right action, it might also be a means to distort truth and a source of misguided action to the status of being wholly condemned.

难度系数： A-

语句结构及读法：

第一层： Under the force of this view, it was perhaps inevitable X.

第二层： X = that the art of rhetoric should pass from the status of being regarded as of questionable worth <Y> to the status of being wholly condemned

第三层： Y = because <Z>, it might also be a means to distort truth and a source of misguided action

第四层： Z = although it might be both a source of pleasure and a means to urge people to take right action

译　文： 在这个观点的作用下，有一点可能是不可避免的，即修辞艺术从被认为具有值得怀疑的价值的状态变为被彻底谴责的状态。修辞艺术被认为具有值得怀疑的价值是因为虽然它可能既是欢乐的源泉又是督促人们做出正确行为的方法，但它可能也是扭曲事实的方法和误导行为的来源。

难点分析：

第一，第一层信息的主语 it 是一个形式主语，它指代后面出现的由 that 引导的一直到句末的从句。

第二，在 X 中，Y 的出现使得原本应紧挨在一起的词组 pass from A to B 变得十分不连贯，令人不清楚 A 究竟变成了什么，割裂了句子意思。

第三，Y 和 Z 中的两个连词 because 和 although 直接连在了一起，虽然两者分属不同的层级，但如果读到这里已经被前面的成分弄晕，那么此处两个连续的连词更会是雪上加霜，甚至导致完全放弃对这个句子的理解。

23

She wished to discard the traditional methods and established vocabularies of such dance forms as ballet and to explore the internal sources of human expressiveness.

难度系数： A-

语句结构及读法：

第一层： X_1 and X_2.

第二层： X_1 = She wished to discard the traditional methods and established vocabularies of such dance forms as ballet

X_2 = she wished to explore the internal sources of human expressiveness

译　文： 她希望抛弃传统的方法和像芭蕾舞这样的舞蹈形式中已经确立的舞蹈语言，并且希望去探索人类表现力的内在源泉。

难点分析：

本句虽然不长，但是绝对算得上是难句。表面上看本句是由两个 and 连接三部分的内容，但是在逻辑上很难说得通。考生一般读到 established 通常会认为其是谓语动词，同前面的 wished 平行，继续往下读，读到第二个 and 时开始犯迷糊，这里的 and to explore 又是干什么的呢？如果说 to explore 和 to discard 平行，那么在语法上完全说不通。实际上，established 这里不是谓语动词，而是过去分词，

168

是形容词用法，修饰 vocabularies。established vocabularies 由此和 the traditional methods 平行，均是"抛弃 (discard)"的宾语。如此一来，第二个 to explore 就容易判断了，确实是和 to discard 平行。

请大家务必把诸如 established 这样的过去分词做形容词的情况记在笔记本上，反复读几遍，在考场上就算第一次没读懂也能尽快反应过来。

24

The idea of an autonomous discipline called "philosophy" distinct from and sitting in judgment on such pursuits as theology and science turns out, on close examination, to be of quite recent origin.

难度系数：A+

语句结构及读法：

第一层：The idea of an autonomous discipline [X] turns out, on close examination, to be of quite recent origin.

第二层：X= discipline is called "philosophy" [Y]

第三层：Y= discipline called philosophy is distinct from and sitting in judgment on such pursuits as theology and science

译　文：如果我们仔细检查，就可以知道"一个叫'哲学'的独立学科有别于并且高高在上地审视类似于神学和科学这些学科"的这一个观点实际上是近来才出现的。

难点分析：

本句不长，但是较难。

第一，整句的谓语动词 turns out 与其主语 the idea 由于定语 X 的插入而相隔很远。

第二，在 Y 中，真正的平行对象是 distinct from 和 sitting in judgment on，两者都是形容词词性，功能上平行。这里是难点，因为通常意义上看到 and 后面出现现在分词，很多有经验的考生都会下意识地去 and 前面找分词，如果找不到，就直接慌神了。

第三，本句中还出现了许多抽象的短词，这些短词的语义不易理解，例如：sit

in judgement on：审视，做出判断；pursuit：从事的事业（此处不指"追求"）；turn out to be：实际上是……

第四，called "philosophy" 和 distinct from and sitting in judgment on such pursuits as theology and science 均是简化的定语从句，修饰 discipline。表示这个学科有两个特点：①叫作"哲学"；②有别于并且高高在上地审视类似于神学和科学这些学科。

25

The broad language of the amendment strongly suggests that its framers were proposing to write into the Constitution not a laundry list of specific civil rights but a principle of equal citizenship that forbids organized society from treating any individual as a member of an inferior class.

难度系数：A-

语句结构及读法：

第一层：The broad language of the amendment strongly suggests X.

第二层：X = that its framers were proposing to write into the Constitution not a laundry list of specific civil rights but a principle of equal citizenship [Y]

第三层：Y = a principle of equal citizenship forbids organized society from treating any individual as a member of an inferior class

译　文：这个修正法案概括性的语言强烈表明：其制定者不是想要把一个具体的民权清单写进宪法，而是要把一个平等公民权的原则写入宪法，这个原则禁止有组织的社会把任何个人当作下等阶级的成员来对待。

难点分析：

本句的难点主要在 X 中。由于 write 的直接宾语太长，所以做了倒装，正常语序为：Its framers were proposing to write not a laundry list of specific civil rights but a principle of equal citizenship into the Constitution。而且这个宾语是一个 not... but... 句型，很长，一口气很难读下来。此外，本句中有大量的法律类词汇，增加了句意的理解难度。

26

Human genes contain too little information even to specify which hemisphere of the brain each of a human's 10^{11} neurons should occupy, let alone the hundreds of connections that each neuron makes.

难度系数：A

语句结构及读法：

第一层：Human genes contain too little information even to specify X, let alone the hundreds of connections that each neuron makes.

第二层：X = which hemisphere of the brain each of a human's 10^{11} neurons should occupy

译　文：人类的基因包含的信息太少以至甚至无法确定一个人的 10^{11} 个神经元应该占据大脑的哪一个半球，更不用说每一个神经元形成的数百个连接了。

难点分析：

第一，X 部分十分晦涩难懂。它其实是一个宾语从句，只不过将自己的宾语倒装到了主语前面，正常语序为：Each of a human's 10^{11} neurons should occupy <u>which hemisphere of the brain</u>。与第一层信息连在一起为：Human genes contain too little information even to specify (that) each of a human's 10^{11} neurons should occupy which hemisphere of the brain.

第二，let alone 的意思是"更不用说……"。这是一个在 GMAT 考试中十分常见的固定搭配，大家需要牢记它的意思。

27

When the object is optimal resource allocation, that combination of legal methods should be used that most nearly yields the allocation that would exist if there were no external costs resulting from allocating resources through market activity.

难度系数：A-

语句结构及读法：

第一层：<X_1>, that combination of legal methods should be used [X_2].

第二层：X₁ = When the object is optimal resource allocation

X₂ = combination of legal methods most nearly yields the allocation [Y]

第三层：Y = the allocation would exist <Z>

第四层：Z = if there were no external costs resulting from allocating resources through market activity

译　　文：当目标是最优资源分配时，应该使用那种法律方法的组合。如果通过市场活动分配资源而没有外部成本的话，那种组合最接近于产生现有的分配。

难点分析：

本句的难点在于出现了三个 that，令人难以确定它们各自的身份。第一个 that 是一个代词，后两个 that 均为引导定语从句的关系词（连词）。当然，本句放在文章里的时候肯定比现在单独看要容易理解得多（至少可以更容易地判断出第一个 that 是代词），但是，我们需要磨炼出在任何情况下都能看懂每一个句子的能力，这样才能在考试中所向披靡。

28

To explain this unfinished revolution in the status of women, historians have recently begun to emphasize the way a prevailing definition of femininity often determines the kinds of work allocated to women, even when such allocation is inappropriate to new conditions.

难度系数： A-

语句结构及读法：

第一层：To explain this unfinished revolution in the status of women, historians have recently begun to emphasize the way [X].

第二层：X = a prevailing definition of femininity often determines the kinds of work [Y] by the way

第三层：Y = the kinds of work are allocated to women, <Z>

第四层：Z = even when such allocation is inappropriate to new conditions

译　　文：为了解释这场关于女性地位的尚未完成的革命，历史学家们近来开始强调一种方法。通过这种方法女性特点的流行定义往往决定分配给女性的工作种类，即使这种分配已经不适用于新的形势。

172

难点分析：

第一，我们比较熟悉的是当先行词在定语从句中充当宾语时，关系词可以被省略的情况。但是在本句中，一是考生可能并没有意识到 the way 后面是一个省略了关系词的定语从句，二是就算有一定经验的考生意识到了这个问题，也会发现这里的 the way 似乎并不是做 determines 的宾语。无论是哪种情况，均会导致无法理解 X 部分的功能。实际上，对 the way 这个词来说，无论其在后面的定语从句中充当何种成分，都经常会省略关系词，例如本句还原为正常的定语从句则有：Historians have recently begun to emphasize the way <u>by which</u> a prevailing definition of femininity often determines the kinds of work.

第二，Y 是一个简化定语从句。由于该定语从句是被动语态，所以此处 allocate 用了过去分词，初学者容易将其理解为谓语动词的过去式，从而错判句子重心。

第三章

如何理解文章

——脑中具象化，纸上搭框架

正如开篇所写的，想要做好阅读理解，既要阅读到位，又要充分理解。

"阅读"部分唯一的技巧就是：逐层级抽主干。即像剥洋葱一样，将一个长长的句子一层层剥开，拆分成一个个单句，再去提取每个单句的主干成分。当我们能准确理解句子三个层级的意思时，这个长句子的大意我们就理解得八九不离十了。

虽然 GMAT 的一篇阅读文章一般最多会给出 4 道考题，但是在题库中这篇文章可能带有 8 道甚至更多的考题，只不过按照当前考生的能力水平只出现其中一部分罢了。因此，文章中的任何一句话，甚至任何一个词都有可能成为考点（一共 200 个词的文章，如果出 8 道题目，那么可想而知，题目所涉及的地方自然几乎涵盖了整篇文章的各个角落）。

既然题目可能涵盖文章的任何部分，那么我们在阅读文章时自然也就不能只读一部分，必须通读全文。GMAT 阅读的文章最长一般不超过 350 个词。虽然词数看起来不多，但是考生在第一次阅读时经常出现完全读不懂的状况，或者不是完全看不懂，而是读着读着就不知道文章在讲什么了、读了后面忘了前面、像读报纸一样很顺利地读完后却什么也没记住、回答问题时需要反复重新阅读文章等。由于 GMAT 考题大多要求深刻理解文意，马马虎虎的理解根本无助于解题，所以在阅读后完成考题时就会遇到很大的麻烦，文章读不懂，任何解题技巧也就都用不上。

之所以会遇到类似的这些问题，很多时候并不是因为不懂单词词义或长难句难以理解，而是因为无法进行有效阅读。有些考生可能会反驳："我从小英语就很不错，经常阅读英文报纸，甚至还在以英语为母语的国家上过学，难道我从来没有进行过有效阅读？"答案是否定的。我们当然进行过有效阅读，但是彼时的有效阅读和在 GMAT 考试中的有效阅读完全不能画等号。要知道，报纸和教科书中文章的目的，就是让你看懂，所以往往主题非常突出；GMAT 阅读文章大多数来源于历史文献、科技论文、科学杂志等，这些文章的特点在于逻辑性较强且信息量较大，加之 GMAC（GMAT 的出题机构，当然，它也不是真正命题的机构，真正命题的机构是美国大学考试中心，简称 ACT）还经常删改、浓缩一些文字使信息容纳量进一步增加，所以这些文章的可读性比报纸和教科书要差得多。自然而然，考生们进行充分理解的难度也随之陡然上升。

那么，如何能在阅读 GMAT 文章时充分理解呢？答案很简单：脑中具象化，纸上搭框架。

3.1 将文章具象化

我们先来给出"理解"的定义：理解指的是将学到的新知识和我们已有的老知识嫁接在一起的过程。举个例子：

假设现在马路上突然出现一个以 60km/h 的速度运动的保温杯，虽然这个场景我们闻所未闻，但相信大部分人都会下意识地躲开。为什么会有这样的举动，这就是因为我们将这个离谱的新事物和脑中已有的旧场景（以 60km/h 的速度运动的车辆）进行了嫁接——如果不避开快速移动的车辆会被撞伤，那么不避开快速移动的保温杯极有可能也会出现类似的后果。

看考试文章也是一样的，如果"硬"读肯定是无法充分理解的，我们需要将其描述的内容和我们看到过的场景、经历过的事情或熟悉的人物进行关联，一旦成功对接，自然更容易理解。

那么该如何具体操作呢？

GMAT 考试的文章通常可以按照文体分为三大类——论证型、解释/计划型和叙事/描述型。

论证型文章是用一个或多个观点作为理由来接受另外的一个或多个观点。其中的有些观点经常没有被明确地表达出来，但却是显而易见的。这些论证型文章可以被理解为放大版的批判性推理考题。具象论证型文章涉及识别推理结构和揣摩论点，主要由以下五个部分组成：

(1) 理解文章结构：首先，识别文章的基本结构，包括论点、论据、反驳和结论。了解作者如何组织论证可以帮助你更好地理解文章的流程和重点。

(2) 识别主要论点：文章的主要论点或论题通常是作者想要证明或论述的中心观点。这通常解决的是主旨题。

(3) 分析论据：注意作者提出的支持主要论点的理由、证据或例证。在阅读时，可以边读边尝试分析这些论据的有效性和可靠性。

有效性指的是论证的推理是否完备，有没有被削弱的漏洞（详细内容可以参考《GMAT 批判性推理：逻辑分类精讲》一书）。

可靠性指的是论证的前提本身是否真实，是否存在虚构，是否符合生活场景。

(4) 寻找反驳和反论：寻找作者如何处理反对意见或反论。一个有力的论证通常会考虑并回应可能的反对观点。

177

(5) 评估逻辑连接：留意文章中的逻辑连接，如因果关系、对比、类比等。

解释 / 计划型文章通常旨在阐释某个概念、事件或现象，抑或是对一些可能发生的情况给出应对策略。具象这类文章涉及对场景的识别以及重要性判断，主要由以下四个部分组成：

(1) 理解核心概念：首先明确文章试图解释或阐述的核心概念或问题。理解这个核心是理解整篇文章的关键。

(2) 关注文章结构：注意文章是如何组织的。解释计划型文章通常会按照某种逻辑顺序（如时间顺序、重要性顺序等）来展开论述。

(3) 理解方法和理论：如果文章包含特定的方法论或理论框架，努力理解这些并考虑它们是如何应用于主题的。

(4) 联系背景知识：将文章内容与你已有的知识和信息联系起来，这有助于更好地理解和记忆文章内容。

叙事 / 描述型文章通常按照时间次序，对相关事件进行描述。阅读时，重点在于理解故事的情节、角色、背景和主题。具象这类文章通常需要：

(1) 关注情节发展：理解故事的起始、发展和结局。这有助于把握故事的整体架构和流程。

(2) 了解角色：关注故事中的主要和次要角色。理解他们各自的性格特点、动机和他们之间的关系如何推动故事发展。

(3) 识别背景和环境：尽可能了解故事发生的时间、地点和社会文化背景。这些因素往往对故事的情节和角色有重要影响。GMAT 文章中出现的背景大多是美国历史、司法体系、经济决策、种族权力等。

(4) 探究主题和信息：思考作者想要通过故事传达什么主题或信息。这可能包括人生教训、社会评论或哲学思考。

(5) 感受语言和风格：体会作者的语言风格和使用的修辞手法，如比喻、拟人等。这些元素往往决定了作者的态度。

(6) 投入情感体验：让自己沉浸在故事中，与角色建立情感联系。这可以增强阅读体验和对故事的理解。

下面我们就来看看该如何使文章具象化。

例文 1

More selective than most chemical pesticides in that they ordinarily destroy only unwanted species, biocontrol agents (such as insects, fungi, and viruses) eat, infect, or parasitize targeted plants or animal pests. However, biocontrol agents can negatively affect nontarget species by, for example, competing with them for resources: a biocontrol agent might reduce the benefits conferred by a desirable animal species by consuming a plant on which the animal prefers to lay its eggs. Another example of indirect negative consequences occurred in England when a virus introduced to control rabbits reduced the amount of open ground (because large rabbit populations reduce the ground cover), in turn reducing underground ant nests and triggering the extinction of a blue butterfly that had depended on the nests to shelter its offspring. The paucity of known extinctions or disruptions resulting from indirect interactions may reflect not the infrequency of such mishaps but rather the failure to look for or to detect them: most organisms likely to be adversely affected by indirect interactions are of little or no known commercial value and the events linking a biocontrol agent with an adverse effect are often unclear. Moreover, determining the potential risks of biocontrol agents before they are used is difficult, especially when a nonnative agent is introduced, because, unlike a chemical pesticide, a biocontrol agent may adapt in unpredictable ways, so that it can feed on or otherwise harm new hosts.

注意，我们在想的时候，可以把任何宏观的概念微观化。比如提到的 plants，可以对应任何一种具体的植物；提到的 insects，可以对应到任何一种具体的昆虫。不必拘泥于文章描述的那个原本的事物，只要能够产生关联，就可以帮助我们进一步理解。

现在，让我们来一句一句地构建场景。

More selective than most chemical pesticides in that they ordinarily destroy only unwanted species, biocontrol agents (such as insects, fungi, and viruses) eat, infect, or parasitize targeted plant or animal pests.

可以对应的场景：

一片玉米地里，一瓶农药（chemical pesticides）洒下去，玉米本身、旁边的杂草和玉米上的害虫可能都死了。但如果引入一种蜻蜓（biocontrol agents），可以只（selective）吃掉害虫（only unwanted species）。

However, biocontrol agents can negatively affect nontarget species by, for example, competing with them for resources: a biocontrol agent might reduce the benefits conferred by a desirable animal species by consuming a plant on which the animal prefers to lay its eggs.

可以对应的场景：

蜻蜓还吃一种草（plant），另一种有益的蝴蝶（desirable animal species）会在这种草上产卵。

Another example of indirect negative consequences occurred in England when a virus introduced to control rabbits reduced the amount of open ground (because large rabbit populations reduce the ground cover), in turn reducing underground ant nests and triggering the extinction of a blue butterfly that had depended on the nests to shelter its offspring.

可以对应的场景：

在英国，引入病毒 → 杀死兔子 → 没有兔子啃草，植被茂盛，没有开阔地 → 地下巢穴的蚂蚁被捂死 → 蓝蝴蝶的卵连带死亡 → 蓝蝴蝶灭绝。

The paucity of known extinctions or disruptions resulting from indirect interactions may reflect not the infrequency of such mishaps but rather the failure to look for or to detect them: most organisms likely to be adversely affected by indirect interactions are of little or no known commercial value and the events linking a biocontrol agent with an adverse effect are often unclear.

可以对应的场景：

案例当中的蝴蝶没什么商业价值，而且连锁反应过长，科学家追溯起来也一脸懵（unclear）。

Moreover, determining the potential risks of biocontrol agents before they are used is difficult, especially when a nonnative agent is introduced, because, unlike a chemical pesticide, a biocontrol agent may adapt in unpredictable ways, so that it can feed on or otherwise harm new hosts.

可以对应的场景：

引入蜻蜓可能有风险：蜻蜓变异（adapt in unpredictable ways），不仅吃害虫，还开始吃别的动植物。

此处我们只用文字为大家尽量描绘出场景，大家在实操的时候，还需要尽量在脑海中想象出一个3D动图。

我们再来看一篇抽象性文章。

例文 2

Much research has been devoted to investigating what motivates consumers to try new products. Previous consumer research suggests that both the price of a new product and the way it is advertised affect consumers' perceptions of the product's performance risk (the possibility that the product will not function as consumers expect and/or will not provide the desired benefits). Some of this research has concluded that a relatively high price will reduce a consumer's perception of the performance risk associated with purchasing a particular product, while other studies have reported that price has little or no effect on perceived performance risk. These conflicting findings may simply be due to the nature of product advertisements: a recent study indicates that the presentation of an advertised message has a marked effect on the relationship between price and perceived performance risk.

Researchers have identified consumers' perception of the credibility of the source of an advertised message—i.e. the manufacturer—as another factor affecting perceived performance risk: one study found that the greater the source credibility, the lower the consumer's perception of the risk of purchasing an advertised new product. However, past research suggests that the relationship between source credibility and perceived performance risk may be more complex: source credibility may interact with price in a subtle way to affect consumers' judgments of the performance risk associated with an advertised product.

场景构建：

Much research has been devoted to investigating what motivates consumers to try new products.

可以对应的场景：

我（consumers）为什么会尝试新的美白护肤品（new products）？

Previous consumer research suggests that both the price of a new product and the way it is advertised affect consumers' perceptions of the product's performance risk (the possibility that the product will not function as consumers expect and/or will not provide the desired benefits).

可以对应的场景：

做攻略的时候，其价格以及其营销的方式（请明星在电视上做广告，或在社交平台上请网红或大 V 做推广）都会成为我评估这款护肤品究竟能否提亮肤色（product's performance risk）的影响因素。

Some of this research has concluded that a relatively high price will reduce a consumer's perception of the performance risk associated with purchasing a particular product, while other studies have reported that price has little or no effect on perceived performance risk.

可以对应的场景：
有些研究表明，价格越高，我觉得越靠谱，而有些研究表明价格影响不大。

These conflicting findings may simply be due to the nature of product advertisements: a recent study indicates that the presentation of an advertised message has a marked effect on the relationship between price and perceived performance risk.

可以对应的场景：
为什么不同的研究表明的内容会不一样，原因可能是：这种护肤品的信息呈现会产生影响价格和风险之间的关系。

Researchers have identified consumers' perception of the credibility of the source of an advertised message—i.e. the manufacturer—as another factor affecting perceived performance risk: one study found that the greater the source credibility, the lower the consumer's perception of the risk of purchasing an advertised new product.

可以对应的场景：
著名品牌（credibility of the source of an advertised message）的护肤品，听起来就比微商的三无护肤品靠谱许多。

However, past research suggests that the relationship between source credibility and perceived performance risk may be more complex: source credibility may interact with price in a subtle way to affect consumers' judgments of the performance risk associated with an advertised product.

可以对应的场景：
过去的研究表明，情况可能会更复杂一些：最终决定要不要买这款护肤品时，我不仅会看谁制造的，还会看对应的价格（比如，著名品牌的护肤品只卖 90 元，我可能也会浅浅怀疑这款产品究竟靠不靠谱）。

练习

请大家尽情发挥想象力，根据下面的文章构建出对应的场景。（大家在练习的时候，不必非得一句一句地想场景。可以将描述同一事件的几句话想成一个场景，归为一个记忆模块。当描述的内容发生改变时，再建立新的场景即可。）

文章 1

Carotenoids, a family of natural pigments, form an important part of the colorful signals used by many animals. Animals acquire carotenoids either directly (from the plants and algae that produce them) or indirectly (by eating insects) and store them in a variety of tissues. Studies of several animal species have shown that when choosing mates, females prefer males with brighter carotenoid-based coloration. Owens and Olson hypothesize that the presence of carotenoids, as signaled by coloration, would be meaningful in the context of mate selection if carotenoids were either rare or required for health. The conventional view is that carotenoids are meaningful because they are rare: healthier males can forage for more of the pigments than can their inferior counterparts. Although this may be true, there is growing evidence that carotenoids are meaningful also because they are required: they are used by the immune system and for detoxification processes that are important for maintaining health. It may be that males can use scarce carotenoids either for immune defense and detoxification or for attracting females. Males that are more susceptible to disease and parasites will have to use their carotenoids to boost their immune systems, whereas males that are genetically resistant will use fewer carotenoids for fighting disease and will advertise this by using the pigments for flashy display instead.

文章 2

In their study of whether offering a guarantee of service quality will encourage customers to visit a particular restaurant, Tucci and Talaga have found that the effect of such guarantees is mixed. For higher-priced restaurants, there is some evidence that offering a guarantee increases the likelihood of customer selection, probably reflecting the greater financial commitment involved in choosing an expensive restaurant. For lower-priced restaurants, where one expects less assiduous service, Tucci and Talaga found that a guarantee could actually have a negative effect: a potential customer might think that a restaurant offering a guarantee is worried about its service. Moreover, since customers understand a restaurant's product and know what to anticipate in terms of service, they are empowered to question its quality. This is not generally true in the case of skilled activities such as electrical work, where, consequently, a guarantee might have greater customer appeal.

For restaurants generally, the main benefit of a service guarantee probably lies not so much in customer appeal as in managing and motivating staff. Staff members would know what service standards are expected of them and also know that the success of the business relies on their adhering to those standards. Additionally, guarantees provide some basis for defining the skills needed for successful service in areas traditionally regarded as unskilled, such as waiting tables.

文章 3

Seeking to decrease costs and improve service, some consumer products companies (for example, sellers of collectibles, clothing, and furniture) have considered installing computerized inventory control systems. Such systems assign each item a unique code as soon as it enters the warehouse and use these codes to monitor the precise location of items in storage in order to optimize the usage of warehouse space. These systems can particularly enhance operations for companies that offer a diverse array of products, place a high priority on ensuring the quality of their products, wish to decrease the number of employees in their warehouses, or possess limited storage space.

Despite these advantages, the introduction of a computerized inventory control system can sometimes create operations inefficiencies rather than alleviate them. The retraining or replacement of employees unfamiliar with the new technology can bring about a long transition period in which many customer orders are lost or fulfilled incorrectly. Managers may need to be reassigned to oversee the installation of the new system, stalling or postponing other important projects. Some companies may cut back on personnel in anticipation of the efficient new system and find themselves unable to keep up with orders during a challenging conversion process. And the systems themselves may not be sufficiently customized to each company's particular needs, negating one of the advantages that this technology offers.

文章 4

Most studies of what causes people to leave their current job (employee turnover) have focused exclusively on full-time employment. Much of this research draws attention to four categories of influence on turnover: work-related factors, such as low job satisfaction; external factors, such as wage-earner status in the household and attractive job alternatives; individual characteristics, such as education and age; and job performance (how well an individual functions in a particular job). A question that arises for industries that rely heavily on part-time labor is whether these factors influence turnover among part-time employees in the same manner that they do among full-time employees. Studies focusing on full-time employment have posited that the higher the employee's educational level, the higher that individual's expectations, leading to greater job dissatisfaction and increased likelihood of turnover. A recent study that focused on turnover among part-time workers suggests that when an individual assumes a part-time job as a secondary activity to supplement household income, it is probable that because of its lower importance, the job will cause considerably less frustration for the individual than will a job that provides a household's primary income. On the other hand, the same study finds support for applying to part-time workers the assertion found in full-time turnover literature that household primary-income earners are less likely than are other workers to leave a job voluntarily.

参考答案

文章 1

> 对应场景（仅供参考）：
>
> 孔雀 (animals) 通过吃蓝色的花（directly）或通过吃昆虫 (indirectly) 来获得蓝色色素（pigments）。雌孔雀喜欢更蓝一些（brighter carotenoid-based coloration）的雄孔雀。传统观点认为：蓝色色素很稀有，浑身肌肉（healthier）的蓝孔雀比弱不禁风（inferior）的蓝孔雀更容易捕获到色素。新观点认为：蓝色色素既可以抵抗感冒（immune system）又可以用来吸引异性，所以天生体弱多病的蓝孔雀只能把蓝色色素用在抵抗感冒上，而天生身体就倍儿好的蓝孔雀可以用蓝色色素使身体更蓝（flashy display）。

文章 2

> 对应场景（仅供参考）：
>
> "服务不好不要钱"这种保证（guarantee of service quality）对于不同餐厅的影响是不一样（mixed）的：如果是人均一千元以上的牛排店（higher-priced restaurants），消费者就很吃这一套；如果是街边的串串香（lower-priced restaurants），消费者可能反而会怀疑老板是不是在瞎扯，毕竟小吃摊能提供什么好的服务。但如果是上门维修电器，这种宣传语还是很有吸引力的。
>
> 这种保证其实更大的作用在于激励员工，有了这种保证，海底捞的员工就知道应该随时给客人续酸梅汤、递擦手毛巾，这样海底捞才能做得更成功。

文章 3

对应场景（仅供参考）：

宜家（consumer products companies）为了减少成本、提高服务，每个家具上都贴了一个二维码，扫一扫即可知道家具的准确位置，这样可以合理利用仓库的空间、精简员工。但是，这个新方法也有缺点：宜家需要重新训练员工如何使用二维码，升级期间新手员工手忙脚乱，客户可能会不耐烦而转头去了隔壁的居然之家（orders are lost）；此外，managers 不得不放下双十一大促活动（other important projects）来监督此次升级；由于裁员，转变期会人手不够；最后，这个系统不够个性化。

文章 4

对应场景（仅供参考）：

一家三口中，当全职教师（full-time employment）的母亲会出于什么原因换工作：当班主任累不累（job satisfaction）、工资够不够养活家庭（wage-earner status）、上了年纪之后精力够不够（age），以及有没有评到优秀班主任称号（job performance）。那对于在星巴克兼职（part-time employees）的女儿来说呢，影响她换工作的因素是否相同？研究发现，母亲是研究生学历，比本科学历（educational level）的父亲更容易换工作。而对于女儿来说，反正只是挣零花钱（supplement household income），就更无所谓（less importance）。另一方面，不管是全职还是兼职，如果是家里的主心骨，就更不愿意主动换工作。

187

3.2 搭建逻辑框架

上一节我们介绍了如何更好地理解文章内容：和现实生活产生连接。但在高度紧张的情况下，尤其遇到长文章，我们难免会顾前不顾后，无法全面记住文章的大意。"好记性不如烂笔头"永不过时，我们可以边读，边在纸上用简写或者符号梳理文章的脉络和框架。这也是强迫自己进行主动阅读的重要方式。需要重点记录的内容，一个是文章中出现观点的部分，一个是出现逻辑关系的部分（包括但不限于因果关系、转折关系、对比关系、举例说明关系等）。因为这两个部分是最容易出宏观题的部分。

不要小看这个看似简单的步骤，它可以帮助我们非常有效地集中注意力，并且对文章的整体架构有一个宏观的认知。至于那些考查细节问题的题目，只需按照文章的架构在对应的位置寻找答案即可。

例文 1

According to a theory advanced by researcher Paul Martin, the wave of species extinctions that occurred in North America about 11,000 years ago, at the end of the Pleistocene era, can be directly attributed to the arrival of humans, i.e. the Paleoindians, who were ancestors of modern Native Americans.

However, anthropologist Shepard Krech points out that large animal species vanished even in areas where there is no evidence to demonstrate that Paleoindians hunted them. Nor were extinctions confined to large animals: small animals, plants, and insects disappeared, presumably not all through human consumption. Krech also contradicts Martin's exclusion of climatic change as an explanation by asserting that widespread climatic change did indeed occur at the end of the Pleistocene. Still, Krech attributes secondary if not primary responsibility for the extinctions to the Paleoindians, arguing that humans have produced local extinctions elsewhere. But, according to historian Richard White, even the attribution of secondary responsibility may not be supported by the evidence. White observes that Martin's thesis depends on coinciding dates for the arrival of humans and the decline of large animal species, and Krech, though aware that the dates are controversial, does not challenge them; yet recent archaeological discoveries are providing evidence that the date of human arrival was much earlier than 11,000 years ago.

下面为可以参考的逻辑框架（高亮部分是需要大家重点关注的地方）：

According to a theory **advanced** by researcher Paul Martin, the wave of species extinctions that occurred in North America about 11,000 years ago, at the end of the Pleistocene era, can be directly attributed to the arrival of humans, i.e. the Paleoindians, who were ancestors of modern Native Americans.

| PM：人→动物灭绝 |

However, anthropologist Shepard Krech **points out** that large animal species vanished even in areas where there is no evidence to demonstrate that Paleoindians hunted them.

| PM：人→动物灭绝 |
| ↑ 反对 |
| SK：没人去捕猎的大型动物也灭绝了 |

Nor were extinctions confined to large animals: small animals, plants, and insects disappeared, presumably not all through human consumption.

| PM：人→动物灭绝 |
| ↑ 反对 |
| SK：①没人去捕猎的大型动物也灭绝了 ②没人去吃的小动物也灭绝了 |

Krech **also contradicts** Martin's exclusion of climatic change as an explanation by **asserting** that widespread climatic change did indeed occur at the end of the Pleistocene.

| PM：人→动物灭绝←天气 |
| ↑ 反对 |
| SK：①没人去捕猎的大型动物也灭绝了 ②没人去吃的小动物也灭绝了 ③天气→动物灭绝 |

Still, Krech **attributes** secondary if not primary responsibility for the extinctions to the Paleoindians, arguing that humans have produced local extinctions elsewhere.

| PM：人→动物灭绝←天气 |
| ↑ 反对（不完全） |
| SK：①没人去捕猎的大型动物也灭绝了 ②没人去吃的小动物也灭绝了 ③天气→动物灭绝 |

189

But, according to historian Richard White, even the attribution of secondary responsibility may not be supported by the evidence. White observes that Martin's thesis depends on coinciding dates for the arrival of humans and the decline of large animal species, and Krech, though aware that the dates are controversial, does not challenge them; yet recent archaeological discoveries are providing evidence that the date of human arrival was much earlier than 11,000 years ago.

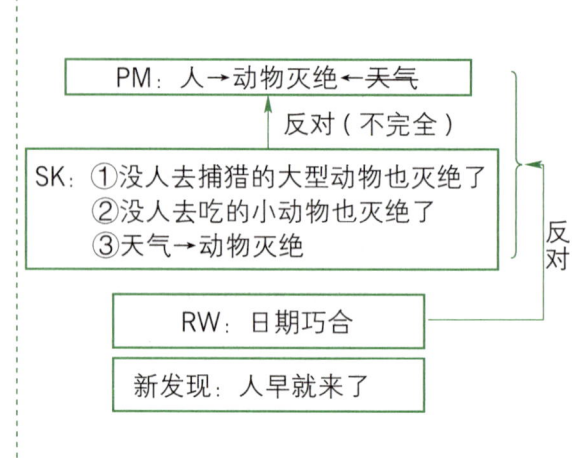

```
PM: 人→动物灭绝←天气
         ↑ 反对（不完全）
SK: ①没人去捕猎的大型动物也灭绝了
    ②没人去吃的小动物也灭绝了     } 反对
    ③天气→动物灭绝

RW: 日期巧合
新发现: 人早就来了
```

注意：为了方便大家理解，笔记中的单词写得比较全，大家在实操的时候可以更简化一些，自己能看明白即可。

例文 2

Acting on the recommendation of a British government committee investigating the high incidence in white lead factories of illness among employees, most of whom were women, the Home Secretary proposed in 1895 that Parliament enact legislation that would prohibit women from holding most jobs in white lead factories. Although the Women's Industrial Defence Committee (WIDC), formed in 1892 in response to earlier legislative attempts to restrict women's labor, did not discount the white lead trade's potential health dangers, it opposed the proposal, viewing it as yet another instance of limiting women's work opportunities.

Also opposing the proposal was the Society for Promoting the Employment of Women (SPEW), which attempted to challenge it by investigating the causes of illness in white lead factories. SPEW contended, and WIDC concurred, that controllable conditions in such factories were responsible for the development of lead poisoning. SPEW provided convincing evidence that lead poisoning could be avoided if workers were careful and clean and if already extant workplace safety regulations were stringently enforced. However, the Women's Trade Union League (WTUL), which had ceased in the late 1880s to oppose restrictions on women's labor, supported the eventually enacted proposal, in part because safety regulations were generally not being enforced in white lead factories, where there were no unions (and little prospect of any) to pressure employers to comply with safety regulations.

逻辑框架：

Acting on the recommendation of a British government committee investigating the high incidence in white lead factories of illness among employees, most of whom were women, the Home Secretary proposed in 1895 that Parliament enact legislation that would prohibit women from holding most jobs in white lead factories.

铅中毒→ HS：禁止女性在铅厂工作

Although the Women's Industrial Defence Committee (WIDC), formed in 1892 in response to earlier legislative attempts to restrict women's labor, did not discount the white lead trade's potential health dangers, it opposed the proposal, viewing it as yet another instance of limiting women's work opportunities.

铅中毒→ HS：禁止女性在铅厂工作
WIDC —反对（此举＝限制女性工作机会）

Also opposing the proposal was the Society for Promoting the Employment of Women (SPEW), which attempted to challenge it by investigating the causes of illness in white lead factories.

铅中毒→ HS：禁止女性在铅厂工作
WIDC —反对（此举＝限制女性工作机会）
SPEW：也反对（表示应该查明原因）

SPEW contended, and WIDC concurred, that controllable conditions in such factories were responsible for the development of lead poisoning.

铅中毒→ HS：禁止女性在铅厂工作
WIDC —反对（此举＝限制女性工作机会）
SPEW：也反对（表示应该查明原因） } 环境 ★

SPEW provided convincing evidence that lead poisoning could be avoided if workers were careful and clean and if already extant workplace safety regulations were stringently enforced.

铅中毒→ HS：禁止女性在铅厂工作
WIDC —反对（此举＝限制女性工作机会）
SPEW：也反对（表示应该查明原因；工人 & 法规） } 环境 ★

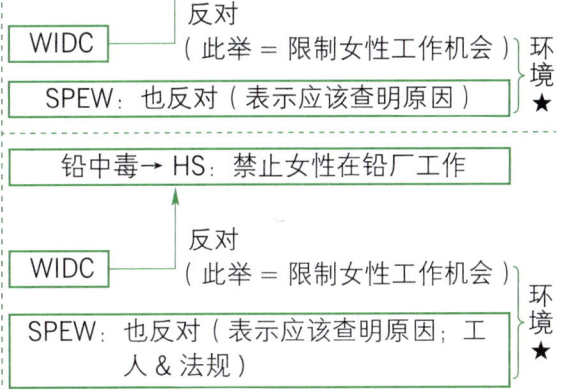

191

However, the Women's Trade Union League (WTUL), which had ceased in the late 1880s to oppose restrictions on women's labor, supported the eventually enacted proposal, in part because safety regulations were generally not being enforced in white lead factories, where there were no unions (and little prospect of any) to pressure employers to comply with safety regulations.

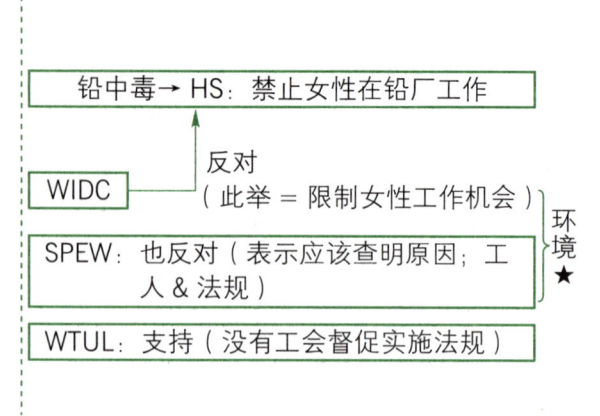

铅中毒 → HS：禁止女性在铅厂工作

WIDC ↑ 反对（此举＝限制女性工作机会）

SPEW：也反对（表示应该查明原因；工人 & 法规）

WTUL：支持（没有工会督促实施法规）

环境 ★

练习

请搭建出下列文章的逻辑框架。

文章 1

In an effort to explain why business acquisitions often fail, scholars have begun to focus on the role of top executives of acquired companies. Acquired companies that retain their top executives tend to have more successful outcomes than those that do not. Furthermore, existing research suggests that retaining the highest-level top executives, such as the CEO (chief executive officer) and COO (chief operating officer), is related more positively to post acquisition success than retaining lower-ranked top executives. However, this explanation, while insightful, suffers from two limitations. First, the focus on positional rank does not recognize the variation in length of service that may exist in top executive posts across companies, nor does it address which particular top executives (with respect to length of service) should be retained to achieve a successful acquisition outcome. Second, the relationship between retained top executives and acquisition outcomes offered by existing research is subject to opposing theoretical explanations related to length of service. The resource-based view (RBV) suggests that keeping acquired company top executives with longer organizational tenure would lead to more successful outcomes, as those executives have idiosyncratic and nontransferable knowledge of the acquired company that would be valuable for the effective implementation of the acquisition. The opposing position, offered by the upper echelons perspective (UEP), suggests that retaining top executives having short organizational tenure would lead to more successful outcomes, as they would have the adaptability to manage most effectively during the uncertainty of the acquisition process.

Responding to these limitations, Bergh conducted a study of executive retention and acquisition outcome that focused on the organizational tenure of retained company top executives in 104 acquisitions, followed over 5 years. Bergh considered the acquisition successful if the acquired company was retained and unsuccessful if it was divested. Bergh's findings support the RBV position. Apparently, the benefits of long organizational tenure lead to more successful outcomes than the benefits of short organizational tenure, while longer tenured top executives may have trouble adapting to change, it appears that their perspectives and knowledge bases offer unique value after the acquisition. Although from the UEP position it seems sensible to retain less tenured executives and allow more tenured ones to leave, such a strategy appears to lower the probability of acquisition success.

文章 2

A small number of the forest species of lepidoptera (moths and butterflies, which exist as caterpillars during most of their life cycle) exhibit regularly recurring patterns of population growth and decline—such fluctuations in population are known as population cycles. Although many different variables influence population levels, a regular pattern such as a population cycle seems to imply a dominant, driving force. Identification of that driving force, however, has proved surprisingly elusive despite considerable research. The common approach of studying causes of population cycles by measuring the mortality caused by different agents, such as predatory birds or parasites, has been unproductive in the case of lepidoptera. Moreover, population ecologists' attempts to alter cycles by changing the caterpillars' habitat and by reducing caterpillar populations have not succeeded. In short, the evidence implies that these insect populations, if not self-regulating, may at least be regulated by an agent more intimately connected with the insect than are predatory birds or parasites.

Recent work suggests that this agent may be a virus. For many years, viral disease had been reported in declining populations of caterpillars, but population ecologists had usually considered viral disease to have contributed to the decline once it was underway rather than to have initiated it. The recent work has been made possible by new techniques of molecular biology that allow viral DNA to be detected at low concentrations in the environment. Nuclear polyhedrosis viruses are hypothesized to be the driving force behind population cycles in lepidoptera in part because the viruses themselves follow an infectious cycle in which, if protected from direct sunlight, they may remain virulent for many years in the environment, embedded in durable crystals of polyhedrin protein. Once ingested by a caterpillar, the crystals dissolve, releasing the virus to infect the insect's cells. Late in the course of the infection, millions of new virus particles are formed and enclosed in polyhedrin crystals. These crystals reenter the environment after the insect dies and decomposes, thus becoming available to infect other caterpillars.

One of the attractions of this hypothesis is its broad applicability. Remarkably, despite significant differences in habitat and behavior, many species of lepidoptera have population cycles of similar length, between 8 and 11 years. Nuclear polyhedrosis viral infection is one factor these disparate species share.

文章 3

Two works published in 1984 demonstrate contrasting approaches to writing the history of United States women. Buel and Buel's biography of *Mary Fish* (1736—1818) make little effort to place her story in the context of recent historiography on women. Lebsock, meanwhile, attempts not only to write the history of women in one southern community, but also to redirect two decades of historiographical debate as to whether women gained or lost status in the nineteenth century as compared with the eighteenth century. Although both books offer the reader the opportunity to assess this controversy regarding women's status, only Lebsock's deals with it directly. She examines several different aspects of women's status, helping to refine and resolve the issues. She concludes that while women gained autonomy in some areas, especially in the private sphere, they lost it in many aspects of the economic sphere. More importantly, she shows that the debate itself depends on frame of reference: in many respects, women lost power in relation to men, for example, as certain jobs (delivering babies, supervising schools) were taken over by men. Yet women also gained power in comparison with their previous status, owning a higher proportion of real estate, for example. In contrast, Buel and Buel's biography provide ample raw material for questioning the myth, fostered by some historians, of a colonial golden age in the eighteenth century but does not give the reader much guidance in analyzing the controversy over women's status.

文章 4

In many instances, the term "developing" is applied to a country with only a rudimentary industrial base and a Gross National Income (GNI) per capita below the world average. This definition gives only a rough-hewn image of those nations in need of international assistance — it measures economic well-being solely by focusing on a country in the midst of economic gains, and one suffering through progressive economic decline.

In response to the crudeness of the traditional measure of development, economists in 1990 created the Human Development Index (HDI), to gauge the development of a country based not only on its GNI, but also on quality of life factors such as life expectancy and education. The UN releases an annual list of HDI values, ranking each country from least developed to most developed on a decimal scale of 0 to 1. However, since HDI only takes into account average income and quality of life, it masks disparities in wealth and well-being among a single nation's citizenry; a country given a "high development" rating may lack motivation to address the gap in income and quality of life between its richest and poorest citizens. Furthermore, countries with low HDI values are rarely able to provide statistics concerning the life expectancy of their citizens, and are prone to both mistake and biases in calculating per capita income. But until economists discover a more inclusive, less ambiguous, indicator of development, the HDI remains the most useful tool in identifying nations in need of international support.

参考答案

文章 1

> P1：收购失败的原因：被收购公司的高级主管（留比不留好；留高级主管比留低级主管好）

> 缺点：
> （1）忽视时长 & 具体留谁？
> （2）两个解释：
> 　① RBV：留任期长的（经验更丰富）
> 　② UEP：留任期短的（适应性更强）

> P2：Bergh 的研究：支持 RBV

文章 2

> P1：lepidoptera 的数量：波动
> 　原因：driving force
> 　如何辨别：
> 　方法 1：测量 agents 造成的死亡率→无效
> 　方法 2：改变栖息地 & 减少毛毛虫数量→无效
>
> P2：猜想：病毒！
> 　旧观点：参与；新观点：发起
>
> P3：此猜想可广泛应用

文章 3

```
两个对立的方法：
Buel：
  ① ~~context~~
  ② 给出大量材料质疑黄金时期，但没有
     给出指导
Lebsock：
  ① 南方社区
  ② 19 世纪 vs 18 世纪女性地位如何变化：
     私人领域↑；经济领域↓
     和男性比↓；和之前比↑
```

共同点：
给读者提供评价女性地位的机会

文章 4

```
"developing"：工业基础差 & GNI < 平均数
        ↓
       片面
        ↓
    HDI：+ 质量
        ↓
缺点：① 忽视国内差距
      ② HDI 低的国家易有偏差
        ↓
但到目前为止，HDI 是最好用的
```

第四章

阅读考题

前几章我们谈到了长难句的阅读，本章将让大家真正感受 GMAT 阅读理解的考题。在 GMAT 语文部分的考试中，我们会碰到三四篇文章，总共 10～14 道阅读考题。GMAT 文章可以分为两类，即长阅读和短阅读。长阅读通常包含 300 个单词以上（通常不超过 350 个词），短阅读通常包含 200～250 个单词。一般来说，考试时会出现三篇短文章和一篇长文章，个别时候，也可能出现两篇短文章和两篇长文章的情况。实际上，我们无须关心文章长短，踏踏实实把题目都做对即可。阅读考题出现时我们需要特别注意三点：

1. 每次只能看到一道题目

实战考试时，文章在屏幕的左边，题目在屏幕的右边，形如：

> Comparable worth, as a standard applied to eliminate inequities in pay, insists that the values of certain tasks performed in dissimilar jobs can be compared. In the last decade, this approach has become a critical social policy issue, as large numbers of private-sector firms and industries as well as federal, state, and local governmental entities have adopted comparable worth policies or begun to consider doing so.
>
> This widespread institutional awareness of comparable worth indicates increased public awareness that pay inequities—that is, situations in which pay is not "fair" because it does not reflect the true value of a job—exist in the labor market. However, the question still remains: have the gains already made in pay equity under comparable worth principles been of a precedent-setting nature or are they mostly transitory, a function of concessions made by employers to mislead female employees into believing that they have made long-term pay equity gains?
>
> Comparable worth pay adjustments are indeed precedent-setting. Because of the principles driving them, other mandates that can be applied to reduce or eliminate unjustified pay gaps between male and female workers have not remedied perceived pay inequities satisfactorily for the litigants in cases in which men and women hold different jobs. But whenever comparable worth principles are applied to pay schedules, perceived unjustified pay differences are eliminated. In this sense, then, comparable worth is more comprehensive than other mandates, such as the Equal Pay Act of 1963 and Title VII of the Civil Rights Act of 1964. Neither compares tasks in dissimilar jobs (that is, jobs across

> According to the passage, comparable worth principles are different in which of the following ways from other mandates intended to reduce or eliminate pay inequities?
>
> ○ Comparable worth principles address changes in the pay schedules of male as well as female workers.
> ○ Comparable worth principles can be applied to employees in both the public and the private sector.
> ○ Comparable worth principles emphasize the training and skill of workers.
> ○ Comparable worth principles require changes in the employer's resource allocation.
> ○ Comparable worth principles can be used to quantify the value of elements of dissimilar jobs.

只有回答完这道题目时，系统才让考生看到下一道题目。也就是说，我们不能先预览所有的题目再读文章，而是必须先读文章，之后再一道一道地完成考题。

2. 题目数量未知

GMAT 不会告诉考生一篇文章后一共会出现几道题目。从一般经验上来说，短文章后会出现三道题，长文章后会出现四道题。

3. 不按文章顺序出题

顾名思义，假设一篇文章有三道题目，那么这三道题目不是第一题问第一段，第二题问第二段，第三题问主旨，而是打乱顺序的。可能第一题就问考生文章主旨，第二题问最后一段的内容，第三题又问回第一段了。

基于 GMAT 阅读的这个特点，请大家千万不要看完一段文章就直接看题，而是要先看完文章中的所有文字，再看题。

阅读部分共有五大类考题，分别为：

主旨大意题（Main Idea）
支持观点题（Supporting Idea）
推断题（Inference）
应用题（Application）
评估题（Evaluation）

4.1 主旨大意题

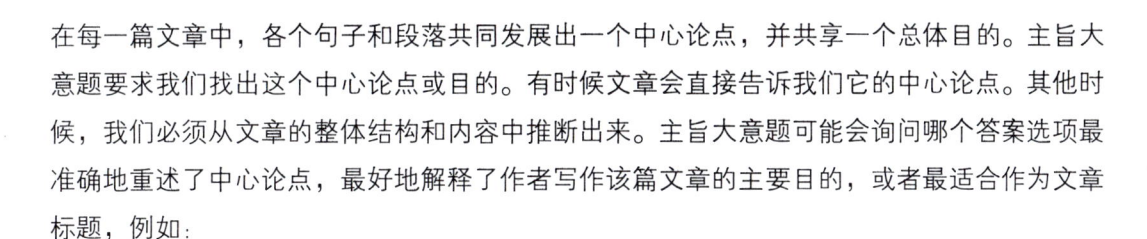

在每一篇文章中，各个句子和段落共同发展出一个中心论点，并共享一个总体目的。主旨大意题要求我们找出这个中心论点或目的。有时候文章会直接告诉我们它的中心论点。其他时候，我们必须从文章的整体结构和内容中推断出来。主旨大意题可能会询问哪个答案选项最准确地重述了中心论点，最好地解释了作者写作该篇文章的主要目的，或者最适合作为文章标题，例如：

The main idea of the second paragraph is that
The author of the passage is primarily concerned with
The primary purpose of the passage is to
…

论证型文章的主旨大意题的正确答案通常会重述或描述中心论点的主要结论。主要结论是整篇文章都给出理由让人接受一个观点，但反过来并不作为接受某些进一步结论的理由。

● 例题

最近的市场研究显示，我们公司的品牌忠诚度在过去两年中有所下降。其中一个明显的原因是竞争对手在产品创新和营销策略上加强了。如果我们不改进我们的产品并更新营销策略，我们可能会继续失去市场份额。因此，我们进行了一系列新产品开发的投资，并且重新设计了我们的广告活动。

经过六个月的努力，新产品线成功吸引了年轻消费者的注意，广告活动也提高了品牌的在线可见性。这表明我们的努力在短期内有效。通过持续的产品创新和精准的营销，我们不仅能够恢复品牌忠诚度，还能够扩大我们的市场份额。为了实现这一长期目标，公司应当继续对产品研发进行投资并采用数据驱动的营销策略，以适应不断变化的市场需求和消费者偏好。

在这篇论证型文章中，"如果我们不改进我们的产品并更新营销策略，我们可能会继续失去市场份额。"是一个中间结论，它是基于市场研究的初步分析。"通过持续的产品创新和精准的营销，我们不仅能够恢复品牌忠诚度，还能够扩大我们的市场份额。"是最终结论，它建立在实施新策略的结果之上。

因此，这篇文章的主旨一定是和文章主结论"通过持续的产品创新和精准的营销，我们不仅能够恢复品牌忠诚度，还能够扩大我们的市场份额。"这句话意思相同的句子。

当文章不是论证型文章的时候，主旨大意题的正确答案通常会说明文章的整体主题或目的。整体主题通常是在不同段落中重复出现的观点；整体目的通常是所有段落共同努力实现的目标。如果文章没有总体主题或目的，正确答案可能只是概括文章。例如，叙事/描述型文章主旨大意题的正确答案可能会概括所描述的事件或说明它们的总体结果。

例题

在一个风和日丽的春日早晨，小镇里的居民们发现了一只迷路的小狗。它在公园里徘徊，看起来又饿又累。小镇里的人们开始尝试找出它的主人是谁。他们张贴了寻狗启事，询问了每一个遇见的人，甚至在社交媒体上发布了关于这只小狗的信息。几天后，一个住在附近城市的家庭看到了这条消息，并且认出了小狗是他们失散多日的宠物。家庭团聚的那一刻，小镇里的居民们感到无比欣慰。这件小事使得小镇里的人们更加团结。

这篇叙事型文章的主旨围绕"社区的力量和团结精神"。答案选项可以为：通过一只迷路的小狗的故事，展示了当一个社区团结一致时可以达到的积极成果。

请注意，干扰选项通常会重复文章中那些不是主要论点的细节，提出看似是主要论点但实际上是不同的主张，或陈述文章中未提及但与之相关的观点。

例题 1

原文：

The idea that equipping homes with electrical appliances and other "modern" household technologies would eliminate drudgery, save labor time, and increase leisure for women who were full-time home workers remained largely unchallenged until the women's movement of the 1970's spawned the groundbreaking and influential works of sociologist Joann Vanek and historian Ruth Cowan. Vanek analyzed 40 years of time-use surveys conducted by home economists to argue that electrical appliances and other modern household technologies reduced the effort required to perform specific tasks, but ownership of these appliances did not correlate with less time spent on housework by full-time home workers. In fact, time spent by these workers remained remarkably constant—at about 52 to 54 hours per week—from the 1920's to the 1960's, a period of significant change in household technology. In surveying two centuries of household technology in the United States, Cowan argued that the "industrialization" of the home often resulted in more work for full-time home workers because the use of such devices as coal stoves, water pumps, and vacuum cleaners tended to reduce the workload of married-women's helpers (husbands, sons, daughters, and servants) while promoting a more rigorous standard of housework. The full-time home workers' duties also shifted to include more household management, child care, and the post Second World War phenomenon of being "Mom's taxi".

题目：

The passage is primarily concerned with

(A) analyzing a debate between two scholars

(B) challenging the evidence on which a new theory is based

(C) describing how certain scholars' work countered a prevailing view

(D) presenting the research used to support a traditional theory

(E) evaluating the methodology used to study a particular issue

这是一篇论证型文章。开篇给出了一个观点（view），后文中 Vanek 和 Cowan 提出各种论据反对开篇的结论。因此，本文的主结论应为"反对开篇的观点"。因此答案为选项（C）。

例题 2

原文:

Historians have identified two dominant currents in the Russian women's movement of the late tsarist period. "Bourgeois" feminism, so called by its more radical opponents, emphasized "individualist" feminist goals such as access to education, career opportunities, and legal equality. "Socialist" feminists, by contrast, emphasized class, rather than gender, as the principal source of women's inequality and oppression, and socialist revolution, not legal reform, as the only road to emancipation and equality.

However, despite antagonism between bourgeois feminists and socialist feminists, the two movements shared certain underlying beliefs. Both regarded paid labor as the principal means by which women might attain emancipation: participation in the workplace and economic self-sufficiency, they believed, would make women socially useful and therefore deserving of equality with men. Both groups also recognized the enormous difficulties women faced when they combined paid labor with motherhood. In fact, at the First All-Russian Women's Congress in 1908, most participants advocated maternity insurance and paid maternity leave, although the intense hostility between some socialists and bourgeois feminists at the Congress made it difficult for them to recognize these areas of agreement. Finally, socialist feminists and most bourgeois feminists concurred in subordinating women's emancipation to what they considered the more important goal of liberating the entire Russian population from political oppression, economic backwardness, and social injustice.

题目:

The passage is primarily concerned with

(A) identifying points of agreement between two groups

(B) advocating one approach to social reform over another

(C) contrasting two approaches to solving a political problem

(D) arguing that the views espoused by one political group were more radical than those espoused by another group

(E) criticizing historians for overlooking similarities between the views espoused by two superficially dissimilar groups

这是一篇论证型文章。第一段在简述两个学派,第二段提出了全文的主结论,其为第一句:...despite antagonism between bourgeois feminists and socialist feminists, the two movements shared certain underlying beliefs. 后文均在论证这两个学派究竟为什么是相通的。答案选项一定要体现该主结论,因此,答案为选项(A)。选项(E)错在原文并未体现"批评"的态度。

例题 3

原文:

Over ten thousand years ago, California's Sonoma Coast lay at the end of a broad coastal terrace. Today, a cluster of mushroom-like outcrops—some nearly sixty feet high—have odd polished areas from ground level to fourteen feet high. These rocks lie near what may have been a terminus for now-extinct megaherbivores (herbivorous mammals exceeding one thousand kilograms) migrating seasonally from valley to coast. The now-submerged coastal savanna attracted mammoths and mastodons from interior pastures, and they may have bathed near the outcrops in what archaeologists suspect is a prehistoric wallow, and then rubbed themselves clean on the outcrops.

Domestic livestock have grazed in the area for over a century, polishing fence posts and rock outcrops to an oily sheen by frequently rubbing against them. This suggests that animals other than megaherbivores could be responsible for the polished areas. However, cows cannot account for rubbings fourteen feet high. Rain and wind weathering has been considered as an explanation, but such weathering would polish the rocks indiscriminately, not just where the rubbing patterns occur.

Recently, researchers analyzed samples of the rubbed rock using microscopes, confirming that the polishing was not caused by weathering. Instead, the scratches worn into the stone closely resemble those on wooden rubbing posts used by zoo elephants to remove grit from their fur after mud baths.

题目:

The primary purpose of the passage is to

(A) impartially compare several hypotheses about the cause of a particular phenomenon

(B) call into question a hypothesis that has been proposed as an explanation of a particular phenomenon

(C) explore the origins of a hypothesis that attempts to explain a particular phenomenon

(D) describe the historical development of a hypothesis that attempts to explain a particular phenomenon

(E) give reason to accept a hypothesis that attempts to explain a particular phenomenon

这是一篇解释型文章。其最终的目的是解释"石头上磨损的划痕与动物园大象洗完泥浴后为了去除皮毛上的沙砾而在木头柱上摩擦留下的划痕非常相似"。因此，主旨应体现这一主要目的。答案为选项（E）。

例题 4

原文：

Ivan Ivanovich Schmalhausen (1884—1963) was a Soviet evolutionary biologist who openly embraced the neo-Darwinian theory of evolution through natural selection, which holds that those organisms with genetic traits that confer advantages in the environment achieve the greatest reproductive success. His views thus conflicted with those of Trofim Denisovich Lysenko (1898—1976), whose neo-Lamarckian theory of evolution was in the ascendant in 1940s Soviet science. In contrast to proponents of natural selection, Lysenko believed that environment could directly alter the heritable qualities of an organism—that the nongenetic traits an individual organism acquires during its lifetime could be passed down to its offspring.

Schmalhausen's career in Soviet science was ruined by his opposition to Lysenko's idea of heritable acquired characteristics. But Schmalhausen's theory about the relationship between heredity and environment, one of the most prescient of his generation, was directly indebted to the challenges posed by the neo-Lamarckian orthodoxy. That is because, unlike evolutionary biologists outside the Soviet Union, who simply dismissed Lysenko's views in favor of neo-Darwinian natural selection, Schmalhausen was forced to take into account the Lysenko agenda. This led him to develop a more nuanced theory of the interpenetration of heredity and environment than was found in either neo-Lamarckian or neo-Darwinian theory at the time.

题目：

The primary purpose of the passage is to

(A) explain Schmalhausen's theory about the relationship between heredity and environment

(B) contrast neo-Darwinian and neo-Lamarckian theories of evolution

(C) criticize the Soviet scientific orthodoxy of the 1940s

(D) describe the historical circumstances that led to Schmalhausen's prescient theory

(E) characterize the contribution of Lysenko to Soviet evolutionary biology

这是一篇描述型文章。文章围绕伊万·伊万诺维奇·施马尔豪森的观点和贡献进行描述。因此，文章的主旨应体现对于伊万的观点和贡献的描述过程，答案为选项（D）。

例题 5

原文：

The Gross Domestic Product (GDP), which measures the dollar value of finished goods and services produced by an economy during a given period, serves as the chief indicator of the economic well-being of the United States. The GDP assumes that the economic significance of goods and services lies solely in their price, and that these goods and services add to the national well-being, not because of any intrinsic value they may possess, but simply because they were produced and bought. Additionally, only those goods and services involved in monetary transactions are included in the GDP. Thus, the GDP ignores the economic utility of such things as a clean environment and cohesive families and communities. It is therefore not merely coincidental, since national policies in capitalist and noncapitalist countries alike are dependent on indicators such as the GDP, that both the environment and the social structure have been eroded in recent decades. Not only does the GDP mask this erosion, it can actually portray it as an economic gain: an oil spill off a coastal region "adds" to the GDP because it generates commercial activity. In short, the nation's central measure of economic well-being works like a calculating machine that adds but cannot subtract.

题目：

The primary purpose of the passage is to

(A) identify ways in which the GDP could be modified so that it would serve as a more accurate indicator of the economic well-being of the United States

(B) suggest that the GDP, in spite of certain shortcomings, is still the most reliable indicator of the economic well-being of the United States

(C) examine crucial shortcomings of the GDP as an indicator of the economic well-being of the United States

(D) argue that the growth of the United States economy in recent decades has diminished the effectiveness of the GDP as an indicator of the nation's economic well-being

(E) discuss how the GDP came to be used as the primary indicator of the economic well-being of the United States

这是一篇描述型文章。整篇文章在描述 GDP 的作用以及关于它的假设。文章最后部分指出，GDP 并不能很准确地描述经济，甚至是有坏处的。因此，文章的主旨可以只概括 GDP 的这个最终结果，即不能准确描述经济，甚至有害。答案为选项（C）。

4.2 支持观点题

支持观点题可能会询问文章表述的任何内容，除了主要论点。要回答一道支持观点题，我们必须理解文章中的各个陈述内容及其在文章中的作用。

支持观点题的答案几乎从不直接引用文章内容。它们通常重述文章中陈述的内容或抽象地描述文章内容。一道支持观点题可能会询问哪个陈述在文章中扮演了特定的角色。例如，它可能会要求我们找出前提、中间结论、被描述的观点、反对意见、正例或反例、因果主张、背景信息、描述性细节，或者解释或叙述的一部分内容。它也可能会询问一个词语或短语在上下文中的含义。

题目可能会问：

Which of the following does the passage mention as providing evidence of the dual nature of quantum objects?

According to the passage, why do the dust particles in a meteor stream eventually surround a comet's original orbit?

The author mentions all of the following as characteristic of world trade in the mid-1940s EXCEPT:

...

例题 1

原文：

The traditional view that a single charismatic leader should set the corporation's direction and make key decisions is rooted in an individualistic worldview. In an increasingly interdependent world, such a view is no longer viable.

题目：

According to the passage, traditional corporate leaders differ from leaders in learning organizations in that the former

(A) encourage employees to concentrate on developing a wide range of skills

(B) enable employees to recognize and confront dominant corporate models and to develop alternative models

(C) make important policy decisions alone and then require employees in the corporation to abide by those decisions

(D) instill confidence in employees because of their willingness to make risky decisions and accept their consequences

(E) are concerned with offering employees frequent advice and career guidance

原文中写道："传统观点是：一个富有魅力的领导应该会设定公司的方向并且做出重要的决策。"本题的答案选项 (C) 是从另一个角度来描述这个传统观点的：传统的企业领导独自做出重要的政策决定，并且之后要求公司的员工们遵守这些决定。此处，"设定公司的方向 (set the corporation's direction)"相当于"要求员工们遵守决定 (require employees in the corporation to abide by those decisions)"。

例题 2

原文：

According to Whig propaganda, women who turned out at the party's rallies gathered information that enabled them to mold party-loyal families, reminded men of moral values that transcended party loyalty, and conferred moral standing on the party. Virginia Democrats, in response, began to make similar appeals to women as well. By the mid-1850's the inclusion of women in the rituals of party politics had become commonplace and the ideology that justified such inclusion had been assimilated by the Democrats.

基于上文可以回答以下两题：

Whig propaganda included the assertion that

(A) women should enjoy more political rights than they did

(B) women were the most important influences on political attitudes within a family

(C) women's reform activities reminded men of important moral values

(D) women's demonstrations at rallies would influence men's voting behavior

(E) women's presence at rallies would enhance the moral standing of the party

本题考查考生对于 information 定语中三个并列句的理解。(A)(B)(D) 在原文中均没有提到过（选项 (B) 中虽然提到了 family，但是其内容和原文中的 mold party-loyal families 相去甚远）。(C) 错在主语 women's reform activities。原文中确实说过 reminded men of moral values，但是并没有说它是妇女改革活动所带来的。(E) 则几乎是原文 women who turned out at the party's rallies gathered information that conferred moral standing on the party 的同义改写。此处，turned out 等于 presence；enhance 等于 confer（授权），所以答案为 (E)。

Which of the following was true of Virginia Democrats in the mid-1850's?

(A) They feared that their party was losing its strong moral foundation.

(B) They believed that the Whigs' inclusion of women in party politics had led to the Whigs' success in many elections.

(C) They created an ideology that justified the inclusion of women in party politics.

(D) They wanted to demonstrate that they were in support of the woman's rights movement.

(E) They imitated the Whigs' efforts to include women in the rituals of party politics.

本题考查考生对于原文后两句的句意理解。(A)(D) 均是原文没有提到过的。(B) 错在原文并没有给出 Virginia Democrats 把妇女包括进来的目的或原因，因此我们不能说 Virginia Democrats 认为把妇女包括进来使 Whig 赢得了选举。(C) 虽然在原文中提到过，但是显然这种意识形态 (ideology) 不是由 Virginia Democrats 创造的（通过最后的 assimilate 也能看出来，这种意识形态是被完全理解和吸收的，说明肯定是学习别人的）。(E) 是原文 "Virginia Democrats, in response, began to make similar appeals to women as well" 的同义改写。此处，make similar appeals 等于 imitate，所以答案为 (E)。

例题 3

原文：

When diatoms are observed under constant conditions in a laboratory, they still display periodic behavior, continuing to burrow on schedule for several weeks.

题目：

According to the passage, the periodic behavior displayed by commuter diatoms under constant laboratory conditions is characterized by which of the following?

(A) Greater unpredictability than the corresponding behavior under natural conditions

(B) A consistent periodic schedule in the short term

(C) No difference over the long term from the corresponding behavior under natural conditions

(D) Initial variability caused by the constant conditions of the laboratory

(E) Greater sensitivity to environmental factors than is the case under natural conditions

(A)(D)(E) 在原文中均没有提到，可以直接排除。(B)(C) 两个选项主要考查考生对于原文中伴随状语 continuing to burrow on schedule for several weeks 的理解。两个选项的区别在于谈及时间的长短，(B) 是 short term，(C) 是 long term。原文中谈及的是 for several weeks（在几周的时间里），是一个较为短期的时间，所以答案为 (B)。此处，short term 等于 for several weeks。

例题 4

原文：

Skepticism about the McKay team's claim remains, however. For example, ALH84001 has been on the Earth for 13,000 years, suggesting to some scientists that its PAHs might have resulted from terrestrial contamination.

题目：

The passage suggests that the fact that ALH84001 has been on the Earth for 13,000 years has been used by some scientists to support which of the following claims about ALH84001?

(A) ALH84001 may not have originated on Mars.

(B) ALH84001 contains PAHs that are the result of nonbiological processes.

(C) ALH84001 may not have contained PAHs when it landed on the Earth.

(D) The organic molecules found in ALH84001 are not PAHs.

(E) The organic molecules found in ALH84001 could not be the result of terrestrial contamination.

本题主要考查考生对于原文最后那句伴随状语的理解。该句表明，ALH84001 在地球上 13 000 年这件事让有些科学家认为其包含的 PAHs 可能来自于地球的"污染"。由此可知，这些科学家认为 ALH84001 刚刚来到地球的时候，可能并不含有 PAHs，在地球上很多年后才含有 PAHs。因此，答案为 (C)。此处，its PAHs might have resulted from terrestrial contamination 等于 may not have contained PAHs when it landed on the Earth。

例题 5

原文：

Most pre-1990 literature on businesses' use of information technology (IT) — defined as any form of computer-based information system — focused on spectacular IT successes and reflected a general optimism concerning IT's potential as a resource for creating competitive advantage.

题目：

Most pre-1990 literature on businesses' use of IT included which of the following?

(A) Recommendations regarding effective ways to use IT to gain competitive advantage

(B) Explanations of the advantages and disadvantages of adopting IT

(C) Information about ways in which IT combined with human resources could be used to increase competitive advantage

(D) A warning regarding the negative effect on competitive advantage that would occur if IT were not adopted

(E) A belief in the likelihood of increased competitive advantage for firms using IT

原文写道："关于 IT 商业应用的文学作品表明了对 IT 具有创造竞争优势的潜力抱有总体乐观态度。"显然，该句表明，大部分的文学作品认为使用 IT 的公司是具有增加竞争优势的可能性的，所以答案为 (E)。此处，"对 IT 具有创造竞争优势的潜力抱有总体乐观态度"等于"认为使用 IT 的公司是具有增加竞争优势的可能性的"。

例题 6

原文：

However, biocontrol agents can negatively affect nontarget species by, for example, competing with them for resources: a biocontrol agent might reduce the benefits conferred by a desirable animal species by consuming a plant on which the animal prefers to lay its eggs.

题目：

Which of the following is mentioned as an effect of using a biocontrol agent?

(A) Reduction of the commercial value of a desirable animal species

(B) An unintended proliferation of a nontarget animal species

(C) An unforeseen mutation in a target species

(D) Diminution of the positive effects conferred by a nontarget animal species

(E) Competition for resources with a largest species

题目问的是哪一项是文中提到的使用生防作用物的影响。答案选项 (D) 实际上就是对原文冒号后的内容的同义改写。原文讲的是生防作用物可能会减少一种动物所提供的收益，答案选项 (D) 讲的是生防作用物会缩减非目标动物的积极影响。显然，此处"缩减 (diminution)"等于"减少 (reduce)"；"积极影响 (positive effects)"等于"收益 (benefits)"。

例题 7

原文：

In a 1918 editorial, W.E.B. Du Bois advised African Americans to stop agitating for equality and to proclaim their solidarity with White Americans for the duration of the First World War. Du Bois believed that African Americans' contributions to past war efforts had brought them some legal and political advances.

题目：

Which of the following is true of the strategy that Du Bois's 1918 editorial urged African Americans to adopt during the First World War?

(A) It was a strategy that Du Bois had consistently rejected in the past.
(B) It represented a compromise between Du Bois's own views and those of Trotter.
(C) It represented a significant redefinition of the long-term goals Du Bois held prior to the war.
(D) It was advocated by Du Bois in response to his recognition of the discrimination faced by African Americans during the war.
(E) It was advocated by Du Bois in part because of his historical knowledge of gains African Americans had made during past wars.

本题的答案选项 (E) 是原文第二句话的同义改写。原文第二句的意思是：Du Bois 相信非洲裔美国人在过去战争中的贡献给他们带来了一些法律和政治上的进展。答案选项 (E) 写的是：部分由于 Du Bois 对于非洲裔美国人在过去战争中获得收益的历史知识。此处，"法律和政治上的进展"等于"收益"。

4.3 推断题

推断题询问文章暗示或支持但没有直接陈述的观点。一道推断题可能会要求我们找到：文章所描述情况的一个可能的原因或结果、文章中一般性描述的具体含义，或者文章中讨论的某人可能会接受或拒绝的陈述。

有时候推断会来自文章的一小部分内容，有时候则有可能依赖于分散在不同段落的几个陈述。

题目可能会问：

It can be inferred from the passage that the Winters doctrine has been used to establish which of the following?

Which of the following statements about the price increases observed in the study is most reasonable to infer from the information in the passage?

推断题一直是 GMAT 阅读中的难点，以下是几个做好推断题的建议：

（1）深入理解文本背景：了解文本的背景信息，如文化和历史背景，可以帮助我们理解作者的意图和文本中的隐含信息。
（2）认识文本结构：理解文章的结构，如引言、主体和结论，可以帮助我们识别关键信息和隐含意义。

（3）注重语言细节：仔细观察作者的语言选择，如明喻、隐喻等，这些都可能隐藏着另外的含义。

（4）理解作者的观点和目的：思考作者为什么写这篇文章，他想要传达什么信息，这有助于揭示隐含信息。可以在阅读时不断问自己："作者为什么会这么说？""这段话暗示了什么？"

（5）联系自己的知识和经验：将文章内容与我们自己的知识和经验联系起来，可以帮助我们理解隐含信息。

（6）寻找文本之间的联系：比较和关联文章中的不同部分，理解它们是如何相互支撑的。

例题 1

原文：

The Chinese, however, made efforts to correct for the errors that had plagued the British. To reduce refraction errors, the Chinese team carried in sea level to within five to twelve miles of Everest's summit, decreasing the amount of air that light passed through on its way to their theodolites.

题目：

It can be inferred from the passage that refraction would be most likely to cause errors in measurements under which of the following conditions?

(A) When there are local variations in sea level
(B) When light passes through humid air
(C) When theodolites are used relatively far from the mountain peak
(D) When weather balloons indicate low air temperature and pressure
(E) When sea level has been carried in to within five to twelve miles of the summit

原文中给出了中国组减少折射误差的方法，即减少光到达它们的经纬仪所需要穿过的空气量。本题的问题要求我们反向理解原文（反义），即哪种情况下的折射可能会引起误差。在逻辑上，由于减少误差的方法是减少光穿过的空气量，那么增加误差的方法肯定就是增加光穿过的空气量。由此可知，答案为 (C)，即当经纬仪被安放在距离山顶很远的地方时（距离山顶越远，距离越长，穿过的空气也就越多）。

215

例题 2

原文：

Most analysts believe that some kind of environmental degradation underlies the demise of many extinct salmon populations. Although some rivers have been recolonized, the unique genes of the original populations have been lost.

Large-scale disturbances in one locale also have the potential to alter the genetic structure of populations in neighboring areas, even if those areas have pristine habitats. Why? Although the homing instinct of salmon to their natal stream is strong, a fraction of the fish returning from the sea (rarely more than 15 percent) stray and spawn in nearby streams. Low levels of straying are crucial, since the process provides a source of novel genes and a mechanism by which a location can be repopulated should the fish there disappear.

题目：

It can be inferred from the passage that the occasional failure of some salmon to return to their natal streams in order to spawn provides a mechanism by which

(A) pristine streams that are near polluted streams become polluted themselves

(B) the particular adaptations of a polluted stream's salmon population can be preserved without dilution

(C) the number of salmon in pristine habitats decreases relative to the number in polluted streams

(D) an environmentally degraded stream could be recolonized by new salmon populations should the stream recover

(E) the extinction of the salmon populations that spawn in polluted streams is accelerated

原文第一段描述了环境退化 (environmental degradation) 是很多三文鱼灭绝的原因。第二段讲到机制时，谈道："如果某地的鱼类消失了，那么这个机制可以让该地区重新出现鱼。"综合这两处信息可知，这个机制应该可以让一个环境退化的地方重新出现三文鱼。答案为 (D)。

例题 3

原文：

The distinction between pheromones and odorants—chemicals that are consciously detected as odors—can be blurry, and some researchers classify pheromones as a type of odorant.

题目：

It can be inferred from the passage that in classifying pheromones as a type of odorant, the researchers posit that

(A) pheromones are perceived consciously

(B) most pheromones are processed by the VNO

(C) most chemical signals processed by the VNO are pheromones

(D) pheromone perception does not occur exclusively between members of the same species

(E) pheromones do not always elicit a specific behavioral or physiological response

原文给出了两个信息：①信息素和有气味的东西可能被混淆；②有气味的东西是一种可以被有意识地检测出来的化学品。综合上述两处信息可以推断出：如果调查者把信息素当成一种有气味的东西，那么他们也一定会认为信息素可以被有意识地感知出来，所以答案为 (A)。

例题 4

原文：

Conventional theories, however, predicted that the distribution of particles would be increasingly dense toward the center of a meteor stream. Surprisingly, the computer-model meteor stream gradually came to resemble a thick-walled, hollow pipe.

Whenever the Earth passes through a meteor stream, a meteor shower occurs. Moving at over 1,500,000 miles per day around its orbit, the Earth would take, on average, just over a day to cross the hollow, computer-model Geminid stream if the stream were 5,000 years old. Two brief periods of peak meteor activity during the shower would be observed, one as the Earth entered the thick-walled "pipe" and one as it exited.

题目：

It can be inferred from the passage that which of the following would most probably be observed during the Earth's passage through a meteor stream if the conventional theories mentioned in the highlighted text were correct?

(A) Meteor activity would gradually increase to a single, intense peak, and then gradually decline.

217

(B) Meteor activity would be steady throughout the period of the meteor shower.

(C) Meteor activity would rise to a peak at the beginning and at the end of the meteor shower.

(D) Random bursts of very high meteor activity would be interspersed with periods of very activity.

(E) In years in which the Earth passed through only the outer areas of a meteor stream, meteor activity would be absent.

文章首先描述了传统观点和电脑模型观点分别猜测的粒子分布特点，即传统观点认为粒子团是中实外空型，电脑模型观点认为粒子团是中空外实型；第二段描述了地球穿过流星群时流星雨的情况，即双峰值型。本题问，如果传统观点正确，那么地球穿过时流星雨会出现什么情况。由于传统观点认为的粒子团模型和电脑模拟的粒子团模型相反，所以流星雨的活动情况也应该相反。流星雨应该是最开始比较弱，然后逐渐在中心部位达到最强，最后再慢慢下降的单峰值情况，所以答案为 (A)。

例题 5

原文：

Will the universe continue to expand indefinitely, or is there enough mass in it for the mutual attraction of its constituents to bring this expansion to a halt? It can be calculated that the critical density of matter needed to brake the expansion and "close" the universe is equivalent to three hydrogen atoms per cubic meter.

题目：

It can be inferred from information presented in the passage that if the density of the universe were equivalent to significantly less than three hydrogen atoms per cubic meter, which of the following would be true as a consequence?

(A) Luminosity would be a true indicator of mass.

(B) Different regions in spiral galaxies would rotate at the same velocity.

(C) The universe would continue to expand indefinitely.

(D) The density of the invisible matter in the universe would have to be more than 70 times the density of the luminous matter.

(E) More of the invisible matter in spiral galaxies would have to be located in their nuclei than in their outer regions.

原文给出的信息是：若密度等于 3 个氢原子每立方米的时候，宇宙将会停止扩张。问题问的是：若密度小于 3 个氢原子每立方米会有什么样的结果。对原文取非：若密度等于 3 个氢原子每立方米，宇宙将会停止扩张，那么密度小于 3 个氢原子每立方米，宇宙将会继续扩张。答案为 (C)。

4.4 应用题

应用题通常问的是文章讨论的情况或想法是如何与文章未提及的其他情况或想法相关联的。

应用题可能会使用像 would，could，might 或 should 这样的词，或者使用 most clearly exemplifies，most similar to 或 most likely ruled out by 这样的短语。

总体来说，有四大类应用题：

第一类应用题要求我们进行类比推理（见《GMAT 批判性推理：逻辑分类精讲》一书）。它们可能会询问几个角色、方法、目标或关系中哪一个最像文章中提到的一个。

第二类应用题要求我们提炼和应用文章里给出的一般规则。例如，它们可能会问哪个行动会违反或遵循文章中陈述的规则。

第三类应用题要求我们扩展文章中的讨论。这类问题可能会要求我们给出最适合的加在文章末尾的新段落的主题，或者给出一个针对作者提出的观点的好例子。

第四类应用题会询问"如果情景"。这类问题可能会问如果某种情况从未出现，那么以下哪件事情是可能会发生的。

请注意，千万不要仅仅因为它们与文章无关就排除答案选项。因为应用题将文章内容与其范围之外的主题联系起来，正确答案往往与文章从未提及的主题有关。例如，关于文章解释水处理过程的类比问题的正确答案可能与书籍出版有关（均需要流程化管理）。

例题 1

原文：

Antonia Castañeda has utilized scholarship from women's studies and Mexican-American history to examine nineteenth-century literary portrayals of Mexican women. As Castañeda notes, scholars of women's history observe that in the United States, male novelists of the period—during which, according to these scholars, women's traditional economic role in home-based agriculture was threatened by the transition to a factory-based industrial economy—define women solely in their domestic roles of wife and mother. Castañeda finds that during the same period that saw non-Hispanic women being economically displaced by industrialization, Hispanic law in territorial California protected the economic position of "Californianas" (the Mexican women of the territory) by ensuring them property rights and inheritance rights equal to those of males.

For Castañeda, the laws explain a stereotypical plot created primarily by male, non-Hispanic novelists: the story of an ambitious non-Hispanic merchant or trader desirous of marrying an elite Californiana. These novels' favorable portrayal of such women is noteworthy, since Mexican-American historians have concluded that unflattering literary depictions of Mexicans were vital in rallying the United States public's support for the Mexican-American War (1846—1848). The importance of economic alliances forged through marriages with Californianas explains this apparent contradiction. Because of their real-life economic significance, the Californianas were portrayed more favorably than were others of the same nationality.

题目：

Which of the following could best serve as an example of the kind of fictional plot discussed by Antonia Castañeda?

(A) A land speculator of English ancestry weds the daughter of a Mexican vineyard owner after the speculator has migrated to California to seek his fortune.

(B) A Californian woman of Hispanic ancestry finds that her agricultural livelihood is threatened when her husband is forced to seek work in a textile mill.

(C) A Mexican rancher who loses his land as a result of the Mexican-American War migrates to the northern United States and marries an immigrant schoolteacher.

(D) A wealthy Californiana whose father has bequeathed her all his property contends with avaricious relatives for her inheritance.

(E) A poor married couple emigrate from French Canada and gradually become wealthy as merchants in territorial California.

这篇文章提供的概念在第二段：一个雄心勃勃的非西班牙裔商人或贸易商渴望与加利福尼亚精英结婚的故事。题目要求我们找到符合这一概念的应用。答案为选项（A），即一位英国血统的土地投机商在墨西哥葡萄园主移居加利福尼亚寻求财富后，与该葡萄园主的女儿结婚。根据文章第一段的描述，第二段中的"加利福尼亚精英"指的是"墨西哥人"。因此，选项（A）中的"一位英国血统的土地投机商"相当于"一个雄心勃勃的非西班牙裔商人"，"加利福尼亚精英"相当于"该葡萄园主的女儿"。

例题 2

原文：

This passage was adapted from an article written in 1990.

Research data indicate that there is a great deal of poverty in the United States among single-parent families headed by women. This problem could result from the fact that women's wages are only 60 percent of men's. Some economists believe that rigorous enforcement of existing equal pay laws would substantially decrease this wage inequity. But equal pay laws are ineffectual when women and men are concentrated in different occupations because such laws require only that women and men doing the same jobs be paid the same. Since gender concentration exists (for example, 80 percent of clerical workers are women), other economists argue that a comparable worth standard, which would mandate that women and men in any jobs that require comparable training and responsibility be paid the same, should be applied instead. But some policy analysts assert that, although comparable worth would virtually equalize male and female wages, many single-parent families headed by women would remain in poverty because many men earn wages that are below the poverty line. These policy analysts believe that the problem is not caused primarily by wage inequity but rather by low wages coupled with single parenthood, regardless of sex. As a solution, they challenge the government's assumption that a family's income should depend primarily on wages and urge the government to provide generous wage supplements (child and housing allowances) to single parents whose wages are low.

题目：

Which of the following is most clearly an example of the policy advocated by the policy analysts mentioned in the highlighted text?

(A) A government provides training to women who wish to move out of occupations in which women are concentrated.
(B) A government supports research that analyzes the connection between wage inequality and poverty among single-parent families headed by women.

(C) A government surveys wages annually to make certain that women and men in the same jobs receive the same pay.

(D) A government analyzes jobs in terms of the education and responsibility they require and publishes a list of jobs that should be considered equivalent for wage purposes.

(E) A government provides large rent subsidies to single parents whose wages are less than half the average worker's wage.

这是一篇典型的计划型文章。高亮部分的政策给出的解决方案是：敦促政府向工资低的单亲父母提供慷慨的补贴（子女补贴和住房补贴）。题目要求我们找到与这一观点对应的例子。答案为选项（E），即政府向工资不到工人人均工资一半的单亲父母提供巨额房租补贴。

4.5 评估题

评估题要求我们评估文章的组织结构和逻辑。这一点和批判性推理考题没有任何区别。它们通常使用 weaken，support，assumption 等逻辑"术语"。另外有些评估题询问文章不同部分的作用。它们可能会问：

The author of the passage mentions the effect of acquisitions on national economies most probably in order to

The author quotes Snyder et al. in the highlighted text most probably in order to

评估题的答案选项往往是抽象的，它们可能不使用文章中的具体词汇或想法。例如，关于段落功能的问题可能会说：它否定了前一段中提出的理论，并提供了任何替代理论需要满足的一些标准。

例题 1

原文：

However, anthropologist Shepard Krech points out that large animal species vanished even in areas where there is no evidence to demonstrate that Paleoindians hunted them. Nor were extinctions confined to large animals: small animals, plants, and insects disappeared, presumably not all through human consumption.

题目：

Which of the following, if true, would most weaken Krech's statement?

(A) Further studies showing that the climatic change that occurred at the end of the Pleistocene era was even more severe and widespread than was previously believed

(B) New discoveries indicating that Paleoindians made use of the small animals, plants, and insects that became extinct

(C) Additional evidence indicating that widespread climatic change occurred not only at the end of the Pleistocene era but also in previous and subsequent eras

(D) Researchers' discoveries that many more species became extinct in North America at the end of the Pleistocene era than was previously believed

(E) New discoveries establishing that both the arrival of humans in North America and the wave of Pleistocene extinctions took place much earlier than 11,000 years ago

本题问的是削弱，但原文中并没有推理，而只有 Shepard Krech 说的两个陈述句。因此，选项仅需要反驳 Shepard Krech 两个陈述句中的某一句即可。答案为 (B)，直接反驳了第二个陈述句。

例题 2

原文：

In addition, the human capital theory explains why there was a high concentration of women workers in certain low-skill jobs, such as weaving, but not in others, such as combing or carding, by positing that because of their primary responsibility in child rearing women took occupations that could be carried out in the home.

题目：

Which of the following, if true, would most weaken the explanation provided by the human capital theory for women's concentration in certain occupations in seventeenth-century Florence?

(A) Women were unlikely to work outside the home even in occupations whose hours were flexible enough to allow women to accommodate domestic tasks as well as paid labor.

(B) Parents were less likely to teach occupational skills to their daughters than they were to their sons.

(C) Women's participation in the Florentine paid labor force grew steadily throughout the sixteenth and seventeenth centuries.

(D) The vast majority of female weavers in the Florentine wool industry had children.

(E) Few women worked as weavers in the Florentine silk industry, which was devoted to making cloths that required a high degree of skill to produce.

推理：

结论：A high concentration of women workers in certain low-skill jobs was because of their primary responsibility in child rearing.

答案方向：削弱题型，结论为因果型，答案需指明有其他导致女性选 weaving 这类工作的原因，或者，在家带孩子和选 weaving 这类工作不会同时出现。

(A) 选项明确指出：即使是工作时间足够灵活，使妇女既能承担家务，又能接受有偿劳动的职业，女性也不愿意接受这样的工作。说明在家带孩子和选工作之间不存在因果关系，可以削弱。(B) 选项不在讨论范围内，我们讨论的是：同样是低技能工作，为什么选 weaving 而不是 combing 或者 carding，此时 skill 的高低就不再是一个影响因素。(C) 选项说的是从事有偿劳动的女性参与度增加，无关。(D) 选项说的是大部分织布女工有孩子，加强了推论。(E) 选项说的是很少的女性做纺织工，推翻了客观事实，错误。

例题 3

原文：

Just as an efficiently higher wage may lower per-unit labor costs, so might judiciously shortened workweeks. Most workweek reductions, such as France's 1998 decision to implement a 35-hour workweek, are meant to ameliorate unemployment.

题目：

The passage implies that the decision to implement a 35-hour workweek in France was based on which of the following assumptions?

(A) Firms will not reduce the wages of the workers who move to a reduced workweek.

(B) Reducing the hours of existing workers will increase the number of available jobs.

(C) Unemployment is more readily subject to amelioration than are other social problems.

(D) A reduction in the workweek is a more effective means of lowering per-unit labor costs than is an increase in wages.

(E) Reducing the workweek will have a number of social and economic benefits, of which a reduction in unemployment is the most important.

推理：

结论：Most workweek reductions are meant to ameliorate unemployment.

答案方向：假设题型，结论为因果型，答案需指明，如果工作时间减少真的能改善失业情况，那么哪个选项一定是正确的。

(A) 选项讨论工资，与题目无关；(C) 选项讨论其他社会问题，与题目无关；(D) 选项将工作时间减少和工资增加做比较，与题目无关；(E) 选项指出减少失业是减少工作时间带来的最重要的好处，与题目无关；(B) 选项指明工作时间减少可以增加岗位，那么就可以进一步改善失业情况，正确。

例题 4

原文：

Wulf suggests that this critique circulated beyond the daughters of the Quaker elite and middle class, whose commonplace books she mines, proposing that Quaker schools brought it to many poor female students of diverse backgrounds.

Here Wulf probably overstates Quaker schools' impact. At least three years' study would be necessary to achieve the literacy competence necessary to grapple with the material she analyzes. In 1765, the year Wulf uses to demonstrate the diversity of Philadelphia's Quaker schools, 128 students enrolled in these schools. Refining Wulf's numbers by the information she provides on religious affiliation, gender, and length of study, it appears that only about 17 poor non-Quaker girls were educated in Philadelphia's Quaker schools for three years or longer.

题目：

Which of the following, if true, would most seriously undermine the author's basis for saying that Wulf overstates Quaker schools' impact?

(A) The information that Wulf herself provided on religious affiliation and gender of students is in fact accurate.

(B) Most poor, non-Quaker students enrolled in Quaker schools had completed one or two years' formal or informal schooling before enrolling.

(C) Not all of the young women whose commonplace books contained copies of poetry critical of marriage were Quakers.

(D) The poetry featured in young women's commonplace books frequently included allusions that were unlikely to be accessible to someone with only three years' study in school.

(E) In 1765 an unusually large proportion of the Quaker schools' student body consisted of poor girls from non-Quaker backgrounds.

推理：

结论：Wulf overstates Quaker schools' impact.

答案方向：文段认为至少三年的学习经历是必要的，而只有17%的贫穷非Quaker女性在Quaker school待了三年或以上，所以Wulf夸大了Quaker school的影响。削弱题型，结论为事件型，答案选项需要指明Wulf不一定夸大了Quaker school的影响。

(A)选项讨论的是Wulf提供的信息是正确的，与题目无关；(C)选项的意思是"某些女性的书籍中包含批判婚姻的诗歌，这些女性并不都是Quakers"，与题目无关；(D)选项讨论的是有些诗歌包含只上了三年学的人无法理解的典故，与题目无关；(E)选项讨论的是Quaker school里有许多贫穷背景的女孩，与题目无关。(B)选项指明大部分贫穷非Quaker学生在入学前已经学习了一到两年，这样她们即使在Quaker school待不够三年，也可以享受到Quaker school带来的正面影响。所以答案选(B)。

例题 5

原文：

Several explanations have been offered for this decline and for the discrepancy in productivity growth between the manufacturing and service sectors…

Yet another explanation blames the federal budget-deficit: if it were lower, interest rates would be lower too, thereby increasing investment in the development of new technologies, which would spur productivity growth in the service sector.

题目：

Which of the following, if true, would most weaken the budget-deficit explanation for the discrepancy mentioned in the highlighted text?

(A) Research shows that the federal budget-deficit has traditionally caused service companies to invest less money in research and development of new technologies.
(B) New technologies have been shown to play a significant role in companies that have been able to increase their service productivity.
(C) In both the service sector and manufacturing, productivity improvements are concentrated in gains in quality.
(D) The service sector typically requires larger investments in new technology in order to maintain productivity growth than does manufacturing.
(E) High interest rates tend to slow the growth of manufacturing productivity as much as they slow the growth of service-sector productivity in the United States.

推理：

结论：Low budget-deficit leads to low interest rates, thereby increasing investment in the development of new technologies, which would spur productivity growth in the service sector.

答案方向：结论的逻辑链是"财政赤字→利率→科技投资→服务业的生产力→制造业生产力和服务业生产力之间的差距"。削弱题型，结论为因果型，所以答案需要指明：有别的因素导致两个行业之间的差距，或者，财政赤字/利率/科技投资/服务业生产力和差距不会同时出现。

(A) 选项讨论的是财政赤字和科技投资之间的关系，与题目无关；(B) 选项讨论的是科技提高服务业的生产力，属于加强项；(C) 选项讨论的是质量，与题目无关；(D) 选项讨论的是服务业需要更多的科技投资，属于加强项；(E) 选项明确指出利率和行业生产力的差距不会同时出现：利率对制造业生产力的影响和对服务业生产力的影响是一样的，正确。

例题 6

原文：

Evidence for differential distribution of wealth is found in burials of the period: some include large quantities of pottery, jewelry, and other artifacts, whereas others from the same sites lack any such materials.

题目：

Which of the following, if true, would most clearly undermine the author's statement in the last sentence of the passage regarding the distribution of wealth in Western Pueblo settlements?

(A) Only community members of exceptional wealth are likely to have been buried with their personal possessions.

(B) Members of communities with extensive agricultural systems are usually buried without personal possessions.

(C) Most artifacts found in burial sites were manufactured locally rather than imported from other communities.

(D) Burial artifacts are often ritual objects associated with religious practices rather than being the deceased's personal possessions.

(E) The quality of burial artifacts varies depending on the site with which they are associated.

推理：

结论：differential distribution of wealth

答案方向：文段认为有些墓葬包含大量的宝物但有些没有，原因可能是财富分配。削弱题型，结论为事件型，所以答案需指明墓葬中的现象并不一定是财富分配导致的。

(A) 选项讨论的是极其富有的人才会带着个人财产下葬，属于加强选项；(B)(C)(E) 选项与题目的讨论无关；(D) 选项指出导致墓葬中的现象的另一种可能原因：宗教，正确。

例题 7

原文：

The dry mountain ranges of the Western United States contain rocks dating back 440 to 510 million years, to the Ordovician period, and teeming with evidence of tropical marine life.

This rock record provides clues about one of the most significant radiations (periods when existing life-forms gave rise to variations that would eventually evolve into entirely new species) in the history of marine invertebrates. During this radiation the number of marine biological families increased greatly, and these families included species that would dominate the marine ecosystems of the area for the next 215 million years. Although the radiation spanned tens of millions of years, major changes in many species occurred during a geologically short time span within the radiation and, furthermore, appear to have occurred worldwide, suggesting that external events were major factors in the radiation. And, in fact, there is evidence of major ecological and geological changes during this period: the sea level dropped drastically and mountain ranges were formed. In this instance, rather than leading to large-scale extinctions, these kinds of environmental changes may have resulted in an enriched pattern of habitats and nutrients, which in turn gave rise to the Ordovician radiation. However, the actual relationship between these environmental factors and the diversification of life forms is not yet fully understood.

题目：

Which of the following best describes the function of the last sentence of the passage?

(A) It points out that the events described in the passage may be atypical.

(B) It alludes to the fact that there is disagreement in the scientific community over the importance of the Ordovician radiation.

(C) It concludes that the evidence presented in the passage is insufficient to support the proposed hypothesis because it comes from a limited geographic area.

(D) It warns the reader against seeing a connection between the biological and geologic changes described in the passage.

(E) It alerts the reader that current knowledge cannot completely explain the relationship suggested by the evidence presented.

高亮句前的大致内容为：自然环境的变化促进了生物进化期。高亮句的大意为：环境变化和生物多样性之间的关系还尚未被完全理解。因此，这里的However明显是一个让步，提醒读者一切都没有盖棺定论，还有待进一步研究，所以答案为(E)。(D)选项的意思为：警告读者不要看出生物和地质变化之间的联系，这个是不正确的。两者之间是有联系的，只不过这个联系需要我们进一步了解。

• 例题 8

原文：

At the same time, a lack of forthrightness on the part of organizations has led to increased cynicism among employees about management's motivation and competence. Employees are

229

now working 15 percent more hours per week than they were 20 years ago, but organizations acknowledge this fact only by running stress-management workshops to help employees to cope. Sales people are being asked to increase sales and at the same time organizations have cut travel, phone, and advertising budgets. Employees could probably cope effectively with changes in the psychological contract if organizations were more forthright about how they were changing it. But the euphemistic jargon used by executives to justify the changes they were implementing frequently backfires; rather than engendering sympathy for management's position, it sparks employees' desire to be free of the organization all together. In a recent study of employees' attitudes about management, 49 percent of the sample strongly agreed that "management will take advantage of you if given the chance".

题目：

Which of the following best characterizes the function of the final sentence of the passage?

(A) It is such as an alternative explanation for phenomenon discussed earlier in the passage.

(B) It provides data intended to correct a common misconception.

(C) It further weakens an argument that is being challenged by the author.

(D) It introduces a specific piece of evidence in support of a claim made at the beginning of the final paragraph.

(E) It answers a question that is implicit in the preceding sentence.

这一段落的大意为：组织缺乏效率，导致员工心生不满，并且组织也没有采取有效的措施来解决问题，反而进一步激发员工想摆脱管理层束缚的意愿。最后一句中提到的调查具体地表明了员工对管理层的不满。所以答案选 (D)，这一调查作为证据，支持了段首提到的现象。

例题 9

原文：

While acknowledging that there are greater employment opportunities for Latin American women in cities than in the countryside, social science theorists have continued to argue that urban migration has unequivocally hurt women's status. However, the effects of migration are more complex than these theorists presume. For example, effects can vary depending on women's financial condition and social class. Brazilian women in the lowest socioeconomic class have relatively greater job opportunities and job security in cities than do men of the same class, although there is no compelling evidence that for these women the move to the city is a move out of poverty. Thus, these women may improve their status in relation to men but at the same time may experience no improvement in their economic standing.

题目：

In the first paragraph, the author refers to the experiences of Brazilian women most probably in order to

(A) support an earlier assertion made by social science theorists about the effects of urban migration

(B) provide an example of one area in which urban migration has failed to improve Latin American women's lives

(C) substantiate the claim that the effects of urban migration cannot be easily characterized

(D) illustrate the effect that urban migration has had on the economic status of Latin American women

(E) compare the effect that urban migration has had on the economic status of Latin American women with its effect on the economic status of Latin American men

作者提到"然而，迁移带来的影响比预想的要更复杂"，它会受例如女性的经济状况和社会阶层的影响。然后列举巴西底层女性经历的例子。由此可见，巴西女性的经历证明了迁移带来的影响不可轻易定义。所以答案为 (C)。

例题 10

原文：

To compete effectively in international markets, a nation's businesses must sustain investment in intangible as well as physical assets. Although an enormous pool of investment capital exists in the United States, the country's capital investment practices put United States companies at a competitive disadvantage.

United States capital investment practices, shaped by sporadic and unpredictable changes in tax policy and high federal budget deficits, encourage both underinvestment and overinvestment. For example, United States companies invest at a low rate in internal development projects, such as improving supplier relations, which do not offer immediate profit, and systematically invest at a high rate in external projects, such as corporate takeovers, that yield immediate profit. Also, United States companies make too few linkages among different forms of investments. Such linkages are important because physical assets, such as factories, may not reach their potential level of productivity unless companies make parallel investments in intangible assets such as employee training and product redesign. In general, unlike Japanese and German investment practices, which focus on companies' long-term interests, United States investment practices favor those forms of investment for which financial returns are most readily available. By making minimal investments in intangible assets, United States companies reduce their chances for future competitiveness.

题目：

Which of the following best describes the purpose of the second paragraph?

(A) To propose a solution to the problem introduced in the first paragraph

(B) To provide support for an argument presented in the first paragraph

(C) To provide data to refute an assertion made in the first paragraph

(D) To discuss the sources of investment capital mentioned in the first paragraph

(E) To discuss the competitiveness of international markets alluded to in the first paragraph

文章第一段给出观点：尽管美国有巨大的资本投资，但其资本投资行为使美国的公司处于竞争劣势。第二段详细阐明具体是什么样的劣势（underinvestment and overinvestment）以及为什么会这样。由此可见，第二段提供了支持第一段观点的证据。所以答案选 (B)。

例题 11

原文：

Even more than mountainside slides of mud or snow, naturally occurring forest fires promote the survival of aspen trees. Aspens' need for fire may seem illogical since aspens are particularly vulnerable to fires; whereas the bark of most trees consists of dead cells, the aspen's bark is a living, functioning tissue that—along with the rest of the tree—succumbs quickly to fire.

题目：

The author of the passage refers to "the bark of most trees" (see the highlighted text) most likely in order to emphasize

(A) the vulnerability of aspens to damage from fire when compared to other trees

(B) the rapidity with which trees other than aspens succumb to destruction by fire

(C) the relatively great degree of difficulty with which aspens catch on fire when compared to other trees

(D) the difference in appearance between the bark of aspens and that of other trees

(E) the benefits of fire to the survival of various types of trees

文章提到，山杨 (aspen) 需要火的这一现象似乎并不科学，因为它的树皮包含很多活的、不耐火的组织，而其他大部分树的树皮包含的是死细胞。通过山杨和其他树的对比，突出了山杨不耐火的特点，进一步凸显山杨需要火的这一奇怪之处。所以答案选 (A)。

第五章

阅读实战

下面就让我们真正开始完成阅读考题吧。阅读练习一共四组,每组四篇文章,均为三短一长。阅读时,请先边读边画逻辑框架,再完成考题。

第一组

Passage 1

In an effort to raise safety standards in air traffic control, some airport control towers have begun to conduct programs including workshops and counseling sessions to help controllers improve their stress management skills. However, a recent report has cast serious doubt on the efficacy of such programs. Researchers used a combination of written questionnaires and physiological measurements to compare the average stress level of controllers who participated in stress reduction programs with that of controllers who did not. Data confirmed that the stress level of controllers who took part in these programs were lower than those of controllers who did not participate in programs. These results indicated that taking part in such programs should have significantly improved the reliability of controllers with regard to safety. When safety records of these controllers were scrutinized, however, researchers reached the conclusion that length of controllers' shifts, frequency of breaks, and amount of overtime worked were more strongly correlated with safety performance than were empirical stress levels.

Stress, as it is traditionally measured, may certainly be among the assortment of fraction affecting air traffic controllers' ability to perform their jobs safely. Nevertheless, evidence shows that targeting controller stress levels exclusively is unlikely to prove an effective strategy in improving air traffic safety.

1. According to the passage, techniques by which stress is measured include

   (A) determining the average length of workers' shifts and the frequency of their breaks

   (B) evaluating workers' safety records

   (C) asking workers questions and administering physical tests

   (D) discussing stress levels during counseling sessions

   (E) charting changes in air traffic control safety standards

2. Which of the following, if true, would most clearly have supported the conclusion referred to in the highlighted text?

(A) Counseling sessions were found to be more effective than workshops in reducing controllers' stress levels.

(B) Controllers' stress levels correlated more highly with controllers' safety records than researchers expected.

(C) Stress-reduction programs were found to be the most effective technique in lowering controllers' stress level.

(D) Controllers' stress levels correlated highly with length of controllers' shift.

(E) Controllers' safety records correlated more highly with amount of overtime worked than with stress levels.

3. According to the passage, before the safety records of the air traffic controllers involved in this study were analyzed, which of the following seemed likely?

(A) That controller who took the most breaks would also have the lowest stress level.

(B) That controller with the lowest stress levels would have the best safety records.

(C) That controller would have either consistently good or consistently poor safety records.

(D) That controller who attended workshops would have lower stress levels than workers who attended counseling sessions.

(E) That effective stress reduction programs would also involve shortening the length of controllers' shifts.

Passage 2

Did the historical period known as the Renaissance (the fourteenth through the seventeenth centuries in Europe) open up the same kinds of social, political, and intellectual possibilities for women as it did for men? Joan Kelly argued in 1977 that it did not, and at the time her insight seemed powerful, for she was the first historian to emphasize certain continuing harsh realities of women's lives during that period: control by fathers and husbands within the family, lack of power within the church, exclusion from educational institutions, and restrictions on women's right to control money or property. None of these facts suggests that women's lives had greatly changed since the Middle Ages. Yet some scholars contend that there are certain aspects of women's experience that Kelly may not have taken into account. One such scholar argues that during the Renaissance many women found in religious life levels of dignity and self-expression that were otherwise unavailable to them. Even if in general the social condition of women improved very little during this period, many women's sense of themselves changed as a result of their spiritual experience; this change is reflected in the religious writings of certain Renaissance women.

4. The passage is primarily concerned with

   (A) pointing out the similarities between two points of view on a particular historical issue
   (B) endorsing a traditional approach to a particular historical period
   (C) describing one scholar's response to another scholar's interpretation of a particular historical period
   (D) resolving a scholarly debate concerning a particular historical period
   (E) questioning the assumption on which scholarly interpretations of a particular historical period have been based

5. According to the scholar mentioned in the highlighted text, during the Renaissance, women found in religious life greater opportunity for

   (A) economic well-being
   (B) political influence
   (C) self-expression
   (D) social power
   (E) formal education

6. The passage suggests that Kelly's thesis "seemed powerful" (see the highlighted text) because Kelly was one of the first historians to

   (A) suggest that the Renaissance had a greater impact on family structure than had previously been thought
   (B) focus on women's role in the church during the Renaissance
   (C) substantiate tentative historical claims about women's social circumstances during the Middle Ages
   (D) focus on the lives of individual women during the Renaissance rather than study the circumstances of women in general
   (E) stress the continuity of the social circumstances of women's lives from the Middle Ages to the Renaissance

Passage 3

The dating project, in one of the largest studies of its kind, has shown that New Zealand was not visited by humans over 2000 years ago, as some previous research suggests.

Yet Dr Opraph, an American archaeologist, based his result on new radiocarbon dating of Pacific rat bones and rat-gnawed seeds and showed that since rat or kiore cannot swim very far, it can only have arrived in New Zealand with people on board their canoes, either as cargo or stowaways. Therefore, the earliest evidence of the Pacific rat in New Zealand must indicate the arrival of people. This result implied a much earlier human contact about 200 BC.

The original old rat bones dates have been hotly debated ever since they were published in *Nature* in 1996. The ages are controversial because there is no supporting ecological or archaeological evidence for the presence of kiore or humans until 1280—1300 AD and the reliability of the bone dating has been questioned. This is the first time that the actual sites involved in the original study have been re-excavated and analyzed. Dr Wilmshurst and her team researchers re-excavated and re-dated rat bones from nearly all of the previously investigated sites. All of their new radiocarbon dates on kiore bones are no older than 1280 AD. The result of Dr Wilmshurst surely suggests that there must be some flaws in the result of Dr Opraph's radiocarbon dating technique. In addition, the dating of the rat bones was also supported by the dating of over a hundred woody seeds, many of which had distinctive tell-tale rat bite marks, preserved in peat and swamp sites from the North and South Islands. The width of the teeth marks left on the woody seeds exactly matches those of a rat's two front teeth, and cannot be mistaken for any other seed predator. Dr Wilmshurst has dated over 100 individual seeds, some rat-gnawed, others intact or bird-cracked, which show that rat-gnawed seeds only occur in both the North and South Islands of New Zealand after about 1280 AD.

With over 165 dates on seeds and bones from a large number of sites, the overwhelming evidence suggests that rats and their human carriers did not reach New Zealand until about 1280 AD.

7. The author of the passage mentions "The width of… other seed predator" most probably in order to

(A) explain why Dr Wilmshurst does the research on 100 individual seeds to determine when the rat gnawed them

(B) give a reason why one can use the dating of woody seeds as a method to infer the arrival of rats and thus of humans

(C) discuss one of the possible flaws made by Dr Opraph about radiocarbon dating technique

(D) suggest that the dating of the rat bones should be replaced by the dating of woody seeds

(E) show the originality of the woody seeds gnawed by rats

8. The statement that the earliest evidence of the Pacific rat in New Zealand must indicate the arrival of people would be most weakened if which of the following were discovered to be true?

    (A) Recent discoveries have found that 2000 years ago, the distance between New Zealand and places where the rats lived was not as far as it is now.
    (B) Carbon dating of wood indicates that people on that time do not usually use canoes to go to other islands.
    (C) New Zealand was not suitable for humans to survive in 200 BC.
    (D) Rats that went to New Zealand relied heavily on cargo rather than stowaways.
    (E) Radiocarbon dating is not the best method to know when the rat emerges on New Zealand.

9. It can be inferred from the passage that in which way Dr Wilmshurst and Dr Opraph are similar in the researching process?

    (A) They use the same radiocarbon dating technique.
    (B) They both assume that there is no other ways to determine the human arrival in New Zealand.
    (C) They follow the same process to date the rat bones.
    (D) They both believe that the rat bones are younger than 1280 AD.
    (E) They ignored dating the woody seeds as a key support to date rat bones.

10. Which of the following is most consistent with Dr Wilmshurst's reasoning as presented in the passage?

    (A) The rat-gnawed seeds in 100 individual seeds can fully represent all rat-gnawed seeds that occurred in both the North and South Islands of New Zealand.

(B) Humans used canoes and visited New Zealand over 2000 years ago.

(C) Dr Opraph's radiocarbon dating technique has some flaws and needs to be revised.

(D) Even if rats swam to New Zealand themselves, one could still use the date of rat bones to determine that of human arrival.

(E) Humans did not arrive in New Zealand until about 200 BC.

Passage 4

Dendrochronology, the study of tree-ring records to glean information about the past, is possible because each year a tree adds a new layer of wood between the existing wood and the bark. In temperate and subpolar climates, cells added at the growing season's start are large and thin-walled, but later the new cells that develop are smaller and thick-walled; the growing season is followed by a period of dormancy. When a tree trunk is viewed in cross section, a boundary line is normally visible between the small-celled wood added at the end of the growing season in the previous year and the large-celled spring wood of the following year's growing season. The annual growth pattern appears as a series of larger and larger rings. In wet years rings are broad; during drought years they are narrow, since the trees grow less. Often, ring patterns of dead trees of different, but overlapping, ages can be correlated to provide an extended index of past climate conditions.

However, trees that grew in areas with a steady supply of groundwater show little variation in ring width from year to year; these "complacent" rings tell nothing about changes in climate. And trees in extremely dry regions may go a year or two without adding any rings, thereby introducing uncertainties into the count. Certain species sometimes add more than one ring in a single year, when growth halts temporarily and then starts again.

11. The passage suggests which of the following about the ring patterns of two trees that grew in the same area and that were of different, but overlapping, ages?

    (A) The rings corresponding to the overlapping years would often exhibit similar patterns.

    (B) The rings corresponding to the years in which only one of the trees was alive would not reliably indicate the climate conditions of those years.

    (C) The rings corresponding to the overlapping years would exhibit similar patterns only if the trees were of the same species.

    (D) The rings corresponding to the overlapping years could not be complacent rings.

(E) The rings corresponding to the overlapping years would provide a more reliable index of dry climate conditions than of wet conditions.

12. In the highlighted text, "uncertainties" refers to

    (A) dendrochronologists' failure to consider the prevalence of erratic weather patterns
    (B) inconsistencies introduced because of changes in methodology
    (C) some tree species' tendency to deviate from the norm
    (D) the lack of detectable variation in trees with complacent rings
    (E) the lack of perfect correlation between the number of a tree's rings and its age

13. The passage is primarily concerned with

    (A) evaluating the effect of climate on the growth of trees of different species
    (B) questioning the validity of a method used to study tree-ring records
    (C) explaining how climatic conditions can be deduced from tree-ring patterns
    (D) outlining the relation between tree size and cell structure within the tree
    (E) tracing the development of a scientific method of analyzing tree-ring patterns

答案及解析

参考答案

1. C   2. E   3. B   4. C   5. C   6. E   7. B
8. A   9. A   10. A   11. A   12. E   13. C

答案解析

Passage 1

逻辑框架：

> 为了安全→开课（提高压力管理技能）→有用
> 但是，其他因素也很重要→只关注压力无助于安全

1. According to the passage, techniques by which stress is measured include

    (A) determining the average length of workers' shifts and the frequency of their breaks

    (B) evaluating workers' safety records

    (C) asking workers questions and administering physical tests

    (D) discussing stress levels during counseling sessions

    (E) charting changes in air traffic control safety standards

题目类型： 支持观点题

题目分析： 问题问我们检测压力的技术包括什么。原文第一段讨论调查者是如何检测出控制者的压力的，即：Researchers used a combination of written questionnaires and physiological measurements to compare the average stress level of controllers who participated in stress reduction programs with that of controllers who did not. 由此可知，本题实际考查的是对这句话的理解，需要在选项中找到这句话的同义句。

选项分析：

(A) 确定工人调换的平均时长和他们休息的频率。问题问的是检测压力的技术是什么，而没问什么因素会改变安全记录。

(B) 评估工人的安全记录。本选项也不是问题问的内容。

243

(C) (Correct) 问工人问题并且给予生理检测。本选项是原文中 a combination of written questionnaires and physiological measurements 的同义改写。

(D) 在辅导课程的环节讨论压力等级。本文没有提到这一点。

(E) 记录航空管制安全标准的变化。本文没有提到这一点。

2. Which of the following, if true, would most clearly have supported the conclusion referred to in the highlighted text?

(A) Counseling sessions were found to be more effective than workshops in reducing controllers' stress levels.

(B) Controllers' stress levels correlated more highly with controllers' safety records than researchers expected.

(C) Stress-reduction programs were found to be the most effective technique in lowering controllers' stress level.

(D) Controllers' stress levels correlated highly with length of controllers' shift.

(E) Controllers' safety records correlated more highly with amount of overtime worked than with stress levels.

题目类型：评估题

题目分析：文中的高亮部分是一个结论，但是它没有前提。也就是说，此处并不是一个论证。由此可知，本题依然着重考查理解句意的能力，直接找到一个可以加强这个句子的选项即可。

选项分析：

(A) 辅导课程在降低控制者的压力方面比研讨会更有效。本选项讨论的是如何降低压力，而高亮部分讨论的是降低压力和其他方面相比哪个更能让控制者保持安全记录。

(B) 控制者的压力等级与其安全记录的关系比研究者认为的更大。本选项能在一定程度上削弱高亮部分，毕竟高亮部分讲的是压力等级与安全记录的关系较小。

(C) 人们发现压力降低项目是降低控制者压力等级最有效的方法。本选项讨论的是降低压力等级的方法，不是讨论降低压力等级和其他方面相比哪个更有效的问题。

(D) 控制者的压力等级与其调换的时长高度相关。本选项讨论的是压力等级与调换的相关度，不是它们和安全记录的相关度。

(E) (Correct) 控制者的安全记录与加班时长的相关度大于其和压力等级的相关度。本选项和高亮部分讲述的内容一致。

3. According to the passage, before the safety records of the air traffic controllers involved in this study were analyzed, which of the following seemed likely?

(A) That controller who took the most breaks would also have the lowest stress level.

(B) That controller with the lowest stress levels would have the best safety records.

(C) That controller would have either consistently good or consistently poor safety records.

(D) That controller who attended workshops would have lower stress levels than workers who attended counseling sessions.

(E) That effective stress reduction programs would also involve shortening the length of controllers' shifts.

题目类型：推断题

题目分析：原文描述了在安全记录出现后，压力、加班、调换等与安全记录的相关度。本题要求我们反向理解原文，选出在安全记录出现以前的情况。

选项分析：

(A) 休息得最多的控制者压力等级会最低。整篇文章没有讨论过压力与休息的关系。

(B) (Correct) 压力等级最低的控制者将会保持最好的安全记录。在安全记录出现后，我们知道压力等级与安全记录的关系不大。因此，在安全记录出现以前，我们会认为压力等级与安全记录的关系较大。

(C) 控制者要么一直保持好的安全记录，要么一直保持差的安全记录。文中没有提过此类信息。

(D) 参加研讨会的控制者比参加辅导课程的控制者压力等级更低。文中没有提过此类信息。

(E) 压力降低项目也会涉及缩短控制者的调换时长。整篇文章没有讨论过压力与调换的关系。

Passage 2

逻辑框架：

```
JK：文艺复兴时期女性地位并没有提升
          ↑ 反对
其他学者：JK 忽视了宗教层面
```

4. The passage is primarily concerned with

   (A) pointing out the similarities between two points of view on a particular historical issue
   (B) endorsing a traditional approach to a particular historical period
   (C) describing one scholar's response to another scholar's interpretation of a particular historical period
   (D) resolving a scholarly debate concerning a particular historical period
   (E) questioning the assumption on which scholarly interpretations of a particular historical period have been based

题目类型：主旨大意题

题目分析：问题问的是文章的中心思想，如果我们将逻辑框架搭对了，那么解决这种类型的题目就会十分简单，检查哪个选项描述了逻辑框架的构造即可。

选项分析：

(A) 指出了针对一个特定历史事件的两个观点的相同点。文章没有出现两个观点的相同之处。

(B) 认同针对某一个特定历史时期的传统途径。文章中描述的是JK和其他学者互相没有认同。

(C) (Correct) 描述一个学者针对另一个学者对一个特定历史时期所做出的解读的回应。这里的一个学者指文中的有些学者；另一个学者指JK；特定历史时期指文艺复兴时期。

(D) 解决一个关于特定历史时期的学术争端。文章仅列出了两种人的观点，最终没有解决他们的争端。

(E) 质疑对一个特定历史时期进行学术解读所基于的假设。文章没有提到过本选项的内容，即没说过有什么假设。

5. According to the scholar mentioned in the highlighted text, during the Renaissance, women found in religious life greater opportunity for

   (A) economic well-being
   (B) political influence
   (C) self-expression
   (D) social power
   (E) formal education

题目类型：支持观点题

题目分析：本题相对比较简单，只要能找到高亮的部分，并且看懂其所在句即可。其所在句的内容为：One such scholar argues that during the Renaissance many women found in religious life levels of dignity and self-expression that were otherwise unavailable to them.

选项分析：

(A) 经济福祉

(B) 政治影响

(C) (Correct) 自我表达

(D) 社会力量

(E) 正式教育

6. The passage suggests that Kelly's thesis "seemed powerful" (see the highlighted text) because Kelly was one of the first historians to

   (A) suggest that the Renaissance had a greater impact on family structure than had previously been thought

   (B) focus on women's role in the church during the Renaissance

   (C) substantiate tentative historical claims about women's social circumstances during the Middle Ages

   (D) focus on the lives of individual women during the Renaissance rather than study the circumstances of women in general

   (E) stress the continuity of the social circumstances of women's lives from the Middle Ages to the Renaissance

题目类型： 支持观点题

题目分析： 本题由于有高亮部分存在，所以定位十分简单，只需在选项中找到高亮部分所在句的同义句，即 for she was the first historian to emphasize certain continuing harsh realities of women's lives during that period。

选项分析：

(A) 表明文艺复兴对于家庭结构的影响比之前大家认为的要显著。文章讲的是女性还是像以前那样艰苦，没有提到家庭结构的问题。

(B) 聚焦文艺复兴时期女性在教堂里的角色。Kelly 确实提到过教堂的角色，但是她说的是女性在教堂里的力量没什么变化。

(C) 证明针对中世纪女性社会环境发表的初步的历史声明。文中完全没有提到过本选项的信息。

247

(D) 聚焦文艺复兴时期个别女性的生活而不是研究总体女性的社会环境。文中完全没有提到过本选项的信息。

(E) (Correct) 强调从中世纪到文艺复兴时期女性生活的社会环境的持续。本选项是对原文定位句的同义改写。

Passage 3

逻辑框架：

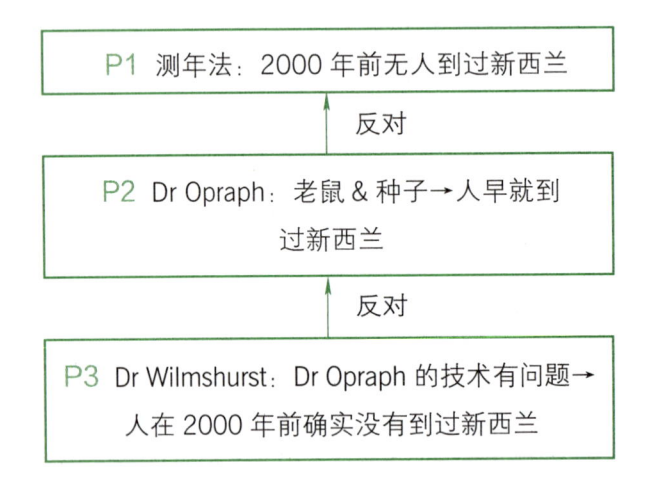

```
P1 测年法：2000 年前无人到过新西兰
              ↑ 反对
P2 Dr Opraph：老鼠 & 种子 → 人早就到过新西兰
              ↑ 反对
P3 Dr Wilmshurst：Dr Opraph 的技术有问题 → 人在 2000 年前确实没有到过新西兰
```

7. The author of the passage mentions "The width of… other seed predator" most probably in order to

   (A) explain why Dr Wilmshurst does the research on 100 individual seeds to determine when the rat gnawed them

   (B) give a reason why one can use the dating of woody seeds as a method to infer the arrival of rats and thus of humans

   (C) discuss one of the possible flaws made by Dr Opraph about radiocarbon dating technique

   (D) suggest that the dating of the rat bones should be replaced by the dating of woody seeds

   (E) show the originality of the woody seeds gnawed by rats

题目类型： 评估题

题目分析： 本题问的是高亮部分的写作目的，定位十分容易。

选项分析：

(A) 解释 Dr Wilmshurst 为什么要调查 100 粒种子来确定老鼠是何时咬它们的。本选项是高度干扰项。请注意，作者确实在这句话之后提到了自己用 100 粒种子做实验，但他并没有认为高亮句是解释提出这个实验的原因。

(B) (Correct) 给出一个可以用木本植物种子的年代测定来推测老鼠和人类何时到来的原因。高亮部分的目的其实是想向读者解释为什么可以用种子的年代测定来推算老鼠和人类到来的时间，而不是为什么要用那 100 粒种子来确定老鼠咬它们的时间。

(C) 讨论 Opraph 在放射性碳年代测定技术上可能犯下的一个错误。这句话和 Opraph 没有什么关系。

(D) 表明应该用木本植物种子的年代测定来替换老鼠骨头的年代测定。这句话表明了用种子来进行年代测定的可能性，但是没有表明测定种子比测定老鼠骨头的年代更好或更坏。

(E) 展示老鼠咬过的木本植物种子的独特性。本句和本选项内容无关。

8. The statement that the earliest evidence of the Pacific rat in New Zealand must indicate the arrival of people would be most weakened if which of the following were discovered to be true?

(A) Recent discoveries have found that 2000 years ago, the distance between New Zealand and places where the rats lived was not as far as it is now.

(B) Carbon dating of wood indicates that people on that time do not usually use canoes to go to other islands.

(C) New Zealand was not suitable for humans to survive in 200 BC.

(D) Rats that went to New Zealand relied heavily on cargo rather than stowaways.

(E) Radiocarbon dating is not the best method to know when the rat emerges on New Zealand.

题目类型： 评估题

题目分析： 结论：The earliest evidence of the Pacific rat in New Zealand must indicate the arrival of people.

答案方向：削弱题型，结论为因果型，答案需指明老鼠出现在新西兰的另一个原因，或者"老鼠出现在新西兰"和"人类到达新西兰"这两个现象不会同时出现。

选项分析：

(A) (Correct) 现在的研究发现在 2000 年以前，新西兰与老鼠居住的地方没有现在相距这么远。若当年老鼠住得离新西兰很近，那么它们可以不凭借船只直接"游"到这里，自然不能表明人类曾经到过新西兰。此选项给出了老鼠出现在新西兰的另一个原因。

(B) 木材的碳年代测定表明在那个时候人类不经常使用独木舟去其他岛屿。人类是否经常用独木舟出行与高亮句无关。

(C) 在公元前 200 年的时候，新西兰不适宜人类生活。本选项和高亮句无关。

(D) 那些去新西兰的老鼠更加可能靠货物运输而不是偷偷乘船。老鼠究竟是通过什么方式乘人类的船到达新西兰的和人类是否到过新西兰无关。

(E) 放射性碳年代测定不是知道老鼠何时出现在新西兰的最好方法。方法是不是最好的，和能不能获知人类到达的时间无关。

9. It can be inferred from the passage that in which way Dr Wilmshurst and Dr Opraph are similar in the researching process?

(A) They use the same radiocarbon dating technique.
(B) They both assume that there is no other ways to determine the human arrival in New Zealand.
(C) They follow the same process to date the rat bones.
(D) They both believe that the rat bones are younger than 1280 AD.
(E) They ignored dating the woody seeds as a key support to date rat bones.

题目类型： 推断题

题目分析： 问题要求我们根据文章信息推断出 Wilmshurst 和 Opraph 的相似之处。可以发现，两者虽然得出的实验数据不同，但是使用的实验方法是相同的。

选项分析：

(A) (Correct) 他们用了相同的放射性碳年代测定技术。虽然实验数据有冲突，但是用的实验技术是相同的。

(B) 他们都认为没有其他方法来确定人类是否到过新西兰。文中没有提及两人是否认为有其他方式确定人类是否到过新西兰这个问题。

(C) 他们测定老鼠骨头年代的步骤是相同的。文中没有提到两人测定老鼠骨头年代的过程。

(D) 他们都认为老鼠骨头的年代在公元后 1280 年之后。这是 Wilmshurst 的说法，不是 Opraph 的。

(E) 他们忽略了用测定木本植物种子的年代作为一个对测定老鼠骨头年代的重要支持。至少 Wilmshurst 并没有忽略这件事，所以本选项不可能是相同点。

10. Which of the following is most consistent with Dr Wilmshurst's reasoning as presented in the passage?

    (A) The rat-gnawed seeds in 100 individual seeds can fully represent all rat-gnawed seeds that occurred in both the North and South Islands of New Zealand.
    (B) Humans used canoes and visited New Zealand over 2000 years ago.
    (C) Dr Opraph's radiocarbon dating technique has some flaws and needs to be revised.
    (D) Even if rats swam to New Zealand themselves, one could still use the date of rat bones to determine that of human arrival.
    (E) Humans did not arrive in New Zealand until about 200 BC.

题目类型：评估题

题目分析：前提：with over 165 dates on seeds and bones from a large number of sites

结论：rats and their human carriers did not reach New Zealand until about 1280 AD

答案方向：加强题型，结论为事件类，答案需指明：如果老鼠和人类真的没有在公元后 1280 年之前到过新西兰，那么哪个选项一定是正确的。

选项分析：

(A) (Correct)100 粒种子中老鼠咬过的种子完全能代表在新西兰北岛和南岛出现的老鼠咬过的所有种子。如果真的能根据 165 dates 推断出人类和老鼠没有在 2000 年前到过新西兰，那么这些种子一定可以代表新西兰出现的老鼠咬过的所有种子。

(B) 人类在 2000 年以前使用独木舟并且到达了新西兰。本选项和 Dr Wilmshurst 的结论不符。

(C) Opraph 的放射性碳年代测定技术有误并且需要修正。本选项确实是 Dr Wilmshurst 同意的内容，但是和他的推理无关。

(D) 就算是老鼠自己游到新西兰的，也会有人用老鼠骨头的时间来确定人类到达的时间。本选项和 Dr Wilmshurst 的推理无关。

(E) 直到大约公元前 200 年人类都没到过新西兰。本选项和 Dr Wilmshurst 的推理无关，也不是 Dr Wilmshurst 推理出的结论。

Passage 4

逻辑框架：

> 年轮学：
> 生长季：大 & 薄壁；后期：小 & 厚壁
> 潮湿：宽；干燥：窄
> 但是，有不确定性（地下水；极度干旱）

11. The passage suggests which of the following about the ring patterns of two trees that grew in the same area and that were of different, but overlapping, ages?

   (A) The rings corresponding to the overlapping years would often exhibit similar patterns.
   (B) The rings corresponding to the years in which only one of the trees was alive would not reliably indicate the climate conditions of those years.
   (C) The rings corresponding to the overlapping years would exhibit similar patterns only if the trees were of the same species.
   (D) The rings corresponding to the overlapping years could not be complacent rings.
   (E) The rings corresponding to the overlapping years would provide a more reliable index of dry climate conditions than of wet conditions.

题目类型： 支持观点题

题目分析： 文章中出现本题信息的句子是：Often, ring patterns of dead trees of different, but overlapping, ages can be correlated to provide an extended index of past climate conditions. 通过这个句子即可得到答案，需要注意对 extended index 的理解。

选项分析：

(A) (Correct) 有重合年份的树木的年轮通常有相似的纹路。在定位句中作者提到，不同年龄的树，只要有共同活着的时间，那么这样的年轮就可以被联系起来提供扩展的气候索引信息。如何能提供"扩展 (extended)"的索引呢？必然，两棵树的年轮在重合年份部分需要有相似的纹路，否则，绝不会产生扩展信息。试想，如果生长在一起且年份有重合的两棵树的年轮完全不同，那么由于年轮会展现气候信息，而这两棵树在重合年份的部分展示出了不同的气候信息，所以这只能表明有一棵树展示的信息是错误的（或者两个都是错的），无法扩展气候索引信息（最好的情况是一对一错，那也只能保持那棵提供正确信息的树的信息，无法进一步扩展）。

(B) 只和其中一棵活着的树年份相符的年轮不能说明那些年的气候情况。只要两棵树有共同活着的年份，那么这棵树其他任何的年轮都可以通过其粗细来显示气候。所以就算在有些年只有一棵树活着，该树的年轮也可以反映那些年的气候。

(C) 只有同种类的树木中有重合年份的树木的年轮才能展示相似的纹路年轮。文中并没有提到一定要同种类的树木。所以该信息属无中生有。

(D) 有重合年份的树木的年轮不可能是充盈的年轮。年轮是否充盈是由水分多少决定的，和本题问的内容无关。

(E) 有重合年份的树木的年轮在湿润的条件下比在干燥的条件下更能可靠地反映当时的气候。这个选项可以定位到 "In wet years rings are broad; during drought years they are narrow, since the trees grow less." 文中没有证据证明湿润气候比干燥气候更加可靠。

12. In the highlighted text, "uncertainties" refers to

    (A) dendrochronologists' failure to consider the prevalence of erratic weather patterns
    (B) inconsistencies introduced because of changes in methodology
    (C) some tree species' tendency to deviate from the norm
    (D) the lack of detectable variation in trees with complacent rings
    (E) the lack of perfect correlation between the number of a tree's rings and its age

题目类型：支持观点题

题目分析：本题考查对于高亮部分所在句的理解，即对 trees in extremely dry regions may go a year or two without adding any rings 的理解。

选项分析：

(A) 树木年代学家并没有考虑盛行的极端天气模式。文中确实提到了树木年代学家没有考虑极端天气模式，但其和高亮部分无关。

(B) 由于方法的改变而引发的不一致。文中没有提到整体方法的改变。

(C) 一些树木种类趋向于背离规范。文章提到过这个选项的内容："Certain species sometimes add more than one ring in a single year, when growth halts temporarily and then starts again."但其和高亮部分无关。

(D) 年轮充盈的树缺乏可发现的变化（湿润与干燥气候）。文章中说到，充盈的年轮本身是不可用的，所以这个不属于 uncertainty。

253

(E) (Correct) 年轮的数目与树龄之间缺乏完美匹配。高亮句的前半句说明了在一定条件下有可能会少一圈或两圈年轮（有一两年没有长年轮），这就造成了年轮的数目与树龄不匹配的问题。选项和这半句是同义句。

13. The passage is primarily concerned with

    (A) evaluating the effect of climate on the growth of trees of different species
    (B) questioning the validity of a method used to study tree-ring records
    (C) explaining how climatic conditions can be deduced from tree-ring patterns
    (D) outlining the relation between tree size and cell structure within the tree
    (E) tracing the development of a scientific method of analyzing tree-ring patterns

题目类型：主旨大意题

题目分析：主旨大意题选择与逻辑框架所描述的结构相同的选项即可。

选项分析：

(A) 评估气候对不同种类的树木生长的影响。文中提及的是气候对年轮生长的影响，没有提到过对树木生长的影响。

(B) 质疑一个研究树木年轮的方法。这个选项有一定的迷惑性，文中的第二段确实提出了这种方法在一些情况下可能不适用，但是作者没有质疑方法的意思。

(C) (Correct) 解释气候条件怎样被反映在树木的年轮中。第一段在文中介绍了原理，第二段提出让步，这两者的结合有效地解释了气候条件在年轮中的反映情况。

(D) 概括树木大小与细胞结构的关系。文中没有提到树木大小与细胞结构的关系。

(E) 探究一个分析年轮模式的科学方法的发展过程。文中没有提及探究分析年轮模式的科学方法的发展过程，只是介绍了原理。

Passage 1

On way to assess whether people reject determinism is to present them with a nontechnical description of a deterministic universe and then gauge their reaction. In one study, a deterministic universe was characterized as follows: "Everything that happens in the universe is completely caused by whatever happened before it. This is true from the very beginning of the universe, so what happened in the beginning of the universe caused what happened next, and so on right up until the present." Determinism is a sophisticated theory of the universe, so none of participants questioned the idea about the universe. Furthermore, the group of people from cross-cultural background was showed another material: "One day John decided to have French fries at dinner. Like everything else, this decision was completely caused by what happened before it. So, if everything in this universe was exactly the same up until John made decision, then it had to happen that John would decide to have French fries." After reading such a description, most of the participants tended to reject the idea that our universe is like this, at least when it comes to human decision-making.

These results from experimental philosophy confirm what many philosophers already maintained: that common sense is committed to indeterminism about decision-making. But the results underscore a puzzling aspect of this common-sense commitment. One explanation with an impressive philosophical pedigree is that people reject determinism because introspection does not reveal a deterministic set of causes of action. Often when we introspect on our reasons for performing an action, the reasons we perceive do not univocally point to a particular action. Also, cognitive scientists widely agree that introspection fails to reveal all of the causal influences on our actions.

1. It can be inferred from the passage that if the rest of the participants (the participants who did not reject the idea) are purely advocators of determinism, they might agree which of the following assertions?

   (A) The introspection may help people to have a better understanding of determinism.
   (B) John's decision of eating French fries was determined by his past days' decisions.
   (C) What happened in the universe may be independent from anything in the past.

(D) Cognitive scientists are not well-supported since introspection determines John's decision on French fries.

(E) Although John belongs to the universe, he and the universe mentioned in the first material follow different theories (determinism or indeterminism) of a deterministic universe.

2. The primary purpose of the passage is to

   (A) contrast the differences between advocators of determinism and of indeterminism
   (B) explore possible explanation for advocators of the universe's determinism
   (C) explain why people may reject the sophisticated theory of the universe
   (D) criticize the participants of admitting the idea that our universe follows the determinism theory
   (E) summarize the study findings and show that the study is valid

Passage 2

Many United States companies believe that the rising cost of employees' health care benefits has hurt the country's competitive position in the global market by raising production costs and thus increasing the prices of exported and domestically sold goods. As a result, these companies have shifted health care costs to employees in the form of wage deductions or high deductibles. This strategy, however, has actually hindered companies' competitiveness. For example, cost shifting threatens employees' health because many do not seek preventive screening. Also, labor relations have been damaged: the percentage of strikes in which health benefits were a major issue rose from 18 percent in 1986 to 78 percent in 1989.

Health care costs can be managed more effectively if companies intervene in the supply side of health care delivery just as they do with other key suppliers: strategies used to procure components necessary for production would work in procuring health care. For example, the make/buy decision—the decision whether to produce or purchase parts used in making a product—can be applied to health care. At one company, for example, employees receive health care at an on-site clinic maintained by the company. The clinic fosters morale, resulting in a low rate of employees leaving the company. Additionally, the company has constrained the growth of health care costs while expanding medical services.

3. The passage is primarily concerned with

   (A) providing support for a traditional theory
   (B) comparing several explanations for a problem
   (C) summarizing a well-known research study
   (D) recommending an alternative approach
   (E) criticizing the work of a researcher

4. The author of the passage asserts which of the following about managing health care costs in an effective manner?

   (A) Educating employees to use health care wisely is the best way to reduce health care costs.
   (B) Allowing employees to select health care programs is the most effective means of controlling health care costs.
   (C) Companies should pass rising health care costs on to employees rather than to consumers of the companies' products.
   (D) Companies should use strategies in procuring health care similar to those used in procuring components necessary for production.
   (E) Companies should control health care costs by reducing the extent of medical coverage rather than by shifting costs to employees.

5. Which of the following, if true, would provide the most support for the author's view about intervening on the supply side of health care?

   (A) Most companies do not have enough employees to make on-site clinics cost-effective.
   (B) Many companies with on-site clinics offer their employees the option of going outside the company's system to obtain health care.
   (C) The costs of establishing and running an on-site clinic are demonstrably higher than the costs of paying for health care from an outside provider.
   (D) Companies with health care clinics find that employees are unwilling to assist in controlling the costs of health care.
   (E) Employees at companies with on-site clinics seek preventive screening and are thus less likely to delay medical treatment.

Passage 3

Although rarer, sleep-intervention studies have begun to suggest physiological mechanisms that might account for deleterious effects of reduced sleep, evidence for such findings, including a shorter life span, has come largely from epidemiological studies. Two years ago, for example, neuroscientist Orfeu Buxton of Brigham and Women's Hospital in Boston and colleagues showed that young men who underwent just a week of reduced sleep had lower responsiveness to the hormone insulin, a decline that is a hallmark of type 2 diabetes.

Our 24/7 society can disrupt our schedules in another way. Humans evolved to be active during the day. Light calibrates the central circadian pacemaker, the body's master clock in the brain. In turn, it helps harmonize molecular clocks in individual tissues so that our physiology and behavior mesh—we get hungry in the morning, for instance, and feel drowsy at night. Studies have suggested that upsetting these circadian rhythms triggers a range of health problems. That's potentially bad news for people who have night jobs or are on rotating shifts, which require them to change work hours frequently; they often have to contend with inadequate sleep and discombobulated circadian cycles.

In their latest sleep study, Buxton and colleagues gauged the physiological impact of this double whammy. For nearly 6 weeks each, 21 study subjects lived in the equivalent of a hotel suite in the hospital's Boston research lab. After storing upon sleep, these people spent 3 weeks on a regimen in which they could sleep for only 5.6 hours in each 24-hour period. Like rotating shift workers, they went to bed at varying times. To throw off their circadian rhythms, the light-dark cycle in the facility lasted 28 hours rather than the usual 24. And to prevent these rhythms from resetting, the researchers kept light levels at the equivalent of twilight or dimmer.

So how did the participants, who went more than a month without Internet access, TV, or contact with anyone outside the facility, cope with these conditions? "Our general impression is that people aren't always their kindest selves when they are sleep restricted." Buxton tactfully notes.

6. According to the passage, if a healthy person usually has night jobs or is on rotating shifts, which of the following, if true, would most likely to occur as a consequence?

   (A) The person may not feel drowsy before he sleeps.
   (B) The person may have lower responsiveness to the hormone insulin.

(C) The person may feel hard to get into sleep and thus have difficulties to get up early.

(D) The person may be chosen as Buxton and colleagues' study subjects.

(E) The person's physiology and behavior may not mesh and the person may have some health problems.

7. The author's claim that "who went more than a month without Internet access, TV, or contact with anyone outside the facility" (see the highlighted text) is primarily in order to do which of the following purposes?

   (A) To suggest that inadequate sleep and discombobulated circadian cycles and relatively low level of physical health are strongly related

   (B) To describe the certain environment in which the participants should be confined in the study

   (C) To explain why the participants are not always their kindest selves when their sleep is restricted

   (D) To show who are qualified to be the subjects in the study conducted by Orfeu Buxton

   (E) To tell apart the participants who cope with certain conditions and the participants who do not cope with the conditions

8. It can be inferred from the first paragraph of the passage that Orfeu Buxton and his colleagues would be most likely to agree which of the following statements?

   (A) Reduced sleep is hard for some young people to avoid.

   (B) That reduced sleep has deleterious effects on physical health is common sense for people.

   (C) Reduced sleep has physiological impact on people, even on young people.

   (D) People who have night jobs have lower responsiveness to the hormone insulin.

   (E) Sleep-intervention studies cannot fully represent deleterious effects of reduced sleep.

9. The primary purpose of the passage is to

   (A) explain the differences between the sleep-intervention studies and the epidemiological studies

   (B) provide three studies and suggest that reduced sleep may lead to a range of health problems

   (C) trace the development of the epidemiological studies of sleep studies

   (D) suggest that people will not be always their kindest selves when their sleep is restricted

(E) present studies that show the impact of inadequate sleep and discombobulated circadian cycles

Passage 4

What kinds of property rights apply to Algonquian family hunting territories, and how did they come to be? The dominant view in recent decades has been that family hunting territories, like other forms of private landownership, were not found among Algonquians (a group of North American Indian tribes) before contact with Europeans but are the result of changes in Algonquian society brought about by the European-Algonquian fur trade, in combination with other factors such as ecological changes and consequent shifts in wildlife harvesting patterns. Another view claims that Algonquian family hunting territories predate contact with Europeans and are forms of private landownership by individuals and families. More recent fieldwork, however, has shown that individual and family rights to hunting territories form part of a larger land-use system of multifamilial hunting groups, that rights to hunting territories at this larger community level take precedence over those at the individual or family level, and that this system reflects a concept of spiritual and social reciprocity that conflicts with European concepts of private property. In short, there are now strong reasons to think that it was erroneous to claim that Algonquian family hunting territories ever were, or were becoming, a kind of private property system.

10. The primary purpose of the passage is to

    (A) provide an explanation for an unexpected phenomenon
    (B) suggest that a particular question has yet to be answered
    (C) present a new perspective on an issue
    (D) defend a traditional view from attack
    (E) reconcile opposing sides of an argument

11. It can be inferred from the passage that proponents of the view mentioned in the first highlighted text believe which of the following about the origin of Algonquian family hunting territories?

    (A) They evolved from multifamilial hunting territories.
    (B) They are an outgrowth of reciprocal land-use practices.
    (C) They are based on certain spiritual beliefs.

(D) They developed as a result of contact with Europeans.

(E) They developed as a result of trade with non-Algonquian Indian tribes.

12. According to the passage, proponents of the view mentioned in the first highlighted portion of text and proponents of the view mentioned in the second highlighted portion of text both believe which of the following about Algonquian family hunting territories?

(A) They are a form of private landownership.

(B) They are a form of community, rather than individual landownership.

(C) They were a form of private landownership prior to contact with Europeans.

(D) They became a form of private landownership due to contact with Europeans.

(E) They have replaced reciprocal practices relating to land use in Algonquian society.

答案及解析

参考答案

| 1. B | 2. C | 3. D | 4. D | 5. E | 6. E |
| 7. A | 8. C | 9. E | 10. C | 11. D | 12. A |

答案解析

Passage 1

逻辑框架：

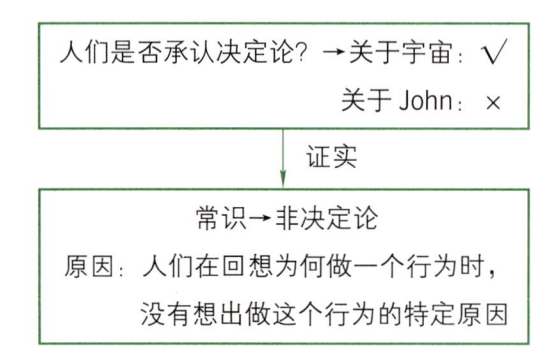

```
人们是否承认决定论？→关于宇宙：√
                    关于 John：×
                        ↓ 证实
常识→非决定论
原因：人们在回想为何做一个行为时，
      没有想出做这个行为的特定原因
```

1. It can be inferred from the passage that if the rest of the participants (the participants who did not reject the idea) are purely advocates of determinism, they might agree which of the following assertions?

   (A) The introspection may help people to have a better understanding of determinism.

   (B) John's decision of eating French fries was determined by his past days' decisions.

   (C) What happened in the universe may be independent from anything in the past.

   (D) Cognitive scientists are not well-supported since introspection determines John's decision on French fries.

   (E) Although John belongs to the universe, he and the universe mentioned in the first material follow different theories (determinism or indeterminism) of a deterministic universe.

   题目类型：推断题

   题目分析：本题较难，考查考生对于文章的反向理解能力。文中描述的是：After reading such a description, most of the participants tended to reject the idea that our universe is like this, at least when it comes to human decision-making. 本题问的是除了这些人外，其余的人会有什么样的反应。在逻辑上，其余的参与者应该继续坚信决定论思想。

选项分析：

(A) 内省可以帮助人们更好地理解决定论。本选项是第二段才讲到的内容，和这些参与者没有联系。

(B) (Correct) John 吃薯条的这个决定是被他过去的决定所决定的。本选项描述的是决定论的内容，正是其余参与者继续坚信的思想。

(C) 宇宙中发生的事情可能和之前发生的事情无关。本选项是非决定论的思想，是大部分参与者被进行薯条试验后应该有的想法。

(D) 因为内省决定 John 吃薯条的决定，所以认知科学家是不被支持的。本选项和原文信息无关。

(E) 虽然 John 属于宇宙，但是他和第一段材料中提到的宇宙遵循不同的确定性宇宙原理（决定论还是非决定论）。本选项不是决定论应该有的内容。

2. The primary purpose of the passage is to

   (A) contrast the differences between advocates of determinism and of indeterminism
   (B) explore possible explanation for advocates of the universe's determinism
   (C) explain why people may reject the sophisticated theory of the universe
   (D) criticize the participants of admitting the idea that our universe follows the determinism theory
   (E) summarize the study findings and show that the study is valid

题目类型： 主旨大意题

题目分析： 主旨大意题选择与逻辑框架所描述的结构相同的选项即可。

选项分析：

(A) 对比决定论倡导者和非决定论倡导者之间的不同。本文没有描述过两者的不同点。

(B) 探寻针对宇宙决定论倡导者的可能解释。本文是想解释为什么人们可能不倡导决定论，而不是解释为什么有决定论的倡导者。

(C) (Correct) 解释人们为什么会否定宇宙中复杂的原理。本选项给出了本文的逻辑结构。

(D) 批判同意宇宙遵循决定论这一说法的参与者。本文没有批判的意思，而是给出一种解释。

(E) 总结研究发现并且展示研究是有效的。我们可以说文章总结了研究的发现，但是文章的第二段没有展示这些研究是否有效，而是解释了研究结果产生的原因。

◦ Passage 2 ◦

逻辑框架：

> P1
> 美国公司认为：
> 健康福利↑→生产成本↑→商品价格↑→全球竞争力↓
> 所以，这些公司↓工资
> 但实际上，损害了竞争力：员工并不愿体检 & 损害劳工关系
>
> P2
> 有效的解决办法：从供给方入手（e.g. 自己开诊所）

3. The passage is primarily concerned with

   (A) providing support for a traditional theory
   (B) comparing several explanations for a problem
   (C) summarizing a well-known research study
   (D) recommending an alternative approach
   (E) criticizing the work of a researcher

题目类型： 主旨大意题

题目分析： 主旨大意题选择与逻辑框架所描述的结构相同的选项即可。

选项分析：

(A) 对传统学说提供支持。这个选项说得不但不全面还说反了。作者可以算是反驳了一个传统的方法。

(B) 比较一个问题的几种解释。文中没有提出任何的解释。

(C) 总结一个有名的研究。作者是根据情况提出了自己的观点，没有总结他人的研究。

(D) (Correct) 推荐另一种方法。第一段偏向于介绍，第二段作者想引出一个可以让 health care 变得更加有效率的方法。

(E) 评价一个研究员的作品。文中没有提到过某研究员的作品。

4. The author of the passage asserts which of the following about managing health care costs in an effective manner?

(A) Educating employees to use health care wisely is the best way to reduce health care costs.

(B) Allowing employees to select health care programs is the most effective means of controlling health care costs.

(C) Companies should pass rising health care costs on to employees rather than to consumers of the companies' products.

(D) Companies should use strategies in procuring health care similar to those used in procuring components necessary for production.

(E) Companies should control health care costs by reducing the extent of medical coverage rather than by shifting costs to employees.

题目类型：支持观点题

题目分析：本题定位原文句：Health care costs can be managed more effectively if companies intervene in the supply side of health care delivery just as they do with other key suppliers: strategies used to procure components necessary for production would work in procuring health care. 关键词十分明显，答案选项也几乎照抄原句。

选项分析：

(A) 教育雇员明智地使用医疗保障是减少医疗保障费用的最好方法。文中没有提及教育雇员这类的方法。

(B) 允许职员去选择医疗项目是控制医疗经费最有效的办法。文中没有提到让员工自主选择医疗项目。

(C) 公司应该给员工增加医疗保障费用而不是给他们的顾客增加医疗保障费用。文中没有涉及给顾客提供医疗保障。

(D) (Correct) 公司应该使用类似采购产品必要组件的策略来"采购"医疗保障。这个选项几乎是照抄原文定位句。

(E) 公司应该通过减少医疗覆盖来控制医疗保障费用而不是将费用转移给雇员。这个选项的后半句是正确的，在文中出现过：cost shifting threatens employees' health because many do not seek preventive screening。但是让其变得更有效的方法不是缩小医疗的覆盖范围（设立定点医院不等同于缩小医疗覆盖范围，医疗覆盖范围多指可医治的疾病数量），文中没有提过缩小医疗范围。

5. Which of the following, if true, would provide the most support for the author's view about intervening on the supply side of health care?

(A) Most companies do not have enough employees to make on-site clinics cost-effective.

(B) Many companies with on-site clinics offer their employees the option of going outside the company's system to obtain health care.

(C) The costs of establishing and running an on-site clinic are demonstrably higher than the costs of paying for health care from an outside provider.

(D) Companies with health care clinics find that employees are unwilling to assist in controlling the costs of health care.

(E) Employees at companies with on-site clinics seek preventive screening and are thus less likely to delay medical treatment.

题目类型：评估题

题目分析：作者对 intervening on the supply side of health care 还是持肯定态度的，即 Health care costs can be managed more effectively if companies intervene in the supply side of health care delivery. 选择支持作者这一态度的选项即可。

选项分析：

(A) 大部分公司都没有足够的员工来使诊所实现成本效益。这个选项是否定的态度，相反，它削弱了作者的观点。

(B) 许多有诊所的公司都给员工提供去公司外的地方享有医疗保障的选择。如果这个选项是正确的，那么作者提出的这个双赢的办法就被削弱了。（有诊所的公司都给员工提供去公司外的地方享有医疗保障的选择——诊所形同虚设。）

(C) 建立和运营诊所比请公司外的机构给员工提供医疗保障花费更大。如果这个花费大于去公司外的地方享有医疗保障的花费，那么省钱的初衷就无法达到了，所以不支持作者的观点。

(D) 有医疗保障诊所的公司发现员工不愿意支持公司控制医疗保障经费。如果员工不支持，那么他们就不会去公司的诊所，以前的问题依旧存在。

(E) (Correct) 有诊所的公司员工会进行预防性筛查，因此不会耽误治疗。员工不愿意进行预防性检查是以前方法的弊病。如果现在可以解决，那无疑是支持了作者的肯定态度。

Passage 3

逻辑框架：

> P1 减少睡眠→影响健康
> P2 睡眠不规律→影响健康
> P3 做实验：减少睡眠 & 睡眠不规律
> P4 →不能展现最好的自己

6. According to the passage, if a healthy person usually has night jobs or is on rotating shifts, which of the following, if true, would most likely to occur as a consequence?

   (A) The person may not feel drowsy before he sleeps.
   (B) The person may have lower responsiveness to the hormone insulin.
   (C) The person may feel hard to get into sleep and thus have difficulties to get up early.
   (D) The person may be chosen as Buxton and colleagues' study subjects.
   (E) The person's physiology and behavior may not mesh and the person may have some health problems.

题目类型： 支持观点题

题目分析： 本题定位在原文第二段。上夜班或者倒班的人是作者列举出的有可能经常会改变自己昼夜节律的人。由此可知，他们应该具有第二段描述的特点。

选项分析：

(A) 这个人可能在睡觉前不会感觉疲乏。没有理由相信一个上夜班的人在睡觉前不会疲乏。原文中讲的是昼夜节律让人在晚上感觉疲乏，而不是睡觉前。

(B) 这个人分泌的胰岛素可能较少。这个例子是作者用来描述一个睡眠较少的人的，不是用来描述昼夜节律改变的人的。

(C) 这个人可能感觉难以入睡并且因此难以早起。文章中没有提过本选项的信息。

(D) 这个人可能会被选出成为 Buxton 和她同事的研究对象。文中没有提及 Buxton 和她的同事选择实验对象的标准。

(E) (Correct) 这个人的生理和行为可能不一致并且这个人可能有一些健康问题。本选项和第二段中所写的句子几乎完全一样。

7. The author's claim that "who went more than a month without Internet access, TV, or contact with anyone outside the facility" (see the highlighted text) is primarily in order to do which of the following purposes?

(A) To suggest that inadequate sleep and discombobulated circadian cycles and relatively low level of physical health are strongly related

(B) To describe the certain environment in which the participants should be confined in the study

(C) To explain why the participants are not always their kindest selves when their sleep is restricted

(D) To show who are qualified to be the subjects in the study conducted by Orfeu Buxton.

(E) To tell apart the participants who cope with certain conditions and the participants who do not cope with the conditions

题目类型：评估题

题目分析：这个高亮部分其实是实验对象的一个定语。作者额外地介绍了一下这些实验对象是因为作者想排除其他一些可能干扰实验结果的因素。

选项分析：

(A) **(Correct)** 为了表明睡眠不足和昼夜周期混乱与低等级的身体健康是有密切关联的。由于这些参与者没有受到高亮部分提出的这些因素的影响，所以高亮部分的目的是证明这些人的身体不健康确实是由睡眠不足和昼夜周期混乱导致的。

(B) 为了描述参与者在研究中被设定的特定环境。本选项具有一定干扰性。高亮部分确实描述了这些参与者所处于的环境，但是这不是它的目的。

(C) 为了解释为什么当参与者的睡眠被限制的时候，他们不会处于自己最好的状态。本选项和高亮部分写作的内容无关。

(C) 为了展示那些能成为 Orfeu Buxton 进行的研究中实验对象的人。本选项和高亮部分写作的内容无关。

(E) 为了区分处理特定情况和不处理特定情况的参与者。所有参与者均需要保证不接触互联网，所以高亮部分不是为了区分参与者的。

8. It can be inferred from the first paragraph of the passage that Orfeu Buxton and his colleagues would be most likely to agree which of the following statements?

   (A) Reduced sleep is hard for some young people to avoid.
   (B) That reduced sleep has deleterious effects on physical health is common sense for people.
   (C) Reduced sleep has physiological impact on people, even on young people.
   (D) People who have night jobs have lower responsiveness to the hormone insulin.
   (E) Sleep-intervention studies cannot fully represent deleterious effects of reduced sleep.

题目类型：推断题

题目分析：本题要求考生综合第一段中两句话给出的信息，做出推断。

选项分析：

(A) 有些年轻人很难避免缺少睡眠。第一段确实提到过有些年轻人缺少睡眠，但是没有提及他们是否可以避免少睡。

(B) 缺少睡眠会对身体产生有害的影响是人们的常识。第一段没有提及本选项的信息。

(C) (Correct) 就算是年轻人也会因为缺少睡眠而影响生理健康。综合第一段中的两句话，可知本选项的信息。

(D) 那些在夜晚工作的人胰岛素分泌较少。第一段只说过一个年轻人缺少睡眠，他的胰岛素分泌较少，并没有说他是不是在夜晚工作的 (他在夜晚工作也可以在白天睡觉，可见，何时工作与睡觉时间多少没有必然联系)。

(E) 睡眠干预研究不能完整地展示缺少睡眠的有害影响。第一段中没有讲过睡眠干预研究是否能展示这种影响，只是说现在睡眠干预研究还不太关注缺少睡眠的有害影响。

9. The primary purpose of the passage is to

   (A) explain the differences between the sleep-intervention studies and the epidemiological studies
   (B) provide three studies and suggest that reduced sleep may lead to a range of health problems
   (C) trace the development of the epidemiological studies of sleep studies
   (D) suggest that people will not be always their kindest selves when their sleep is restricted
   (E) present studies that show the impact of inadequate sleep and discombobulated circadian cycles

题目类型：主旨大意题

题目分析：主旨大意题选择与逻辑框架所描述的结构相同的选项即可。

选项分析：

(A) 解释睡眠干预研究和流行病学研究的区别。只有第一段提到过本选项的信息，显然不是整个文章的主旨。

(B) 提供三个研究并且表明缺少睡眠可能引发一系列的健康问题。第一段后面几段着重写的并不是缺少睡眠，而是睡眠失调，所以本选项也不是文章的主旨。

(C) 探索关于研究睡眠的流行病学研究的发展。只有第一段提到过流行病学研究睡眠，所以本选项不是文章的主旨。

(D) 表明当睡眠被限制时，人们将不能表现最好的自己。人们不能表现最好的自己只是最后一段讲到的一个影响。

(E) (Correct) 展示表现睡眠不足和昼夜混乱的影响的研究。本文的重心在于对睡眠不足和昼夜混乱的研究。

◦ Passage 4 ◦

逻辑框架：

> Algonquian 的财产权是什么样的以及怎么来的？
>
> 主流观点：私人 & 和欧洲人接触之后
>
> 另一个观点：私人 & 和欧洲人接触之前
>
> 最近观点：非私人

10. The primary purpose of the passage is to

    (A) provide an explanation for an unexpected phenomenon

    (B) suggest that a particular question has yet to be answered

    (C) present a new perspective on an issue

    (D) defend a traditional view from attack

    (E) reconcile opposing sides of an argument

题目类型： 主旨大意题

题目分析： 主旨大意题选择与逻辑框架所描述的结构相同的选项即可。

选项分析：

(A) 提供一个针对意外现象的解释。文中提到的现象就是 property rights 现象，但作者并没有说这是个意外现象。

(B) 表明一个特定的问题尚未有答案。文中提到唯一的问题是 how did they come to be。在文中这个问题已经被回答，只是作者认为回答得不正确。

(C) (Correct) 展示对待一个事件的全新视角。作者对文章一开始提出的问题做了一个全新的回答。前面驳斥的两个观点也是作者为了提出自己的观点而做出的铺垫。

(D) 防止一个传统的观点被攻击。作者在文中攻击两个传统观点，而不是保护传统观点。

(E) 调和争论的双方。作者没有调和以往的争论，而是提出自己的观点。

11. It can be inferred from the passage that proponents of the view mentioned in the first highlighted text believe which of the following about the origin of Algonquian family hunting territories?

   (A) They evolved from multifamilial hunting territories.

   (B) They are an outgrowth of reciprocal land-use practices.

   (C) They are based on certain spiritual beliefs.

   (D) They developed as a result of contact with Europeans.

   (E) They developed as a result of trade with non-Algonquian Indian tribes.

   题目类型：推断题

   题目分析：本题的答案出现在文中两个高亮部分之间，从选项中找到意思与其相同的部分即可。

   选项分析：

   (A) 它们从多家庭狩猎领地中进化而来。本选项是作者的观点（即第三个观点）。

   (B) 它们是土地使用实践的回馈结果。land-use 是在作者最后提出自己的观点时才出现的，不是第一个观点的内容。

   (C) 它们基于特定的精神信条。第一个观点中没有提到精神信条。

   (D) (Correct) 它们是由于与欧洲人的接触而发展起来的。文中第一个观点的主要意思就是与欧洲人接触的结果。

   (E) 它们是由于和非 Algonquian 的印度部落交易而发展起来的。文中没有提到和其他部落交易的信息。

12. According to the passage, proponents of the view mentioned in the first highlighted portion of text and proponents of the view mentioned in the second highlighted portion of text both believe which of the following about Algonquian family hunting territories?

   (A) They are a form of private landownership.

   (B) They are a form of community, rather than individual landownership.

   (C) They were a form of private landownership prior to contact with Europeans.

   (D) They became a form of private landownership due to contact with Europeans.

   (E) They have replaced reciprocal practices relating to land use in Algonquian society.

   题目类型：推断题

题目分析： 本题需要考生根据两个观点提到的信息，推断出两者的相同点。两个观点都提到了 landownership，即这两个观点争论的地方不是 landownership 本身，而是这样的 landownership 到底是因何而形成的。因此，它们的共同点就是都承认 landownership。

选项分析：

(A) (Correct) 它们都是一种私有土地所有制的形式。这是两个观点的相同点。

(B) 它们是一种社区形式，而不是个人的土地所有制。本选项是作者的观点，不是两个高亮部分的观点。

(C) 它们是在和欧洲人接触以前形成的一种私人土地所有制形式。本选项是第二个观点的内容，不是两者的共同观点。

(D) 它们是一个由于和欧洲人接触而形成的私人土地所有制。本选项是第一个观点的内容，不是两者的共同观点。

(E) 它们替代了与 Algonquian 社会的土地使用相关的实际回馈机制。本选项的内容在作者的观点中讲到过。

第三组

Passage 1

The usual descriptions of how the brain processes information rely on the same model that engineers have used to design electrical circuits. Just as electrons flow along the wires in a circuit, the neurons in the brain relay information along structured pathways, passing messages across specific points called synapses. According to this model, information does not leave the neuronal circuitry.

But there is increasing evidence that neurons can also communicate by means of "volumetransmission", which does not involve the relaying of information across synapses. Volumetransmission is not an alternative to the traditional view, commonly called wiring or synaptictransmission, but a complement to that established theory. Neurons do relay information quickly and efficiently across synapses, but experiments show that neurons can also release chemical signals into the fluid-filled space between the cells of the brain; these signals are not necessarily detected by neighboring cells but by cells in a different part of the brain, in the same way that hormones released by a gland into the bloodstream can have effects on cells faraway. These processes occur on much longer time scales than does synaptic transmission, and they probably play a distinct role, perhaps regulating or modulating the brain's response to synaptic signals.

1. The primary purpose of the passage is to

   (A) note similarities between two ways in which the brain processes information
   (B) propose a new model as an analogy for the structure of the brain
   (C) suggest that the brain uses more than one method to process information
   (D) explain why one theory about brain processes has been more influential than another theory
   (E) examine data challenging a new theory about the way in which the brain processes information

2. The passage suggests which of the following about the "usual descriptions" (see the highlighted text) of the brain's processing of information?

   (A) They provide a misleading analogy for the way in which synaptic transmission occurs.

(B) They incorrectly assume that information is conveyed exclusively through the neuronal circuitry.
(C) They underestimate the speed at which the transfer of information across synapses occurs.
(D) They are based on an analogy to the way in which hormones function to control the body.
(E) They acknowledge the existence of volume transmission but underestimate its importance in regulating brain responses.

3. The passage mentions which of the following as a possible function of volume transmission in the brain?

(A) Facilitating the release of hormones in different parts of the body
(B) Transmitting different types of sensory information than does synaptic transmission
(C) Serving to regulate the brain's response to synaptic signals
(D) Enhancing the brain's response to external stimuli
(E) Regulating different bodily functions than does synaptic transmission

Passage 2

More selective than most chemical pesticides in that they ordinarily destroy only unwanted species, biocontrol agents (such as insects, fungi, and viruses) eat, infect, or parasitize targeted plant or animal pests. However, biocontrol agents can negatively affect nontarget species by, for example, competing with them for resources: a biocontrol agent might reduce the benefits conferred by a desirable animal species by consuming a plant on which the animal prefers to lay its eggs. Another example of indirect negative consequences occurred in England when a virus introduced to control rabbits reduced the amount of open ground (because large rabbit populations reduce the ground cover), in turn reducing underground ant nests and triggering the extinction of a blue butterfly that had depended on the nests to shelter its offspring. The paucity of known extinctions or disruptions resulting from indirect interactions may reflect not the infrequency of such mishaps but rather the failure to look for or to detect them: most organisms likely to be adversely affected by indirect interactions are of little or no known commercial value and the events linking a biocontrol agent with an adverse effect are often unclear. Moreover, determining the potential risks of biocontrol agents before they are used is difficult, especially when a nonnative agent is introduced, because, unlike a chemical pesticide, a biocontrol agent may adapt in unpredictable ways so that it can feed on or otherwise harm new hosts.

4. The passage is primarily concerned with

   (A) explaining why until recently scientists failed to recognize the risks presented by biocontrol agents
   (B) emphasizing that biocontrol agents and chemical pesticides have more similarities than differences
   (C) suggesting that only certain biocontrol agents should be used to control plant or animal pests
   (D) arguing that biocontrol agents involve risks, some of which may not be readily discerned
   (E) suggesting that mishaps involving biocontrol agents are relatively commonplace

5. According to the passage, which of the following is a concern that arises with biocontrol agents but not with chemical pesticides?

   (A) Biocontrol agents are likely to destroy desirable species as well as undesirable ones.
   (B) Biocontrol agents are likely to have indirect as well as direct adverse effects on nontarget species.
   (C) Biocontrol agents may change in unforeseen ways and thus be able to damage new hosts.
   (D) Biocontrol agents may be ineffective in destroying targeted species.
   (E) Biocontrol agents may be effective for only a short period of time.

6. The passage suggests which of the following about the blue butterfly mentioned in the highlighted text?

   (A) The blue butterfly's survival was indirectly dependent on sustaining a rabbit population of a particular size.
   (B) The blue butterfly's survival was indirectly dependent on sustaining large amounts of vegetation in its habitat.
   (C) The blue butterfly's survival was threatened when the ants began preying on its offspring.
   (D) The blue butterfly was infected by the virus that had been intended to control rabbit populations.
   (E) The blue butterfly was adversely affected by a biocontrol agent that competed with it for resources.

Passage 3

Ethnohistoric documents from sixteenth-century Mexico suggesting that weaving and cooking were the most common productive activities for Aztec women may lead modern historians to underestimate the value of women's contributions to Aztec society. Since weaving and cooking occurred mostly (but not entirely) in a domestic setting, modern historians are likely to apply to the Aztec culture the modern Western distinction between "private" and "public" production. Thus, the ethnohistoric record conspires with Western culture to foster the view that women's production was not central to the demographic, economic, and political structures in sixteenth-century Mexico.

A closer examination of Aztec culture indicates that treating Aztec women's production in Mexico in such a manner would be a mistake. Even if the products of women's labor did not circulate beyond the household, such products were essential to population growth. Researchers document a tenfold increase in the population of the valley of Mexico during the previous four centuries, an increase that was crucial to the developing Aztec political economy. Population growth — which could not have occurred in the absence of successful household economy, in which women's work was essential — made possible the large-scale development of labor-intensive chinampa (ridged-field) agriculture in the southern valley of Mexico which, in turn, supported urbanization and political centralization in the Aztec capital.

But the products of women's labor did in fact circulate beyond the household. Aztec women wove cloth, and cloth circulated through the market system, the tribute system, and the redistributive economy of the palaces. Cotton mantles served as a unit of currency in the regional market system. Quantities of woven mantles, loincloths, blouses, and skirts were paid as tribute to local lords and to imperial tax stewards and were distributed to ritual and administrative personnel, craft specialists, warriors, and other faithful servants of the state. In addition, woven articles of clothing served as markers of social status and clothing fulfilled a symbolic function in political negotiation. The cloth that was the product of women's work thus was crucial as a primary means of organizing the flow of goods and services that sustained the Aztec state.

7. The author of the passage would be most likely to agree with which of the following statements about the documents mentioned in the first sentence of the passage?

   (A) They contain misleading information about the kinds of productive activities Aztec women engaged in.

(B) They overlook certain crucial activities performed by women in Aztec society.

(C) They provide useful information about the way that Aztec society viewed women.

(D) They are of limited value because they were heavily influenced by the bias of those who recorded them.

(E) They contain information that is likely to be misinterpreted by modern-day readers.

8. According to the passage, Aztec women's cloth production enabled Aztec society to do which of the following?

   (A) Expand women's role in agriculture
   (B) Organize the flow of goods and services
   (C) Develop self-contained communities
   (D) Hire agricultural laborers from outside the society
   (E) Establish a higher standard of living than neighboring cultures

9. Which of the following best describes the function of the third paragraph of the passage?

   (A) It attempts to reconcile conflicting views presented in the previous paragraphs.
   (B) It presents evidence intended to undermine the argument presented in the second paragraph.
   (C) It provides examples that support the position taken in the first sentence of the second paragraph.
   (D) It describes the contents of the documents mentioned in the first paragraph.
   (E) It suggests that a distinction noted in the first paragraph is valid.

10. The passage is primarily concerned with

    (A) using modern understanding of cultural bias to challenge ethnohistoric documents
    (B) evaluating competing descriptions of women's roles in Aztec society
    (C) comparing the influence of gender on women's roles in Aztec society and in modern society
    (D) remedying a potential misconception about the significance of women's roles in Aztec society
    (E) applying new evidence in a reevaluation of ethnohistoric documents

Passage 4

American telecoms firms are clamoring for more wireless spectrum. Hence the interest in LightSquared, a firm which had hovered up a chunk of airwaves formerly used by satellite operators, will boost. It planned to build a high-speed terrestrial network and rent it out to others. But the America's Federal Communications Commission (FCC) said no.

The FCC's announcement was prompted by a report from another government body, the National Telecommunications and Information Administration (NTIA), which conclude that LightSquared's technology would interfere with navigation equipment used by planes and other moving things. The company protests that the test process the NTIA has used is deeply flawed. It is hoping to convince the FCC to take the NTIA's findings "with a generous helping of salt".

Its efforts are likely to prove futile. Last year, NTIA gave a report about the potential health threat of a LTE program when a company called Spance is initializing that program. Spance insisted that the program had as little impact on human as possible and Spance would provide additional precaution around the LTE base station. But FCC ignored all of Spance's statement. As for LightSquared, the situation was even worse. If the FCC does not relent, there will be a serious blow to LightSquared, which has invested almost $ 4 billion to develop its business.

LightSquared could turn to the courts to challenge the regulator, but the firm may not want a costly legal battle. Much will depend on what impact the FCC's decision has on the many firms that have already inked deals with LightSquared to use its spectrum. If they abandon it in droves, it will be big trouble. All eyes will be on Sprint Nextel, a large wireless firm, which has an agreement with LightSquared to build and operate its network.

11. The primary purpose of the passage is to

 (A) describe a dilemma that some companies face and give solutions to that dilemma
 (B) describe LightSquared's plan and discuss the difficulties the company faces when it wants to implement that plan
 (C) explain why the plan LightSquared gives is at fault
 (D) propose a plan and give a possible reason to explain why LightSquared chooses that plan
 (E) discuss the bad effect about the LightSquared's plan

12. It can be inferred from the passage that "with a generous helping of salt" means

    (A) not analyzing the NTIA's report deeply
    (B) not taking seriously about the NTIA's report
    (C) changing the way of analyzing the NTIA's report
    (D) using the NTIA's report with the aid of some other sources
    (E) checking the NTIA's report clearly

13. The authors' suggestion that "its efforts are likely to prove futile" would be most weakened if which of the following were discovered to be true?

    (A) NTIA sometimes gives reports that are seriously flawed and the reports can not be used by any agencies such as FCC.
    (B) FCC always rejects some of the program it deals with.
    (C) Spance is less common than any other company that has at least some advantages in specific field.
    (D) Both LightSquared and Spance are controlled and managed by the same person who holds different political views with FCC's executive.
    (E) If LightSquared's effort were likely to prove futile, its executive would find additional evidence about the potential failure.

答案及解析

▶ 参考答案

1. C　　2. B　　3. C　　4. D　　5. C　　6. A　　7. E
8. B　　9. C　　10. D　　11. B　　12. C　　13. C

▶ 答案解析

◎ **Passage 1** ◎

逻辑框架：

> P1 人脑传递信息 = 电路
> P2 volume transmission：补充方式

1. The primary purpose of the passage is to

   (A) note similarities between two ways in which the brain processes information
   (B) propose a new model as an analogy for the structure of the brain
   (C) suggest that the brain uses more than one method to process information
   (D) explain why one theory about brain processes has been more influential than another theory
   (E) examine data challenging a new theory about the way in which the brain processes information

题目类型：主旨大意题

题目分析：主旨大意题选择与逻辑框架所描述的结构相同的选项即可。

选项分析：

(A) 记录大脑处理信息的两种方式的相同点。本文更多的是指出第二种方式与第一种的不同，并且介绍第二种方式。

(B) 提出一个类似大脑结构的新模型。本文没有提及任何模型。

(C) (Correct) 表明大脑用了不止一种方法来处理信息。文章给出了大脑处理信息的两种方法，并且着重介绍了第二种。

(D) 解释为什么一个关于大脑处理信息的原理比另外一个更有影响力。本文并没有说这两个原理哪个更好，而是说两者互相补充。

(E) 检测对关于大脑处理信息方法的新原理提出质疑的数据。本文没有说到过此方面的内容。

2. The passage suggests which of the following about the "usual descriptions" (see the highlighted text) of the brain's processing of information?

   (A) They provide a misleading analogy for the way in which synaptic transmission occurs.
   (B) They incorrectly assume that information is conveyed exclusively through the neuronal circuitry.
   (C) They underestimate the speed at which the transfer of information across synapses occurs.
   (D) They are based on an analogy to the way in which hormones function to control the body.
   (E) They acknowledge the existence of volume transmission but underestimate its importance in regulating brain responses.

   题目类型： 支持观点题

   题目分析： 第一段描述了 usual descriptions 的信息。文章在段末提到：According to this model, information does not leave the neuronal circuitry.

   选项分析：

   (A) 它们给突触传递方式提供了一个错误类比。"一般的描述"只是没有提到突触传递而已，并没有误导。

   (B) (Correct) 它们错误地假设了信息仅通过神经元回路传递。本选项是第一段最后一句的同义改写。信息不离开回路 = 信息仅通过神经元回路传递。

   (C) 它们低估了突触传递信息的速度。"一般的描述"就没有提到过用突触传递信息，自然也不会低估或高估它的速度。

   (D) 它们基于一种类似于荷尔蒙控制身体的方法。荷尔蒙控制身体的方法是靠突触传递的，而"一般的描述"没有提到突触传递。

   (E) 它们承认音量传递的存在，但是低估了它的重要性。"一般的描述"没有提到过用音量传递信息。

3. The passage mentions which of the following as a possible function of volume transmission in the brain?

   (A) Facilitating the release of hormones in different parts of the body

(B) Transmitting different types of sensory information than does synaptic transmission

(C) Serving to regulate the brain's response to synaptic signals

(D) Enhancing the brain's response to external stimuli

(E) Regulating different bodily functions than does synaptic transmission

题目类型：支持观点题

题目分析：第二段的最后写出了 volume 传递在脑信息传递中扮演的角色，即：These processes occur on much longer time scales than does synaptic transmission, and they probably play a distinct role, perhaps regulating or modulating the brain's response to synaptic signals.

选项分析：

(A) 促进身体不同部位的荷尔蒙释放。

(B) 传递与突触传递不同种类的感觉信息。

(C) (Correct) 调节大脑对突触信号的反应。

(D) 增强大脑对外部刺激的反应。

(E) 调节与突触传递不同的身体机能。

Passage 2

逻辑框架：

> biocontrol agents
> 和化学杀虫剂相比：只消灭不想要的物种
> 　　　　　　　　　但会负面影响非目标物种
> 例子：①竞争资源；② virus → 兔子↓ → 开阔地↓
> 　　　　→ 蚂蚁的巢穴↓ → 蓝蝴蝶↓
> 现在的困境：①不易察觉；②难以预测

4. The passage is primarily concerned with

   (A) explaining why until recently scientists failed to recognize the risks presented by biocontrol agents

   (B) emphasizing that biocontrol agents and chemical pesticides have more similarities than differences

   (C) suggesting that only certain biocontrol agents should be used to control plant or animal pests

(D) arguing that biocontrol agents involve risks, some of which may not be readily discerned

(E) suggesting that mishaps involving biocontrol agents are relatively commonplace

题目类型： 主旨大意题

题目分析： 主旨大意题选择与逻辑框架所描述的结构相同的选项即可。

选项分析：

(A) 解释为什么直到现在科学家们还不能识别出生物制剂的风险。文中作者的确说明了不能识别出生物制剂的风险，但是作者并没有解释为什么不能识别。

(B) 强调生物制剂和化学农药的相同点多于不同点。本文主要写了生物制剂可能的不良影响，并没有说生物制剂和化学制剂的相同点多于不同点。

(C) 提出只有一定种类的生物制剂可以被用来防治植物或动物害虫。作者在文中所说的内容全部面向所有生物制剂的种类，并没有提出只有某些特定的生物制剂可以被用来防治植物或动物害虫。

(D) (Correct) 提出生物制剂有风险，其中一些风险也许不能被很容易察觉出来。文中除了最后一句话都在说生物制剂可能的风险，最后一句话说明了风险可能不容易被发现 (a biocontrol agent may adapt in unpredictable ways so that it can feed on or otherwise harm new hosts)。

(E) 提出生物制剂的失误相对来说是常见的。文章没有体现这层意思，通篇也没有提及这些失误是否常见。

5. According to the passage, which of the following is a concern that arises with biocontrol agents but not with chemical pesticides?

(A) Biocontrol agents are likely to destroy desirable species as well as undesirable ones.

(B) Biocontrol agents are likely to have indirect as well as direct adverse effects on nontarget species.

(C) Biocontrol agents may change in unforeseen ways and thus be able to damage new hosts.

(D) Biocontrol agents may be ineffective in destroying targeted species.

(E) Biocontrol agents may be effective for only a short period of time.

题目类型： 支持观点题

题目分析： 原文最后提到了生物制剂和化学药品的不同之处，即：Unlike a chemical pesticide, a biocontrol agent may adapt in unpredictable ways so that it can feed on or otherwise harm new hosts.

283

选项分析：

(A) 生物制剂有可能在消灭不满意的物种的同时也消灭了满意的物种。从文中的第一句话可以看出，生物制剂的好处就在于可以消灭特定的物种。也就是说化学制剂可能会消灭其他不应该被消灭的物种。后文又提到，生物制剂也可能会对其他物种产生影响。因此，甚至可以说，这点是两者的相同点而不是不同点。

(B) 生物制剂有可能对非目标生物造成直接和间接的影响。生物制剂不能直接影响非目标生物。第一句就阐明了生物制剂不会影响其他生物，但是后文阐述了会有间接的影响。

(C) (Correct) 生物制剂可能会有不可预见的变化并且有能力消灭新的物种。

(D) 生物制剂也许会对消灭目标物种无效。文中没有讨论消灭目标物种的有效性问题。

(E) 生物制剂也许只在一段时间内有效。文中没有提到生物制剂是否长期有效。

6. The passage suggests which of the following about the blue butterfly mentioned in the highlighted text?

(A) The blue butterfly's survival was indirectly dependent on sustaining a rabbit population of a particular size.

(B) The blue butterfly's survival was indirectly dependent on sustaining large amounts of vegetation in its habitat.

(C) The blue butterfly's survival was threatened when the ants began preying on its offspring.

(D) The blue butterfly was infected by the virus that had been intended to control rabbit populations.

(E) The blue butterfly was adversely affected by a biocontrol agent that competed with it for resources.

题目类型： 支持观点题

题目分析： 理解了高亮部分的所在句就可以回答本题，即：Another example of indirect negative consequences occurred in England when a virus introduced to control rabbits reduced the amount of open ground (because large rabbit populations reduce the ground cover), in turn reducing underground ant nests and triggering the extinction of a blue butterfly that had depended on the nests to shelter its offspring.

选项分析：

(A) (Correct) 蓝蝶的生存间接依赖于维持在一定数量的兔子种群。原文说蓝蝶依靠蚂蚁的巢穴生存（保护后代）：一定数量的兔子 = 一定数量的蚂蚁巢穴。

(B) 蓝蝶的生存间接依赖于其栖息地大量的植被。文中明确说明了蓝蝶依靠兔子造的巢穴生存。如果没有兔子，植被再多也没法造巢穴。

(C) 蓝蝶的生存在蚂蚁开始捕食蓝蝶的后代时受到了威胁。文中没有提到蚂蚁和蓝蝶的关系，无法证明本选项。

(D) 蓝蝶感染了被用来控制兔子数量的病毒。文中没有提到蓝蝶感染病毒。

(E) 蓝蝶因生物制剂与其抢夺资源而受到不利影响。文中定位部分说得很清楚，蓝蝶是因为没有了兔子，才没有了哺育后代的地方，和生物制剂是否与它们抢夺资源无关。

Passage 3

逻辑框架：

> P1 文献：女性编织和烹饪 → 低估女性贡献
> P2 P1 的低估是错误的
>   只在家庭内有贡献：女性工作→家庭经济↑→
>   人口↑→农业↑→城镇化 & 政治集权↑
> P3 不止在家庭内：女性生产的产品 = 在各个系统里
>   流通 & 货币 & 贡品 & 社会地位 & 政治协商

7. The author of the passage would be most likely to agree with which of the following statements about the documents mentioned in the first sentence of the passage?

(A) They contain misleading information about the kinds of productive activities Aztec women engaged in.

(B) They overlook certain crucial activities performed by women in Aztec society.

(C) They provide useful information about the way that Aztec society viewed women.

(D) They are of limited value because they were heavily influenced by the bias of those who recorded them.

(E) They contain information that is likely to be misinterpreted by modern-day readers.

题目类型： 支持观点题

题目分析：定位原文句：Ethnohistoric documents from sixteenth-century Mexico suggesting that weaving and cooking were the most common productive activities for Aztec women may lead modern historians to underestimate the value of women's contributions to Aztec society. 即，这些档案导致现代历史学家低估了女性对于阿兹特克社会的贡献。

选项分析：

(A) 它们对于阿兹特克女性从事的生产活动存在误导信息。这个选项较易错选。定位文章的第一句话，其意思是"人种史学档案中说的纺织和烹饪是阿兹特克女性最一般的生产活动可能会让现代的史学家贬低阿兹特克女性对社会的贡献"。作者的意思是这些信息会让现代的历史学家产生误会。并不是其信息本身含有什么错误，或有什么误导信息。

(B) 它们忽略了女性在阿兹特克社会中完成的几项重要活动。从作者行文来看，下文肯定了阿兹特克女性这两个主要的生产活动，只是现代的历史学家对这两个生产活动的理解不到位。并不是第一段所指的档案忽略了什么。

(C) 它们提供了关于阿兹特克社会评价女性的方法的有用信息。文中没有提到阿兹特克社会对其女性的观点。

(D) 它们的价值有限是因为记录者的偏见对它们影响很深。文中没有提到16世纪墨西哥人的这个档案有什么他人的偏见因素在其中。

(E) (Correct) 它们包含的信息有可能被现代的读者误解。这些信息可能会让别人误解，而非信息本身的问题。

8. According to the passage, Aztec women's cloth production enabled Aztec society to do which of the following?

   (A) Expand women's role in agriculture
   (B) Organize the flow of goods and services
   (C) Develop self-contained communities
   (D) Hire agricultural laborers from outside the society
   (E) Establish a higher standard of living than neighboring cultures

题目类型：支持观点题

题目分析：本题的答案出现在文中最后一段提及cloth的位置上。

选项分析：

(A) 在农业方面扩大女性的作用。文章中提到了女性在农业方面的内容，不过作者说的是女性对家庭的贡献会使人口上升，继而使某些农业得到发展。这和cloth无关。

(B) (Correct) 组织商品和服务的流动。文中最后一段写道:"The cloth that was the product of women's work thus was crucial as a primary means of organizing the flow of goods and services that sustained the Aztec state."本选项为该句的重复。

(C) 发展自给自足的社会。文中没有提到发展自给自足的社会的问题。

(D) 雇用他们社会外的农民。这个选项的内容和 cloth 无关,而且文中也没有提到雇用其他农民的信息。

(E) 建立一个比邻近社会文明更高层次的生活标准。文中没有提及是否有更高层次的生活水平的问题。

9. Which of the following best describes the function of the third paragraph of the passage?

(A) It attempts to reconcile conflicting views presented in the previous paragraphs.

(B) It presents evidence intended to undermine the argument presented in the second paragraph.

(C) It provides examples that support the position taken in the first sentence of the second paragraph.

(D) It describes the contents of the documents mentioned in the first paragraph.

(E) It suggests that a distinction noted in the first paragraph is valid.

题目类型: 评估题

题目分析: 从逻辑框架上可以看出,这段在加强前面的论点,第二段说的是"就算是只在家庭范围内",第三段开头就点明,"何况不仅限于家庭范围内"。

选项分析:

(A) 它试图调和前面段落的争论之处。文章通篇都没有争论之处,只是作者对于现代历史学家的误解提出质疑并给出解释。

(B) 它提出了试图削弱第二段所提出的论点的证据。第三段其实恰恰是对第二段开头句这个论点的一个加强,没有提出削弱的证据。

(C) (Correct) 它列举了支持第二段第一句的例子。

(D) 它描述了第一段提到的档案的内容。档案只在第一段被引入过一次,此后作者都没有对该档案继续做出评价。

(E) 它提出第一段表明的区别是有根据的。其实作者通篇想说的是西方的区别是不应该用在阿兹特克女性身上的,所以第三段不可能是本选项描述的作用。

10. The passage is primarily concerned with

    (A) using modern understanding of cultural bias to challenge ethnohistoric documents
    (B) evaluating competing descriptions of women's roles in Aztec society
    (C) comparing the influence of gender on women's roles in Aztec society and in modern society
    (D) remedying a potential misconception about the significance of women's roles in Aztec society
    (E) applying new evidence in a reevaluation of ethnohistoric documents

题目类型： 主旨大意题

题目分析： 主旨大意题选择与逻辑框架所描述的结构相同的选项即可。

选项分析：

(A) 用对于文化偏见的现代理解来挑战人种史学档案。这个历史的档案本身没有问题，是现代历史学家对其的理解有问题，作者通过文章希望可以更正这种错误的理解。

(B) 评估对阿兹特克社会女性地位所进行的一些存有分歧的描述。文章中只有一种描述，就是 underestimate 的描述，其是由研究者的误解造成的。主旨不是评估各种描述。

(C) 将阿兹特克社会和现代社会中性别对于女性地位的影响相比较。作者在文中没有提及现代社会的女性作用和地位，所以不是比较"阿兹特克"时代和现代。

(D) (Correct) 减少对阿兹特克社会女性地位的潜在误解。作者是想更正被人们误解的阿兹特克女性的地位。第一段总起，后面两段都在证明第一段说的内容。

(E) 在重新评估人种史学档案时使用新的证据。作者并没有想重新评估这个档案，而是想纠正以前人们对这个档案的解读。

                                              ◎ Passage 4 ◎

逻辑框架：

P1	LS 建立地面网络，但 FCC：no
P2	原因：NTIA 的报告认为干扰了航空信号
	LS 认为 NTIA 有误，希望 FCC 重新考虑
P3	LS 的希望不会成功，类比了 Spance
P4	LS 的其他手段

11. The primary purpose of the passage is to

    (A) describe a dilemma that some companies face and give solutions to that dilemma
    (B) describe LightSquared's plan and discuss the difficulties the company faces when it wants to implement that plan
    (C) explain why the plan LightSquared gives is at fault
    (D) propose a plan and give a possible reason to explain why LightSquared chooses that plan
    (E) discuss the bad effect about the LightSquared's plan

    题目类型：主旨大意题

    题目分析：主旨大意题选择与逻辑框架所描述的结构相同的选项即可。

    选项分析：

    (A) 描述某些公司遇到的窘境并且给出针对这个窘境的解决方案。本文没有给出任何有效解决窘境的方法。
    (B) (Correct) 描述 LS 的计划并且讨论公司想要实施那个计划时遇到的困难。本文首先描述了计划，之后给出了这个计划在实施过程中可能会遇到的种种难题。
    (C) 解释为什么 LS 的计划是错误的。作者没有认为 LS 的计划是错误的，而是说这个计划实施起来有些困难。
    (D) 提出一个计划并且给出 LS 选择那个计划的可能原因。本文没有给出 LS 选择计划的任何原因。
    (E) 讨论 LS 计划带来的不良影响。本文没有讨论一个计划的影响。

12. It can be inferred from the passage that "with a generous helping of salt" means

    (A) not analyzing the NTIA's report deeply
    (B) not taking seriously about the NTIA's report
    (C) changing the way of analyzing the NTIA's report
    (D) using the NTIA's report with the aid of some other sources
    (E) checking the NTIA's report clearly

    题目类型：推断题

    题目分析：通过高亮部分的所在句和其前文的关系，我们可以猜测出 LS 肯定是希望 FCC 重新考虑方案的可行性，所以这个 with a generous helping of salt 肯定是 LS 希望 FCC 换一种分析 NTIA 报告的方式。

    选项分析：

    (A) 不要深刻地分析 NTIA 的报告。高亮部分不是不让 FCC 分析，而是让它换一个角度分析。

(B) 不要对 NTIA 的报告太过重视。本选项错误同 (A)。

(C) (Correct) 改变分析 NTIA 报告的方式。本选项完整地回答了高亮部分的目的。

(D) 用其他资源作为辅助分析 NTIA 的报告。第二段没有给出任何的其他资源。

(E) 清晰地检查 NTIA 的报告。第二段没有提到本选项的信息。

13. The authors' suggestion that "its efforts are likely to prove futile" would be most weakened if which of the following were discovered to be true?

    (A) NTIA sometimes gives reports that are seriously flawed and the reports can not be used by any agencies such as FCC.

    (B) FCC always rejects some of the program it deals with.

    (C) Spance is less common than any other company that has at least some advantages in specific field.

    (D) Both LightSquared and Spance are controlled and managed by the same person who holds different political views with FCC's executive.

    (E) If LightSquared's effort were likely to prove futile, its executive would find additional evidence about the potential failure.

题目类型： 评估题

题目分析： 前提：Spance 的项目有潜在威胁
结论：its efforts are likely to prove futile
答案方向：削弱题型，结论为事件类，答案需指明，即使 Spance 的项目有潜在威胁，LS 的努力也不见得是白费的（LS 的项目不一定会有潜在威胁）。

选项分析：

(A) NTIA 有时会给出具有严重错误的报告，并且这个报告不能被诸如 FCC 这样的机构使用。本选项没有提到类比的两个案例。

(B) FCC 总是会拒绝一些它处理的项目。本选项没有提到类比的两个案例。

(C) (Correct) Spance 和一些在某些领域具有优势的公司来比的话，还不是那么普遍。本选项虽然没有直接提到 LS，但是显然 LS 是具有优势的公司，所以 LS 的努力不一定就是白费的（其项目不见得有潜在威胁）。

(D) LS 和 Spance 都是由同一个和 FCC 执行官持不同政治观点的人管理的。本选项给出的是两个案例的相似点，可以加强，不能削弱。

(E) 如果 LS 的努力被证明是白费的，那么它的执行者会发现一些额外的关于潜在失败的证据。本选项没有提到 Spance。

第四组

Passage 1

Traditional social science models of class groups in the United States are based on economic status and assume that women's economic status derives from association with men, typically fathers or husbands, and that women therefore have more compelling common interest with men of their own economic class than with women outside it. Some feminist social scientists, by contrast, have argued that the basic division in American society is instead based on gender, and that the total female population, regardless of economic status, constitutes a distinct class. Social historian Mary Ryan, for example, has argued that in early-nineteenth-century America the identical legal status of working-class and middle-class free women outweighed the differences between women of these two classes: married women, regardless of their family's wealth, did essentially the same unpaid domestic work, and none could own property or vote. Recently, though, other feminist analysts have questioned this model, examining ways in which the condition of working-class women differs from that of middle-class women as well as from that of working-class men. Ann Oakley notes, for example, that the gap between women of different economic classes widened in the late nineteenth century: most working-class women, who performed wage labor outside the home, were excluded from the emerging middle-class ideal of femininity centered around domesticity and volunteerism.

1. The primary purpose of the passage is to

    (A) offer social historical explanations for the cultural differences between men and women in the United States
    (B) examine how the economic roles of women in the United States changed during the nineteenth century
    (C) consider differing views held by social scientists concerning women's class status in the United States
    (D) propose a feminist interpretation of class structure in the United States
    (E) outline specific distinctions between working-class women and women of the upper and middle classes

2. It can be inferred from the passage that most recent feminist social science researches on women and classes seek to do which of the following?

(A) Introduce a divergent new theory about the relationship between legal status and gender
(B) Illustrate an implicit middle-class bias in earlier feminist models of class and gender
(C) Provide evidence for the position that gender matters more than wealth in determining class status
(D) Remedy perceived inadequacies of both traditional social science models and earlier feminist analyses of class and gender
(E) Challenge the economic definitions of class used by traditional social scientists

3. Which of the following statements best characterizes the relationship between traditional social science models of class and Ryan's model, as described in the passage?

(A) Ryan's model differs from the traditional model by making gender, rather than economic status, be the determinant of women's class status.
(B) The traditional social science model of class differs from Ryan's in its assumption that women are financially dependent on men.
(C) Ryan's model of class and the traditional social science model both assume that women work, either within the home or for pay.
(D) The traditional social science model of class differs from Ryan's in that each model focuses on a different period of American history.
(E) Both Ryan's model of class and the traditional model consider multiple factors, including wealth, marital status, and enfranchisement, in determining women's status.

Passage 2

Most climatologists believe that ice ages have occurred in cycles in part because the Earth sways while orbiting the Sun, causing fluctuations in the intensity of sunlight reaching the Northern Hemisphere. This theory, proposed by the astronomer Milutin Milankovitch, gained acceptance in the 1980's after the oceanographer John Imbrie discovered supporting evidence in oxygen isotopes contained in shells deposited many thousands of years ago in ocean sediments.

A new study, however, suggests that ancient climates warmed and cooled independently of the Milankovitch orbital cycles. In a study of mineral calcite taken from the walls of Devil's Hole, a deep, freshwater-filled fissure in the Nevada desert, the geochemist Isaac Winograd analyzed the rate of decay of uranium into thorium and determined that the Devil's Hole data differ significantly from the ocean sediment data, suggesting that warm periods between ice ages lasted twice as long as previously thought. Based on his data, Winograd concluded that ice ages waxed and waned due to complex interactions among oceans, ice sheets, and atmosphere.

Some scientists believe that Winograd's data must be wrong. Imbrie, however, while asserting the correctness of the Milankovitch theory, suggests that the studies' different data concerning climate change may be due to geographical variations in climate and differences between marine and freshwater studies.

4. The passage suggests that the evidence discovered by Imbrie supports which of the following conclusions?

    (A) Fluctuations in the Earth's position as it orbits the Sun have resulted in the occurrence of ice ages.
    (B) The atmosphere and the oceans both play a role in determining when an ice age will end.
    (C) The reliability of data on oxygen isotopes found in shells from ocean sediments is questionable.
    (D) Milankovitch did not consider sufficiently the differences between marine and freshwater environments when developing his theory of ice age cycles.
    (E) Climates on the Earth many thousands of years ago became warmer and cooler independently of the Earth's orbital cycles.

5. According to the passage, Milankovitch's theory was not widely subscribed to by scientists prior to a study of which of the following?

    (A) Oxygen isotopes in shell deposits
    (B) Mineral calcite in a freshwater fissure
    (C) Geographical variations in climate
    (D) The rate at which uranium decays into thorium
    (E) The interaction among the atmosphere, oceans, and ice sheets

6. The primary purpose of the passage is to

    (A) criticize the methodology of a scientist's research
    (B) report evidence that challenges a geochemist's theory
    (C) explain why a widely accepted theory about ancient climates was abandoned

(D) describe some recent research on ice age cycles

(E) propose an innovative explanation for variations in oceanographic data

Passage 3

The view has prevailed for the better part of the twentieth century that small firms do not perform an important role in Western economies. Official policies in many countries have favored large units of production because there were strong reasons to believe that large firms were superior to small firms in virtually every aspect of economic performance—productivity, technological progress, and job security and compensation. However, in the 1970s, evidence began to suggest that small firms in some countries were outperforming their larger counterparts. Perhaps the best example of this trend was in the steel industry, where new firms entered the market in the form of "mini-mills," and small-firm employment expanded, while many large companies shut down plants and reduced employment. Although no systematic evidence exists to determine unequivocally whether smaller units of production are as efficient as large firms or are, in fact, more efficient, some researchers have concluded that the accumulated evidence to date indicates that small firms are at least not burdened with an inherent size disadvantage.

Thus, an alternative view has emerged in the economics literature, arguing that small firms make several important contributions to industrial markets. First, small firms are often the source of the kind of innovative activity that leads to technological change. Small firms generate market turbulence that creates additional dimensions of competition, and they also promote international competition through newly created niches. Finally, small firms in recent years have generated the preponderant share of new jobs.

However, empirical knowledge about the relative roles of large and small firms is generally based upon anecdotal evidence and case studies, and such evidence has proved inadequate to answer major questions concerning the role of small firms across various industries and nations. An additional difficulty is that it is not obvious what criteria one should use to distinguish small firms from large ones. While a "small firm" is often defined as an enterprise with fewer than 500 employees, research studies of small firms use a wide variety of definitions.

7. The passage is primarily concerned with

(A) dismissing a challenge to a traditional viewpoint

(B) suggesting a new solution to a long-standing problem

(C) resolving a conflict between two competing viewpoints

(D) discussing the emergence of an alternative viewpoint

(E) defending an alternative viewpoint against possible counterevidence

8. The passage suggests which of the following about the empirical study of small firms' role?

    (A) Anecdotal evidence does not support the theory that small firms' role is significant.

    (B) Degrees of market turbulence are the primary indicator of small firms' role.

    (C) An examination of new niches created by small firms has provided important data for the analysis of such firms' role.

    (D) Case studies have provided reliable evidence to answer major questions concerning small firms' role.

    (E) A more precise definition of the term "small firm" is crucial to making a conclusive analysis about small firms' role.

9. Which of the following best describes the organization of the first paragraph of the passage?

    (A) A viewpoint is introduced, counterevidence is presented, and a new perspective is suggested.

    (B) Opposing viewpoints are discussed, and evidence is provided that refutes both of those viewpoints.

    (C) A hypothesis is described, supported with specific evidence, and then reaffirmed.

    (D) An alternative viewpoint is presented, criticized, and dismissed in light of new evidence.

    (E) Opposing viewpoints are presented, discussed, and then found to be more similar than previously supposed.

10. According to the passage, an important contribution of small firms to industrial markets is that small firms

    (A) operate more efficiently than large firms

    (B) offer high job security and compensation

    (C) cause international competition to decrease

    (D) help prevent market turbulence from affecting competition

    (E) frequently undertake activities that result in technological change

Passage 4

Pine Island Glacier in West Antarctica is hemorrhaging ice at an alarming rate. But it's happening far beyond the reach of human eyes— 3,000 feet below the ocean's surface, beneath a shelf of floating ice as thick as two Empire State Buildings would be tall.

Autosub 3, a robotic submarine, visited this remote spot in 2009. It explored 30 miles under Pine Island's ice shelf, using sonar to map the seafloor below and ice ceiling above. While the sub worked, the research vessel *Nathaniel B. Palmer* measured a worrying process: Strengthening ocean currents are bringing deeper, warm water into contact with thinning ice, melting 19 cubic miles of the ice shelf's underside in 2009 alone and causing the glacier to flow faster into the ocean. Since 1974 Pine Island has thinned by 230 feet and accelerated by more than 70 percent.

Hundreds of miles of Antarctica's coastline are now subject to the same forces, which are expected to drive the increase in ice loss for decades to come. It's difficult but vital to monitor what's happening to the ice shelf's weak underbelly, says Stanley Jacobs of the Lamont-Doherty Earth Observatory, who led the international expedition along with Adrian Jenkins of the British Antarctic Survey. The information gathered from beneath the Pine Island's bottom is essential to making accurate predictions about the Earth sea-level rise.

11. Which of the following is an assumption underlying the last sentence of the passage?

    (A) Although it is difficult to monitor the ice shelf's underbelly, oceanographers are able to find ways to estimate what's happened about it.
    (B) Pine Island Glacier is not a special island glacier which contacts especially much warm water in Antarctica.
    (C) In each year between 1974 and 2009, the robotic submarine visited the island and collected data of warm water.
    (D) There are no other reasons except warm water that melt the ice on Pine Island.
    (E) The information collected by the submarine is not the only source, from which analysts could get data, of information about the Pine Island Glacier.

12. It can be inferred from information presented in the passage that if *Nathaniel B. Palmer's* worrying process continues without any controlling methods, which of the following would be true as a consequence?

    (A) Environmentalists and oceanographers will at least come up with a useful method to control the worrying process.
    (B) Ice will disappear on the Earth and some of cities in the world will be inundated by sea water.
    (C) Pine Island Glacier will not be the last glacier island on the Earth.
    (D) The ice in Pine Island Glacier will drift on the ocean and even disappear finally.
    (E) More robotic submarines will visit Pine Island Glacier to collect data used by analysts in order to pursue the origin of the warm water.

答案及解析

▶参考答案

| 1. C | 2. D | 3. A | 4. A | 5. A | 6. D |
| 7. D | 8. E | 9. A | 10. E | 11. B | 12. D |

▶答案解析

Passage 1

逻辑框架：

```
传统模型：基于经济地位→与同阶层男
        性有更多共同兴趣
              ↑ 反对
一些女权社会主义科学家：基于性别→
不同阶层女性之间的相似点＞不同点
              ↑ 反对
其他分析学家：不同阶层女性之间的gap
              在增大
```

1. The primary purpose of the passage is to

   (A) offer social historical explanations for the cultural differences between men and women in the United States
   (B) examine how the economic roles of women in the United States changed during the nineteenth century
   (C) consider differing views held by social scientists concerning women's class status in the United States
   (D) propose a feminist interpretation of class structure in the United States
   (E) outline specific distinctions between working-class women and women of the upper and middle classes

   题目类型： 主旨大意题

   题目分析： 主旨大意题选择与逻辑框架所描述的结构相同的选项即可。

   选项分析：

   (A) 对美国男性和女性的文化差异提供社会历史解释。文中没有提到过男性和女性的文化差异，通篇讲的是女性的社会阶层问题。

298

(B) 分析 19 世纪美国女性的经济地位是如何改变的。文章开始确实提到了经济状况决定女性的阶层，不过没有涉及女性经济地位的改变。

(C) (Correct) 考虑社会学家对于美国女性阶层地位的不同观点。文章通篇都在讲述各种社会学家怎么划分女性的社会阶层，没有在文中展示个人思想。

(D) 提出一个男女平等主义者对于美国阶层结构的解读。文章并不是讲美国的阶层结构，而是讲女性属于哪个阶层。

(E) 具体概括工人阶级女性与上层和中产阶级女性的不同。文中的三个观点只有一个观点是这个选项的内容，即传统观点。属于文章的细节而不属于主旨。

2. It can be inferred from the passage that most recent feminist social science researches on women and classes seek to do which of the following?

(A) Introduce a divergent new theory about the relationship between legal status and gender
(B) Illustrate an implicit middle-class bias in earlier feminist models of class and gender
(C) Provide evidence for the position that gender matters more than wealth in determining class status
(D) Remedy perceived inadequacies of both traditional social science models and earlier feminist analyses of class and gender
(E) Challenge the economic definitions of class used by traditional social scientists

题目类型：推断题

题目分析：本题问的是近来女权主义者喜欢做哪件事。实际上，本题要求我们推断文章最后提到的女权主义者的观点。

选项分析：

(A) 介绍一个关于法律地位与性别之间关系的不同的新理论。文章中只有 Ryan 的观点提到法律地位，传统观点所涉及的是经济地位。而法律地位和性别属于同一类观点 (Ryan 提到了法律状态，是按照性别区分阶层的一个例子)，是早期社会学家的观点。

(B) 说明在关于阶层和性别的早期女权模式中暗含的一个中产阶级偏见。文中的第三个观点说的是工人阶级女性的地位与同阶层的男性和不同阶层的女性的地位都不相同，与是否有中产阶级偏见无关。

(C) 提出支持"性别比财富更能决定阶层地位"这一说法的证据。现代女权主义者的研究不是支持前面所述的两个观点的其中一个，而是说这两个观点都有不足。

(D) (Correct) 修正传统的社会科学模型和早期女权主义者关于阶层和性别的观点的不全面之处。现代的观点与前述的两个都不同，指出了那两个观点的不足 (examining ways in which the condition of working-class women differs from that of middle-class women as well as from that of working-class men)。

(E) 攻击传统社会学家使用的关于阶层的经济定义。本选项说得不够全面，要说第三个观点攻击什么，也是直接攻击早期女权主义者的观点（文中说现代女权主义者质疑早期女权主义者提出的模型）。其实第三个观点主要是修正前两个观点的不足，不完全是用经济地位来划分阶层，但也不完全由性别来划分阶层。

3. Which of the following statements best characterizes the relationship between traditional social science models of class and Ryan's model, as described in the passage?

   (A) Ryan's model differs from the traditional model by making gender, rather than economic status, be the determinant of women's class status.
   (B) The traditional social science model of class differs from Ryan's in its assumption that women are financially dependent on men.
   (C) Ryan's model of class and the traditional social science model both assume that women work, either within the home or for pay.
   (D) The traditional social science model of class differs from Ryan's in that each model focuses on a different period of American history.
   (E) Both Ryan's model of class and the traditional model consider multiple factors, including wealth, marital status, and enfranchisement, in determining women's status.

   题目类型：评估题

   题目分析：原文中第一和第二个观点之间的一句话阐述了两者的关系，即：Some feminist social scientists, by contrast, have argued that the basic division in American society is instead based on gender, and that the total female population, regardless of economic status, constitutes a distinct class. Ryan 作为 some feminist social scientists 的一个例子，其作用是支持"性别决定阶层地位"这一观点的。而这一观点是不同于传统模型的，所以 Ryan 也是反对传统模型的。

   选项分析：

   (A) (Correct) Ryan 的模型与传统模型的不同在于其认为性别，而不是经济地位，决定了女性的阶层地位。
   (B) 关于阶层的传统社会科学模型和 Ryan 的模型的不同之处在于其假设女性的经济依赖于男人。传统观点确实假设了女性的经济依赖于男人，但是早期的社会学家并没有反驳这个观点，而是从性别上给出了另外的解读。

(C) Ryan 的关于阶层的模型和传统社会科学模型都假设了女性的工作要么在家中，要么是为了赚钱。Ryan 说过，女性 did essentially the same unpaid domestic work。这句话说明 Ryan 没有假设过女性在家可以赚钱。

(D) 关于阶层的传统社会科学模型和 Ryan 的模型不同是因为它们针对美国不同的历史时期。文中没有提到不同时期的问题。

(E) Ryan 的关于阶层的模型和传统模型都考虑到决定女性阶层的许多因素，包括财富、婚姻状况和选举权。本选项所说的这些因素 Ryan 的模型都提到过，但是没有证据显示传统观点也考虑到了这些因素。

Passage 2

逻辑框架：

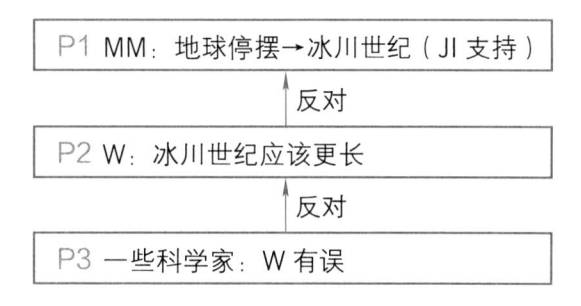

P1 MM：地球停摆→冰川世纪（JI 支持）
↑反对
P2 W：冰川世纪应该更长
↑反对
P3 一些科学家：W 有误

4. The passage suggests that the evidence discovered by Imbrie supports which of the following conclusions?

(A) Fluctuations in the Earth's position as it orbits the Sun have resulted in the occurrence of ice ages.

(B) The atmosphere and the oceans both play a role in determining when an ice age will end.

(C) The reliability of data on oxygen isotopes found in shells from ocean sediments is questionable.

(D) Milankovitch did not consider sufficiently the differences between marine and freshwater environments when developing his theory of ice age cycles.

(E) Climates on the Earth many thousands of years ago became warmer and cooler independently of the Earth's orbital cycles.

题目类型：推断题

题目分析：原文最后给出了 Imbrie 的话，即：Imbrie, however, while asserting the correctness of the Milankovitch theory, suggests that the studies' different data concerning climate change may be due to geographical variations in climate and differences between marine and freshwater studies. 从中可知 Imbrie 是同意 Milankovitch 的观点的。文中第一段提到了 Milankovitch 的观点，即："...ice ages have occurred in cycles in part because the Earth sways while orbiting the Sun, causing fluctuations in the intensity of sunlight reaching the Northern Hemisphere."

选项分析：

(A) (Correct) 地球在其轨道周围的晃动导致了冰河世纪的出现。综合两句，可以推断出本选项。

(B) 大气和海洋在决定冰河世纪什么时候结束方面都起了作用。这是 Winograd 的观点，不是 Imbrie 或 Milankovitch 的观点。

(C) 在海洋沉淀物的贝壳中发现的氧元素同位素的数据的可靠性是值得质疑的。Milankovitch 的观点就是基于这些同位素的，所以 Imbrie 不可能质疑它们。

(D) Milankovitch 在提出关于冰河世纪周期的理论时没有充分考虑到海水和淡水的不同。Imbrie 是同意 Milankovitch 的观点的，而不是质疑他。

(E) 地球几千年前的气候变得更暖和、更凉快，这与地球轨道循环无关。本选项不是 Milankovitch 的观点。

5. According to the passage, Milankovitch's theory was not widely subscribed to by scientists prior to a study of which of the following?

   (A) Oxygen isotopes in shell deposits
   (B) Mineral calcite in a freshwater fissure
   (C) Geographical variations in climate
   (D) The rate at which uranium decays into thorium
   (E) The interaction among the atmosphere, oceans, and ice sheets

   题目类型： 支持观点题

   题目分析： 原文第一段最后部分描述了本选项的内容，即：This theory, proposed by the astronomer Milutin Milankovitch, gained acceptance in the 1980's after the oceanographer John Imbrie discovered supporting evidence in oxygen isotopes contained in shells deposited many thousands of years ago in ocean sediments.

   选项分析：

   (A) (Correct) 贝壳沉积物中的氧同位素。本选项和题目分析中提到的内容相同。
   (B) 淡水裂缝中的矿物方解石。

(C) 不同区域的环境变化。

(D) 铀分解成钍的速率。

(E) 大气、海洋和冰层之间的交换。

6. The primary purpose of the passage is to

   (A) criticize the methodology of a scientist's research

   (B) report evidence that challenges a geochemist's theory

   (C) explain why a widely accepted theory about ancient climates was abandoned

   (D) describe some recent research on ice age cycles

   (E) propose an innovative explanation for variations in oceanographic data

题目类型： 主旨大意题

题目分析： 主旨大意题选择与逻辑框架所描述的结构相同的选项即可。

选项分析：

(A) 批判一个科学家的研究方法。本文没有批判哪个科学家的意思，只是在展示科学家不同的观点。

(B) 报告一个挑战地球化学家理论的证据。本文没有批判哪个原理的想法。

(C) 解释为什么一个广为接受的关于古代的气候原理会被放弃。文章没有提到被放弃的古代气候原理。

(D) (Correct) 描述一些最近的有关冰河时代循环的研究。原文描述了三位科学家各自的研究成果。

(E) 提出一个针对海洋地理数据变化的新潮的解释。本选项和文章的内容无关。

◎ **Passage 3** ◎

逻辑框架：

```
┌─────────────────────────────────────┐
│      P1 观点1：小公司不重要          │
│              ↑ 反对                  │
│      1970s（举例：钢铁工业）         │
└─────────────────────────────────────┘

┌─────────────────────────────────────┐
│ P2 观点2：小公司重要：①技术革新；②竞争；③新工作 │
└─────────────────────────────────────┘
              ↑ 指出问题
┌─────────────────────────────────────┐
│  P3 研究不充分 & 定义"small"的标准是什么？  │
└─────────────────────────────────────┘
```

303

7. The passage is primarily concerned with

    (A) dismissing a challenge to a traditional viewpoint

    (B) suggesting a new solution to a long-standing problem

    (C) resolving a conflict between two competing viewpoints

    (D) discussing the emergence of an alternative viewpoint

    (E) defending an alternative viewpoint against possible counterevidence

题目类型： 主旨大意题

题目分析： 主旨大意题选择与逻辑框架所描述的结构相同的选项即可。

选项分析：

(A) 驳回一个攻击传统观点的观点。其实作者通篇认为传统观点是有问题的，所以提出一个新的观点，最后一段只是指出这个新的观点还有待完善，并不是要驳回它。

(B) 针对一个一直存在的问题提出一个新解决方案。文中没有提到一个一直存在的问题，更不用说作者提出解决方案了。

(C) 解决两个存有分歧的观点的争端。作者倾向于对第二个观点做出论证，第一个观点只是针对第二个观点所做的一个对比，并不注重这两个观点的争端。

(D) (Correct) 讨论另一个观点的出现。整个文章都围绕着这个"另一个观点"，作者的目的是讨论这个观点。

(E) 针对可能存在的"反对证据"为另一个观点辩护。文中第三段也只是提出另一个观点存在的不足（反对证据），并没有为其做辩护的意思。

8. The passage suggests which of the following about the empirical study of small firms' role?

    (A) Anecdotal evidence does not support the theory that small firms' role is significant.

    (B) Degrees of market turbulence are the primary indicator of small firms' role.

    (C) An examination of new niches created by small firms has provided important data for the analysis of such firms' role.

    (D) Case studies have provided reliable evidence to answer major questions concerning small firms' role.

    (E) A more precise definition of the term "small firm" is crucial to making a conclusive analysis about small firms' role.

题目类型： 支持观点题

题目分析： 原文最后一段描述了 empirical study 的一些不足。这表明，文章是承认这些不足的，并且也应该承认这些不足被改进之后会更好。

选项分析：

(A) 轶事证据不支持小公司的地位很重要的这个理论。第三段第一句话就提到轶事证据是不足以支持而不是不支持。

(B) 市场变动的等级是小公司地位重要性的主要指示物。市场变动与经验研究无关。

(C) 对小公司创造的特定市场的检验为分析这些公司的地位提供了重要的信息。本选项的关键词都出现在第二段，与第三段的经验研究无关。

(D) 案例研究提供了可靠的证据来回答与小公司地位有关的主要问题。案例研究提供的证据不足以证明小公司的地位。

(E) (Correct) 一个对小公司更加精确的定义对于结论性分析小公司的地位很重要。文中最后部分说明了另一个困难就是无法准确划分小公司。因此，一个更加精确的划分细则是很重要的。

9. Which of the following best describes the organization of the first paragraph of the passage?

   (A) A viewpoint is introduced, counterevidence is presented, and a new perspective is suggested.

   (B) Opposing viewpoints are discussed, and evidence is provided that refutes both of those viewpoints.

   (C) A hypothesis is described, supported with specific evidence, and then reaffirmed.

   (D) An alternative viewpoint is presented, criticized, and dismissed in light of new evidence.

   (E) Opposing viewpoints are presented, discussed, and then found to be more similar than previously supposed.

题目类型： 评估题

题目分析： 第一段的结构比较简单，即提出一个观点，然后提出反对的证据，最后从另一个角度看待问题。

选项分析：

(A) (Correct) 介绍一个观点，展示反对证据，提出新视角。

(B) 讨论了反对观点，提出反对那两个观点的证据。第一段中提出的证据是偏向第二个观点的，所以不能说是反对两个观点。

(C) 描述一个定理，用具体的证据来支持这个定理，而后重新确定。第一段中的第一个定理被反对，但并没有被重新确定。

(D) 另一个论点被展示、被批评，最后被新的证据驳回。作者并没有批评第一个论点（这段只提到了这一个论点），只是说新的证据支持从另一个角度看问题。

(E) 反对观点被展示、被讨论，最后被发现比以前认为的更加相似。首先，文中没有提到和"以前认为的"更加相似。其次，作者在第一段中没有展示不同的观点（第二段才展示第二个观点）。

10. According to the passage, an important contribution of small firms to industrial markets is that small firms

(A) operate more efficiently than large firms
(B) offer high job security and compensation
(C) cause international competition to decrease
(D) help prevent market turbulence from affecting competition
(E) frequently undertake activities that result in technological change

题目类型： 支持观点题

题目分析： 原文第二段着重讨论了小公司对市场的贡献。

选项分析：

(A) 比操作大公司更加高效。本选项的信息在第一段出现过，即：Although no systematic evidence exists to determine unequivocally whether smaller units of production are as efficient as large firms or are, in fact, more efficient. 由此可知,效率高是没有得到证明的。

(B) 提供高性能的工作安全和补偿。文中没有提到工作安全和补偿问题。

(C) 降低国际竞争。本选项说反了。

(D) 帮助防止市场变动影响竞争。本选项说反了，原文讲的是："Small firms generate market turbulence that creates additional dimensions of competition."

(E) (Correct) 经常举办导致技术变革的活动。第二段写道："First, small firms are often the source of the kind of innovative activity that leads to technological change."

Passage 4

逻辑框架：

> P1 P 岛的冰融化快
> P2 A3 去查 → 令人担忧的过程
> P3 其他地方相似 → P 岛的数据很重要

11. Which of the following is an assumption underlying the last sentence of the passage?

    (A) Although it is difficult to monitor the ice shelf's underbelly, oceanographers are able to find ways to estimate what's happened about it.
    (B) Pine Island Glacier is not a special island glacier which contacts especially much warm water in Antarctica.
    (C) In each year between 1974 and 2009, the robotic submarine visited the island and collected data of warm water.
    (D) There are no other reasons except warm water that melt the ice on Pine Island.
    (E) The information collected by the submarine is not the only source, from which analysts could get data, of information about the Pine Island Glacier.

题目类型： 评估题

题目分析： 结论：利用 Pine Island 水下的情况可以准确预测整个地球海洋水位的情况。
答案方向：假设题型，结论为事件类，答案需指明：如果 Pine Island 真的可以代表整个地球海洋水位的情况，那么哪个选项一定是正确的。

选项分析：

(A) 虽然很难观察冰层下的情况，但是海洋学家有能力找到方法来估计它发生了什么。本选项没有提及样本。

(B) (Correct) 松岛冰川不是一个与南极洲暖水接触特别多的特殊冰川。本选项指出 the Pine Island 是具有代表性的。

(C) 在 1974 至 2009 年的每一年中，机器人潜艇都会去岛屿收集暖水的数据。本选项没有提及样本。

(D) 除了暖水外，没有其他因素可以融化 Pine Island 的冰。样本是 Pine Island 的融化，而不是其融化方式。

(E) 由潜水艇收集的信息并不是分析学家获得的关于松岛冰川信息唯一来源。本选项没有提及样本。

12. It can be inferred from information presented in the passage that if *Nathaniel B. Palmer's* worrying process continues without any controlling methods, which of the following would be true as a consequence?

(A) Environmentalists and oceanographers will at least come up with a useful method to control the worrying process.

(B) Ice will disappear on the Earth and some of cities in the world will be inundated by sea water.

(C) Pine Island Glacier will not be the last glacier island on the Earth.

(D) The ice in Pine Island Glacier will drift on the ocean and even disappear finally.

(E) More robotic submarines will visit Pine Island Glacier to collect data used by analysts in order to pursue the origin of the warm water.

题目类型：推断题

题目分析：文章在第二段讲到了这个 *Nathaniel B. Palmer's* worrying process，即：Strengthening ocean currents are bringing deeper, warm water into contact with thinning ice, melting 19 cubic miles of the ice shelf's underside in 2009 alone and causing the glacier to flow faster into the ocean. Since 1974 Pine Island has thinned by 230 feet and accelerated by more than 70 percent. 综合提到这个过程的两句话的信息，可以选出本题的答案。

选项分析：

(A) 环境学家和海洋学家将会至少提出一个有用的方法来控制这个令人担心的过程。文章中没有提到环保学家是否能提出这样的一个方法。

(B) 冰将会在地球上消失并且有些城市可能会被海水淹没。如果放任这个令人担忧的现象不管，那么终有一天，松岛冰川将会消失。但是，没有理由认为地球上所有的冰都会和松岛冰川相同。

(C) 松岛冰川不会是地球上最后一块冰川。从原文中无法得出本选项的信息。

(D) (Correct) 松岛冰川将会漂在海上并且最后消失。如果放任这个令人担忧的现象不管，那么终有一天，松岛冰川将会消失。

(E) 为了追查暖水的源头，更多的潜艇将会去松岛冰川收集数据以供分析学家使用。从原文中无法得出本选项的信息。